Chinese Communists and Hong Kong Capitalists

Also by Cindy Yik-yi Chu

Meigui xiunü (The Maryknoll Sisters). (2010).

Edited, *The Diaries of the Maryknoll Sisters in Hong Kong, 1921–1966*. New York: Palgrave Macmillan, 2007.

Edited, *Foreign Communities in Hong Kong, 1840s–1950s*. New York: Palgrave Macmillan, 2005.

The Maryknoll Sisters in Hong Kong, 1921–1969: In Love with the Chinese. New York: Palgrave Macmillan, 2004. (Chinese edition, 2007).

Edited with Ricardo K. S. Mak, *China Reconstructs*. (2003).

Edited with Lam Kai-yin, *Yapian zhanzheng de zai renshi* [A reappraisal of the Opium War]. (2003).

Chinese Communists and Hong Kong Capitalists: 1937–1997

Cindy Yik-yi Chu

First published in 2010 by
PALGRAVE MACMILLAN®
in the United States – a division of St. Martin's Press LLC,
175 Fifth Avenue, New York, NY 10010.

Where this book is distributed in the UK, Europe and the rest of the world,
this is by Palgrave Macmillan, a division of Macmillan Publishers Limited,
registered in England, company number 785998, of Houndmills, Basingstoke,
Hampshire RG21 6XS.

Palgrave Macmillan is the global academic imprint of the above companies
and has companies and representatives throughout the world.

Palgrave® and Macmillan® are registered trademarks in the United States,
the United Kingdom, Europe and other countries.

ISBN: 978–0–230–10799–1

Library of Congress Cataloging-in-Publication Data

Chu, Cindy Yik-yi.
    Chinese communists and Hong Kong capitalists : 1937–1997 /
Cindy Yik-yi Chu.
        p. cm.
    Includes bibliographical references.
    ISBN 978–0–230–10799–1 (alk. paper)
    1. China—Relations—China—Hong Kong.   2. Hong Kong (China)—
Relations—China.   3. Communists—China—History—20th century.
4. Capitalists and financiers—China—Hong Kong—History—20th century.
5. Businessmen—China—Hong Kong—History—20th century.   6. Elite
(Social sciences)—China—Hong Kong—History—20th century.   7. China—
Foreign relations—20th century.   8. Constitutional law—China—Hong
Kong—History—20th century.   9. Hong Kong (China)—Economic
conditions—20th century.   10. Hong Kong (China)—History—Transfer
of Sovereignty from Great Britain, 1997.   I. Title.
    DS740.5.G6H633 2010
    324.251'0750951250904—dc22
                                                                        2010013318

A catalogue record of the book is available from the British Library.

Design by MPS Limited, A Macmillan Company

First edition: October 2010

10 9 8 7 6 5 4 3 2 1

Printed in the United States of America.

To Professor Stephen Uhalley, Jr.

Contents

Preface

This book studies the activities of the Chinese Communists in Hong Kong from the outbreak of the Sino-Japanese War in 1937 to the handover in 1997. It points out that Hong Kong had been a special item on the Communists' agenda—from being their station to the overseas audience to being the icon of the achievements of China's national unification. Throughout the period, the Chinese Communists carried out a consistent united front policy in Hong Kong, which was very different from their practice on the mainland. The Communists sought alliance with the Hong Kong capitalists, who were the main targets of the united front effort. The history of the Chinese Communists in Hong Kong differed significantly from that of their past campaigns on the mainland. Therefore, this book traces a unique part of Chinese Communist history, and six decades of astonishing united front between the Chinese Communists and Hong Kong upper-class capitalists.

The present study aims at contributing to modern and contemporary Chinese history. It examines the policies of the Chinese Communists (and even the Nationalist government) toward Hong Kong and overseas Chinese. In addition, it highlights an important aspect of the Sino-Japanese War, namely, how the Communists and Nationalists in Hong Kong competed for external resources for the war effort. This book critically evaluates six decades of Chinese Communist activities in the territory. Importantly, it looks at the Communist presence from a new perspective—through the cooperation between the Chinese Communists and Hong Kong capitalists. It also enhances our understanding of the role of the upper-class capitalists in Hong Kong history.

I have been very appreciative of the education I received from Professor Stephen Uhalley, Jr., Professor Sharon Minichiello, and the late Professor Herbert F. Margulies. Also, I would like to thank my assistants Wong Yiu-chung and Lai Tat-li for their diligent work.

Cindy Yik-yi Chu
April 1, 2010

Abbreviations

ACR	Asian Commercial Research Limited
BLCC	Basic Law Consultative Committee
BLDC	Basic Law Drafting Committee
BPF	Business and Professionals Federation
BPG	Business and Professional Group
CCP	Chinese Communist Party
CPPCC	Chinese People's Political Consultative Conference
CRC	Co-operative Resources Centre
DAB	Democratic Alliance for the Betterment of Hong Kong
Exco	Executive Council
HK Xinhua	Hong Kong Branch of the Xinhua News Agency
HKMAO	Hong Kong and Macao Affairs Office of the State Council
HKMWC	Hong Kong and Macao Work Committee
Legco	Legislative Council
NPC	National People's Congress
PLA	People's Liberation Army
PRC	People's Republic of China
PWC	Preliminary Working Committee
SAR	Special Administrative Region
UN	United Nations

I

Introduction

1. The Historical Question of Hong Kong

When Governor Sir Murray MacLehose visited Beijing in 1979, Deng Xiaoping told him privately that the Chinese government must recover its sovereignty over Hong Kong.[1] This incident marked the beginning of the 1997 question, which Beijing regarded as "a question left over from history." At the end of the Opium War with the signing of the Treaty of Nanjing in 1842, China ceded Hong Kong to Britain. After British and French troops occupied Beijing in 1859 and 1860, and destroyed the Summer Palace, the Qing government had no choice but to sign the Beijing Convention, which granted Britain the Kowloon Peninsula and Stonecutters Island. In 1898, following the French, who had demanded a ninety-nine year lease of Guangzhou Bay, the British asked for a similar lease of the New Territories, which included 235 islands and two bays, up to the year 1997.[2] The Chinese Communists never recognized the above treaties that the Qing government signed with the British. The expiration of the lease of the New Territories on June 30, 1997, however, forced Beijing to finally settle the Hong Kong question.

Although the 1969 *Vienna Convention on the Law of Treaties* and the International Court of Justice recognized the inequality of the treaties, this did not necessarily make them invalid.[3] Beijing insisted that they were void, leading to controversy over their validity. While Beijing considered British control over Hong Kong to be unlawful, it allowed the colonial presence as the problem was of international concern, and any imprudent move would arouse criticism overseas. In 1949, the People's Liberation Army (PLA) did not move into Hong Kong but stopped near Shenzhen River. On May 6, the editorial of Hong Kong's *Wenhuibao* stated, "Discuss Sino-British Relations and the Future of Hong Kong," and noted that Hong Kong was in a most advantageous situation as trade would drastically increase after the establishment of New China. It said, "If Hong Kong is frightened by this unprecedented good luck, and does not actively seek the friendship of New China . . . this will be historically unwise. . . . If British politicians do not take advantage of the situation, the opportunity will soon fade away."[4] The Hong Kong government got the message. In 1950, the British recognized China to preserve the colony and the economic benefits related to connections to the mainland.

In 1951, Politburo member Peng Zhen stated that it would be unwise for the Chinese Communists to be ill-prepared and impetuous in dealing with Hong Kong,[5] where they could obtain foreign supplies and earn foreign currency. British recognition enhanced Communist China's position abroad. The Chinese Communists did not close the mainland–Hong Kong border until the outbreak of the Korean War, at which time illegal smuggling began as China suffered from the blockade by the United States and its allies.

From 1950 to 1959, China's cumulative trade surplus against Hong Kong was US$772.83 million; from 1960 to 1969, the figure was US$3,202.83 million. Such a large surplus and its rapid increase within two decades were unquestionably of great significance to China.[6] In May 1963, Beijing's vice minister of foreign trade emphasized Hong Kong's contribution to China's foreign trade, and to "a valuable source of foreign exchange."[7] Observers stated that China was determined to earn as much foreign currency as possible from Hong Kong.[8]

In March 1972, Beijing's representative to the United Nations (UN) wrote to the special committee on colonization, reiterating Beijing's stance on Hong Kong. China claimed that Hong Kong and Macao were a part of its territory, which had been occupied by Britain and Portugal, respectively. Hong Kong and Macao were an issue of Chinese sovereignty, and did not fall into the category of colonies. After Beijing's protest, the UN removed the two territories from the list of colonies.[9] While China never gave up its claim of sovereignty over Hong Kong and was uncompromising in this regard, the Chinese Communists did not want to rush the matter and preferred to handle it with caution, to avoid unwanted response abroad. Thus, Beijing was disinclined to raise the matter unless it recognized possible encroachments on its position. MacLehose's visit to Beijing in 1979 reopened the historical question of Hong Kong.

In the early 1980s, Sino-British talks focused on the drafting of the Joint Declaration, which laid out the terms of the agreement on the future of Hong Kong. From 1984 to 1997, Hong Kong was in a period of transition, as the Chinese and British governments prepared for the handover of the territory to China. This period was characterized by debates over the Basic Law, which would be the mini-constitution of the Hong Kong Special Administrative Region (SAR) after the handover, and the pace of local democratization. In addressing the 1997 question, scholars have focused on three actors—China, Britain, and Hong Kong. While some have argued that the Chinese and British governments betrayed the people of Hong Kong, others have been sympathetic toward the British. The scholarly literature focuses on why Hong Kong was denied a more democratic government. The ultimate concern is the implementation of the "one country, two systems" concept.

2. The Purpose of This Book

This is a history book, and this introductory chapter discusses different theses related to the 1997 question, highlighting the respective roles of China, Britain, and Hong Kong. In doing so, it addresses a number of questions. Do existing studies provide us with a good understanding of the Hong Kong situation after the 1997 handover? Under what circumstances did they appear? What was the background of the scholarship? What factors affected the assessment of the Hong Kong problem, with particular reference to the "one country, two systems" concept?

This chapter argues that the scholarly literature reflects the political atmosphere in which it appeared, for intellectuals were influenced by and responded to political events and debates. As the political climate changed, so did scholarly concerns. Academic interpretations matured over time, especially in the case of "recent history." There is a strong correlation between the existing circumstances and the resulting scholarship. At the time of the Sino-British Joint Declaration in 1984, there was a great deal of speculation about the Hong Kong problem. During the drafting of the Basic Law in the second half of the 1980s, scholars focused on Sino-British relations, and argued that the Beijing and London governments dictated the future of the territory. They concentrated on the interactions between the two governments, and regarded Hong Kong people as "passive recipients" in the entire process. As the scholarship evolved, researchers asked whether Hong Kong people would be deprived of a democratic government after 1997, and if so, who would be responsible.

This book argues that there should be further study of (1) the local population and (2) the relation of external forces to Hong Kong society. This introductory chapter shows that the scholarly work on Hong Kong politics has tended to focus on Sino-British relations or the external forces of China and Britain. More importantly, there has been inadequate study of the relations between significant external forces, such as the Chinese Communists or Beijing, and the local people.

Through an examination of research into the 1997 question, this book develops another way of looking at the issue—*a historical perspective*—and discusses how the Chinese Communists approached and worked with the local people from the 1930s up to the eve of the handover. Such is the purpose of this book. In investigating Hong Kong's relations with the Chinese Communists during the 1937–1997 period, it attempts to answer the following questions: How does the 1997 question relate to the history of the Chinese Communists in Hong Kong? How can the implementation of the "one country, two systems" concept be better understood through the study of the united front strategy of the Chinese Communists in Hong Kong following the outbreak of the Sino-Japanese War in 1937?

This book shows that the Chinese Communists were involved with Hong Kong capitalists throughout the period from 1937 to 1997. Communication and cooperation between them and mutual interests constitute the manifestation of a united front effort throughout the decades. Sociologist Alvin Y. So suggests in *Hong Kong's Embattled Democracy* that Beijing would not have reached out to Hong Kong's business people had there been no economic interests or connection between mainland China and Hong Kong in the late 1980s.[10] A journal article examines Beijing's collaboration with the local socioeconomic elite from the 1984 Joint Declaration to the eve of the 1997 handover.[11] Christine Loh's recent book, *Underground Front: The Chinese Communist Party in Hong Kong*, also discusses the Communists' collaboration with the business elite from the 1980s onward.[12] In *Keeping Democracy at Bay*, Suzanne Pepper mentions that the united front "was still used by leftists themselves with reference to their search for new friends and allies" in the first half of the 1990s.[13]

The present book, however, takes a longer view. First, it argues that the Chinese Communists were more accommodating of Hong Kong and open to working with Hong Kong capitalists than some analysts and commentators might think. Second, it points out that Chinese Communists and Hong Kong capitalists had worked together since 1937, a point in time earlier than most journalists and China observers have mentioned. Third, it emphasizes Premier Zhou Enlai's directives to Communists in Hong Kong, which were reiterated from the 1930s through the mid-1960s, to strive for a united front with the local capitalists as the main target. Thus, this book contributes to a new understanding of the history of the territory by pointing out that the Chinese Communists were familiar with Hong Kong's situation for many decades before the handover.

Historian Chan Lau Kit-ching examines Chinese Communist activities in Hong Kong in an earlier period in her book, *From Nothing to Nothing: The Chinese Communist Movement and Hong Kong, 1921–1936*.[14] Chan says that Hong Kong "was greatly involved in the [Chinese Communist] movement from its earliest beginning until its culmination in the establishment of the People's Republic of China."[15] She remarks that the Guangdong

Communists were, however, very isolated, and that their activities were seriously weakened by the time of the Long March (1934–1935). She states that Communist activities in Guangdong and Hong Kong "had almost come to a complete halt" by 1936,[16] leading to the title of her book, *From Nothing to Nothing*, which recounts the founding of the Chinese Communist Party (CCP) and the beginning of its activities in Hong Kong in 1921 to their termination in 1936.

The present book fills the gap in the understanding of the Chinese Communist presence in Hong Kong after 1937. The outbreak of the Sino-Japanese War on July 7, 1937, offered the Chinese Communists the rationale and opportunity to once again use Hong Kong as an outpost linking them to the outside world. Hence, 1937 marked a significant turning point. From then on, the Chinese Communists took advantage of various channels to befriend Hong Kong capitalists. This phenomenon was unique in the history of the Chinese Communists, as Hong Kong itself was a special item on the Communist agenda. Leaders including Zhou Enlai considered Hong Kong a separate entity, and therefore to be treated differently from regions in mainland China. As this book studies the history from 1937 to 1997, the introductory chapter discusses only the literature describing the events taking place during this period.

3. The Accusation Thesis

In 1979, MacLehose visited Beijing and brought up the 1997 question with the Chinese leadership. The governor had discussed the issue with his advisers, who cautioned him not to mention it. In his meeting with Deng Xiaoping, however, MacLehose asked whether the Hong Kong government could issue commercial leases beyond 1997. Caught off guard, Deng stressed that Hong Kong was a part of China and would be returned to China. He added that Hong Kong businessmen should "put their hearts at ease."[17] From that time, Beijing and London squabbled about the future settlement of the territory. Chinese nationalism was running high, and Beijing was not willing to compromise on matters concerning sovereignty. At the same time, the British prime minister Margaret Thatcher hoped to trade sovereignty for administration after 1997. From the Chinese perspective, sovereignty could not be compromised, and any deals would inflict only further humiliation upon the Chinese people. The British had to yield, and the first round of Sino-British talks to decide the future of the territory started in July 1983. In December 1984, the Joint Declaration laid out the transfer of Hong Kong to China.

From 1984 onward, the Chinese and British had another concern—no longer was the issue whether Hong Kong would be returned to China, but rather how it should be returned in 1997, and how it would continue thereafter. There were different opinions about Hong Kong's political development after the Joint Declaration. Beijing was suspicious of the British intention to start a local democratization process, and worried that this could create severe difficulties for Chinese governance after the handover. Regarding the political change, the focus was the content of the Basic Law, which would be the mini-constitution of the Hong Kong SAR. Scholars believed that China, Britain, and Hong Kong had different understandings of their needs and the circumstances, and emphasized that conflicts were irresolvable.

Showing no faith in the future of Hong Kong, analysts concluded that attempts to resolve the conflicts would fail. They accused both the Chinese and British governments of failing the Hong Kong people. Robert Cottrell raised the alarm, describing Hong Kong's return to China as leading to *The End of Hong Kong*, the title of his book of the years from the late 1970s up to 1993.[18] He looked at the "abandoned attempts to introduce democracy to Hong Kong under British rule."[19] In the 1980s, the British accommodated Beijing's idea of "convergence," namely, that Hong Kong's political system after 1997 be determined in the forthcoming Basic Law, and that "the British Hong Kong government should only alter the Hong Kong political system prior to 1997 in ways which brought it more closely into conformity with the prescriptions of the Basic Law."[20] China and Britain established limits to the progression of local democracy in this transitional period.[21] After the arrival of Governor Christopher Patten in 1992, there was concern over the increasing tensions among China, Britain, and Hong Kong, and how they could be resolved.

This message was repeated in other books that flooded the market before the handover. Mark Roberti offered a pessimistic view in *The Fall of Hong Kong*, arguing that the Joint Declaration did not result from a resolution of differences between China and Britain. Rather, the two sides disagreed on the form of government for Hong Kong after 1997, but hid their disagreement underneath vague promises of freedoms in the Joint Declaration. By not providing democracy for the people of Hong Kong, the document was only a partial agreement. According to Roberti, the subsequent years witnessed the Chinese triumph over and British betrayal of the local population.[22] Beijing insisted on pushing through its own agenda, and the British wanted only to retreat from the scene without taking further responsibility for the people of Hong Kong. Roberti concluded that a "new power elite," a pro-China group of local businessmen, was notably united and strong on the eve of the handover.

In *The Politics of Hong Kong's Reversion to China*, David Wen-wei Chang and Richard Y. Chuang argued that "China dictated the terms of the Joint

Declaration."[23] In *A People Misruled*, Albert H. Yee even suggested a need to renegotiate the Basic Law.[24] Differences existed, but the British did not want to prolong bargaining, as time was running out. Whereas the British tried simply to "smooth the edges" of the Chinese demands, Beijing insisted on pursuing its own agenda.[25] Both the Chinese and British governments were guilty of ignoring the demands of Hong Kong people, according to these analysts, and hence the "one country, two systems" concept was doomed to failure, for which Beijing and London would be jointly responsible.

4. The "Historical Tragedy" Thesis

Other scholars thought that the British should not be blamed. While they agreed that Beijing and London had enormous differences, they believed that the British had tried their best to fight for the local population. These scholars were sympathetic toward the British government, and believed that the "one country, two systems" concept would fail. This "historical tragedy" thesis differs from the "accusation" view in arguing that China was solely responsible for the failure of the "one country, two systems" policy.

In *A History of Hong Kong*, Frank Welsh argued that the Joint Declaration was "a remarkable document," "the result of much patient negotiation" as Beijing allowed Hong Kong to remain capitalist after the handover.[26] He stated that the British did not have much interest in the territory, which had always been of "peripheral concern."[27] In *The Final Years of British Hong Kong*, John Flowerdew argued that the British "had very little real power to affect the outcome of the transition."[28] According to him, Hong Kong's economic success was a result of the "rule of law," free trade, and the benevolence of British rule.[29] He maintained that it was possible that "the degree of democratic government allowed [in the territory after 1997] would have been considerably less than British might have preferred."[30] Gerald Segal, however, was prepared to predict what would happen. In *The Fate of Hong Kong*, he portrayed Hong Kong as moving toward a model of "convergence."[31] In this model, local political development would have to slow down to the pace desired by the Chinese government, and the settlement of differences would involve compromises on the part of Hong Kong people.

Steve Tsang was the most critical, charging that China was a "totalitarian communist" regime.[32] He said that the concerns of the British government and the Hong Kong people were the same.[33] To him, the troublemaker was Beijing, which upheld "socialist China's 'democratic' standards"[34] and was obsessed with the issue of sovereignty. Tsang shared the pessimism of his fellow scholars as he had little hope that the "one country, two systems" policy would succeed. In another work, he described Britain as "the declining force," China as "the rising force," and Hong Kong people as "the ineffective force" in the transitional period.[35] Jamie Allen was also very distrustful of the Beijing government, and described the 1997 handover as the "recolonization" rather the "decolonization" of Hong Kong.[36] According to Allen in *Seeing Red,* Hong Kong would become "*Xianggang*" (Putonghua) rather than remaining "*Heunggong*" (the Cantonese pronunciation of the two Chinese characters).[37] He stated that the Basic Law was a weak constitution. Although proponents of the accusation and historical tragedy theses both pointed to the British accommodation with Beijing regarding Hong Kong, they differed on whether the British were able to alter the decisions being made. The former believed that the British could do so, whereas the latter argued the opposite.

5. The "Chinese Realism" Thesis

Some scholars focused on China's reform, and contended that Hong Kong was crucial to its success. The practical value of Hong Kong ensured that Beijing would implement the "one country, two systems" policy. Those taking the "Chinese realism" viewpoint paid more attention to the policies and role of the Chinese government during the recent period. In *Deng Xiaoping and the Making of Modern China,* Richard Evans touched upon Hong Kong, and mentioned Deng's determination not to become "another Li Hongzhang," who was responsible for the 1898 lease of the New Territories to the British.[38] In his book, Evans described Hong Kong as a source of information for mainland China. Kevin P. Lane argued that China tried to accommodate the British in the Hong Kong situation, writing: "in the long history of the Hong Kong question, Chinese policy makers have pursued similar goals and have responded in similar ways to incentives presented by Hong Kong's unusual status."[39] Michael Yahuda is a Sinologist who focuses on contemporary China. In *Hong Kong: China's Challenge,* he argued that Hong Kong's future was a test for China.[40] His only fear was that Beijing would interfere in the local economy and create problems.

In her article "Overt and Covert Functions of the Hong Kong Branch of the Xinhua News Agency, 1947–1984," Cindy Yik-yi Chu argued that the CCP "took a practical view of Hong Kong and the local capitalists long before Beijing openly advocated the concept of 'one country, two systems,'"[41] and that the Hong Kong Branch of the Xinhua News Agency was "an important conduit of relations" between China and Hong Kong, serving as "a diplomatic liaison and collaborator with Hong Kong capitalists"[42] while carrying out "united front" activities in the territory. Chu also explained China's united front strategy in the formation of the Basic Law committees in the 1980s,[43] noting that it focused on consolidating support from the upper-class business elite and gaining the good will of the middle class.

6. Evaluation of the Existing Literature

On the eve of the handover in 1997, observers were most concerned about the future political freedom of Hong Kong. The most pessimistic felt that the "one country, two systems" concept would not work, and that the days of Hong Kong were numbered. They had no faith in the Beijing government, Communist ruling style, or Basic Law. They believed that a "Communist dictatorship" and "capitalism" were incompatible and thus that the Hong Kong SAR was doomed to failure. Although they were confident about the Hong Kong government and economy, they argued that Beijing would interfere in local matters and create problems. These scholars contributed to the accusation and "historical tragedy" theses. The former were critical of both the Chinese and British governments, whereas the latter held that China should bear all of the blame for the (would-be) failure of the "one country, two systems" policy.

In contrast, those who had more faith in the future of the territory contributed to the "Chinese realism" thesis. Before 1997, academics emphasized the Greater China phenomenon, which was then an exciting research topic, and the economic integration of mainland China, Hong Kong, and Taiwan. The subtitle of David Shambaugh's edited volume—*Greater China: The Next Superpower?*—indicates their optimism.[44] Similarly, Hong Kong experts were amazed by the rapid growth of Greater China, flourishing Hong Kong real estate market, and promise of the regional economy. They argued that Hong Kong was then the focus of Greater China, the center of the integration process, and that the economic achievement of the former was the most reliable guarantee for the future of the latter. They held that Beijing would not be stupid enough to kill the goose that laid the golden eggs.

More than a decade after the handover, the pessimistic scenarios have not taken place. Although the foregoing work was well researched, the predictions of these scholars did not come true. They focused on the politics of the Beijing and London governments, and neglected the study of Hong Kong society. Compared to the case prior to 1997, the Beijing government, since the handover, has remained comparatively quiet on Hong Kong matters, or chosen the right time to give encouragement to the Hong Kong economy (and people). This contrasts the transitional period from the early 1980s to 1997, during which time the Chinese leaders made every effort to counteract the work of the British. The years from the early 1980s to 1997 were a self-contained period in which Beijing had to be strong and assertive, or it would appear to be yielding to foreign pressure.

This self-contained history reflects on post-1997 events, as Beijing has continued its united front in Hong Kong. In *The Dynamics of Beijing-Hong Kong Relations*, Sonny Shiu-Hing Lo identified the times at which Beijing has employed united front tactics. For example, he pointed to the readjustment of tactics after the mass protest on July 1, 2003. According to Lo, Beijing used certain people as spokespersons to emphasize the importance of patriotism among Hong Kong people and to isolate opponents, and carried out such a strategy again in 2004.[45] Lo claimed that in Hong Kong, the "resurrection of the debate over patriotism" has characterized Beijing's united front work.[46] In short, Beijing-Hong Kong relations have historically been a united front endeavor.

7. The "New Era's Patriotic United Front"

This book argues that the implementation of the "one country, two systems" policy can be better understood through the study of *Chinese Communist activities in Hong Kong over the six decades before the 1997 handover*. It argues that Hong Kong always occupied a unique position on the Communists' agenda—from being their outpost to the outside world and the source of foreign currency, to being the symbol of the success of China's national unification.

Throughout the decades, the Chinese Communists adopted a consistent united front policy in Hong Kong, in a manner entirely different from their policies on the mainland. They strove to create and maintain alliances with Hong Kong's "big capitalists," who had been the chief targets of their united front work. Such efforts differed greatly from their ideology, propaganda, and campaigns in mainland China. Tracing the six decades of the astounding united front between the Chinese Communists and the Hong Kong tycoons and upper-class business elite, this book brings to light a distinctive part of the history of the Chinese Communists.

Before reviewing the book chapters, it is essential to examine the "new era's patriotic united front" and the characteristics of the united front strategy in Chinese Communist history to gain a historical perspective of the united front phenomenon.

In December 1978, the Third Plenum of the Eleventh Central Committee of the CCP met. It stressed reform and abandoned the former revolutionary course. Deng Xiaoping spoke about the Four Modernizations and problems inherited from the past, which were blamed on Lin Biao and the Gang of Four.[47] The Plenum abandoned slogans including "class struggle as the principle" and "the continuous revolution under the dictatorship of the proletariat," shifting the emphasis to Socialist modernization.[48] Importantly, it asked "the Taiwan, Hong Kong and overseas Chinese compatriots" to embrace patriotism and contribute to the effort. In June 1979, Deng proclaimed that the "revolutionary united front" had entered a new stage of development,[49] and that the united front was a widespread alliance between Socialist laborers and Socialist patriots under the leadership of the working class, with the worker-peasant alliance as its foundation.[50] Two months later, the united front became the "revolutionary patriotic united front," with two objectives—the Four Modernizations and the country's unification. Deng called for all forces to be united to accomplish these tasks.[51]

In 1981, the new era's united front became the "patriotic united front" with the word "revolutionary" removed.[52] In 1982, the "patriotic united front" appeared in the newly adopted constitution.[53] Deng said that the "patriotic united front" was extensive, including not only Socialist laborers but also patriots embracing Socialism and other patriots supporting the country's unification. It is important to emphasize here that he was referring to not only Socialist supporters but also non-Socialist patriots.[54]

According to the CCP, China's united front had maintained for a long time two mutually supportive alliances: (1) the basic worker-peasant alliance, which included other laborers and revolutionary intellectuals, and (2) the alliance between laborers and cooperative nonlaborers, the latter being the "national bourgeoisie."[55] However, the "patriotic united front" had undergone certain changes. The "national bourgeoisie" no longer existed as a class, and individual industrialists and entrepreneurs entered the alliance instead. Then, the two alliances merged into one and formed the united front, which comprised patriots, whether or not they supported Socialism. Patriots were not only mainland Chinese but also Chinese in Taiwan, Hong Kong, Macao, and overseas.

An official from the United Front Department of the Beijing City Committee explained that the "new era's patriotic united front" resembled "riding cars on both sides" [*liangmian xingche*], with those supporting national reunification comprising two groups: Socialist laborers and non-laborers, and Socialist and non-Socialist patriots. According to the official, the collaboration [*lianmeng*] was political in nature and not a class alliance.[56]

The 1981 "Resolution on Certain Questions in the History of Our Party since the Founding of the People's Republic of China" stated that the "patriotic united front" would broadly unite all possible forces, and would not prevent groups or individuals from entering the alliance.[57] It was upon such a basis that the "one country, two systems" concept was developed. Thus, the "patriotic united front" would continue to expand after the return to Chinese sovereignty of Hong Kong and Macao, whose social systems and stratification would remain in place for some time.[58]

The "patriotic united front" laid out the framework for China's handling of Hong Kong. The primary task was the Four Modernizations, and the fundamental guidelines were the Four Cardinal Principles, namely, the supremacy of the Socialist path, dictatorship of the proletariat, leadership of the Communist Party, and Marxist-Leninism and Mao's thought. In 1982, CCP General Secretary Hu Yaobang called for collaboration with non-CCP people, embracing the principles of "long-term co-existence, mutual supervision" and "mutual understanding and mutual support" [*changqi gongcun, huxiang jiandu; gandan xiangzhao, rongru yugong*].[59] The second principle was an expansion of the first, which Mao Zedong had talked about in 1956[60]: with the inclusion of Chinese in Hong Kong, Macao, Taiwan, and overseas, the "patriotic united front" would become the "most extensive, widespread, and broadest" [*zui guangfan*] united front in the history of the Chinese Communists.[61]

8. The United Front as a Historical Phenomenon: The Past and the Present

The united front frequently appeared in the history of the Chinese Communists, their domestic and foreign policies, their perceptions of themselves, friends, and enemies, and their propaganda at home and abroad. The "new era's patriotic united front" shared many historical characteristics, including the following.

(1) *The united front has always catered to the CCP's platform and policies at different times.* As the policies of the Chinese Communists have changed, so have the nature, objectives, and even name of the united front. The united front phenomenon dates back to the early years of the CCP, which praised it for being one of the "three great magic weapons" [*san da fabao*] in the history of the seizing of power.[62] J. D. Armstrong wrote that the united front enjoyed the same significance as the CCP and the PLA.[63]

In *Enemies and Friends: The United Front in Chinese Communist History*, Lyman P. Van Slyke considered the united front "a protean theme" that penetrated through Chinese Communist history, revealing its unique features.[64] He believed that the united front represented a "dialectical generation of Chinese Communist thought: from practice to ideology and back to practice."[65] In response to circumstances, the Chinese Communists developed the united front, which in turn became the foundation of their thought and practice.[66]

The first Guomindang (Nationalist Party/Nationalists)-CCP united front (1923–1927) had its ideological origins in Lenin's support for bourgeois-nationalist uprisings in Asia. Lenin believed that Asians should develop their own Communist parties, with their own organization and leadership.[67] In China, the Comintern needed to build a strong CCP on the one hand and help strengthen Guomindang on the other. In its alliance with Guomindang, "the CCP would eventually grow strong enough to take over the nationalist movement from the inside, ousting the 'bourgeois' elements whom it no longer needed."[68]

At the beginning of the Sino-Japanese War (1937–1945), the second Guomindang-CCP united front was part of "an anti-Japanese policy."[69] The Communists then increased the level of their military strength and the amount of territory and number of people that they governed, and changed the united front policy to an anti-Guomindang one. They divided Chinese society into three blocks, namely, the left wing, intermediate section, and right wing.[70] The left wing comprised the Communist-led people, including the proletariat, peasants, and urban petty bourgeoisie; the intermediate section was composed of the national bourgeoisie and upper section of the petty bourgeoisie; and the right wing included the big landlords and big bourgeoisie. It was always the priority of the Communists to broaden and consolidate the core members of their united front, which at that time, meant the left wing. In *The Chinese Communists' Road to Power: The Anti-Japanese National United Front, 1935–1945*, Shum Kui-Kwong attributed the ultimate Communist victory to the contribution of the anti-Japanese united front.[71]

(2) *The united front has operated on many different levels in its theory and practice, domestic and foreign policies, and official propaganda and popular culture.* In *Civil War in China: The Political Struggle, 1945–1949*, Suzanne Pepper saw the civil war as a struggle for political power between the CCP and Guomindang.[72] She argued that the CCP carried out a united front policy, encouraging any sympathizers and potential ones. The CCP was clever enough to recognize the contribution of students to society. Therefore, the students' refusal to cooperate with the Guomindang government reduced the level of political support for the latter. The CCP seemed to be quite respectful of intellectuals and their work. Ultimately, the Communist victory ended whatever hopes the intellectuals had for Guomindang. Of course, the CCP attributed its success mostly to the peasants' unwavering assistance.

In the latter part of the 1960s, the CCP applied its traditional united front policy to foreign relations, which demonstrated the versatility of the united front. In *Revolution and Chinese Foreign Policy: Peking's Support for Wars of National Liberation*, Peter Van Ness studied the foundations of Chinese revolutionary foreign policy.[73] He pointed out that China's world-view changed in 1965, with China shifting its focus to the "anti-imperialist struggle" in Asia, Africa, and Latin America.[74] In May 1965, Peng Zhen declared that the principal conflict was between the "oppressed nations" of Asia, Africa, and Latin America on the one side, and American imperialism on the other.[75] In commemoration of the twentieth anniversary of the end of the Sino-Japanese War, national defense minister Lin

Biao proclaimed, "Long Live the Victory of People's War!" Lin extended the guerilla strategy to foreign relations: "Comrade Mao Tse-tung's theory of the establishment of rural revolutionary base areas and the encirclement of the cities from the countryside is of outstanding and universal practical importance."[76] The Communists called for the encirclement of "the cities of the world"—North America and Western Europe—by "the rural areas of the world"—Asia, Africa, and Latin America.[77] In other words, Beijing was seeking a united front with developing countries against the Western democratic camp.

The united front history is correlated with the Four Cardinal Principles. The "new era's patriotic united front" applied to both domestic and foreign realms, ultimately promoting the Four Modernizations. It also formed the basis for the "one country, two systems" concept, which allows the presence of capitalist entities within the main Socialist body.

As a part of Communist culture, the united front expresses itself in many ways. For example, there is a united front department in every Chinese province, and universities have publications on the united front. Locally, Hong Kong has witnessed the presence of Chinese Communist organizations and investment, left-wing media, and spokespersons. To many Hong Kong people, these constitute the Chinese Communist united front effort and propaganda.

(3) *From its inception to the present, the united front has identified the primary objective of a specific time, and offered the means to achieve it.* Its work has involved, among other things, the classification of people into categories, with different labels and treatment. In the 1980s, the "new era's patriotic united front" identified targets and divided them into ten groups—democratic parties, independent personalities (mainly patriots), non-CCP intellectual cadres, former Guomindang political and military figures (who had joined the revolution), former industrialists and entrepreneurs, the upper class of ethnic minorities, patriotic religious leaders, people with a Taiwan linkage (with relatives and friends there), friends in Hong Kong and Macao, and Chinese compatriots (both returning home and staying abroad).[78]

The "patriotic united front" served propaganda purposes and revealed the nature of Chinese policy, for its targets shared some similar features. Those who had a high level of education, significant scientific and technical knowledge, and rich management experience comprised the intellectual group. Some had more widespread social connections than the average mainland Chinese, not only within China but also abroad, whereas others had indispensable connections in Hong Kong, Macao, and Taiwan, which were useful for attracting foreign investment, advanced technology, and human resources, expanding China's influence, and promoting the prospects of the country's unification. Finally, all were highly supportive of the Four Modernizations.[79]

In 1995, an official of the United Front Department of the Beijing City Committee claimed that Beijing had recently added "the eleventh target of united front work." This was private enterprises, which included private companies and cooperatives on the mainland, and private capital overseas.[80] He emphasized private enterprises in South China, and believed that private capital was instrumental to the development of the "productive power" of the country.

9. The United Front Strategy and the "One Country, Two Systems" Concept

The united front has always involved collaboration among diverse elements to achieve highly propagandized goals. It has embraced many objectives simultaneously, with priorities changing according to circumstances. This was the case for the first and second Guomindang-CCP united fronts. The proposed "third CCP-Guomindang collaboration" originated from the desire of the Chinese Communists to counteract the effects of American support for Taiwan. It continued through the development of the "one country, two systems" concept, which in theory accepted capitalist components within the main Socialist structure.

Chinese leaders claimed that the "one country, two systems" concept would be a workable solution to the Taiwan question. Two mainland China sources have traced its origins and outlined three phases of its development.[81] The first stage began on the eve of the Third Plenum of the Eleventh Central Committee in December 1978, when Deng Xiaoping proposed "the third CCP-Guomindang collaboration" to achieve the unification of the country. He said Taiwan's socioeconomic system, lifestyle, and foreign investment would remain unchanged, while its military forces would become the local militia. In January 1979, Deng claimed that China would no longer call for the liberation of Taiwan. Instead, it would ask Taiwan to return, and respect the latter's existing system. In this speech, Deng outlined the concept that he would later call "one country, two systems."[82]

On September 30, 1981, Ye Jianying's nine-point policy marked the beginning of the second stage of development. Ye was chairman of the Standing Committee of the National People's Congress (NPC). He called for negotiations between the CCP and Guomindang on an equal footing to implement their third collaboration and together fulfill the task of national unification. Ye said that after China's unification, Taiwan could become an SAR, enjoying a high degree of autonomy and retaining its military. Beijing would not interfere with local affairs. He stated that Taiwan's socioeconomic system, lifestyle, and overseas economic and cultural relations would be unaffected. The right to possess and inherit private capital, housing, land, and corporations would be respected, as would the existing foreign investment.[83]

In January 1982, the "one country, two systems" concept appeared when Deng talked about Ye's nine points. Eight months later, Deng applied the "one country, two systems" concept to the Hong Kong situation in a talk with British Prime Minister Margaret Thatcher.[84] In June 1983, Deng met with Professor Yang Liyu from the United States, and during their discussion asserted that Taiwan would become an SAR. He said that its government would have the right to determine its own internal policies, and that as an SAR, Taiwan would have powers that were not given to provinces, cities, or autonomous regions. In return, it would not take actions detrimental to national unification.[85]

Accepting Deng's report in June 1984, the NPC formally adopted the "one country, two systems" policy, giving it legal recognition. The Sino-British Joint Declaration of 1984 represented the first step in putting the policy into practice. In October 1984, the third stage began with the publication in *Liaowang* of Deng's article, "A Concept of Great Meaning—Deng Xiaoping Talks About 'One Country, Two Systems.'" Chinese sources claim that the "one country, two systems" concept had now become a complete, systematic, and scientific theory. Although it started as a response to the Taiwan problem, it was to be implemented in Hong Kong.[86]

The "new era's patriotic united front" was to operate in Hong Kong. Although Beijing's recovery of sovereignty over Hong Kong in 1997 was a certainty, China faced problems, including the absence of guiding precedents, a reluctant population, legacies of British rule, local opposing and critical opinions, and unavoidable world attention. United front work has been especially important in times of uncertainty, with the need to gain support, identify friends and enemies, and determine the level of intimacy or hostility. Real power depends on a viable administration and high degree of legitimacy. As Beijing had promoted the principle of "Hong Kong people governing Hong Kong" [*Gangren zhi Gang*], staunch supporters were required in Hong Kong and a suitable leadership for the future SAR, which would help maintain the authority of the central government while retaining the confidence in the territory.

10. The Chapters of this Book

This book makes several contributions to the field. First, it fills a gap in the research into Hong Kong's history by offering an in-depth examination of Chinese Communist activities in the territory. Importantly, it looks at the

Communist presence from a new angle—through the united front of the Chinese Communists and Hong Kong capitalists. This also enriches our knowledge of the role of Chinese capitalists in the history of the territory. Second, it sheds light on an aspect of the Sino-Japanese War, namely, how the Communists and the Nationalists (Guomindang) in Hong Kong sought outside support and funding for the war effort. Third, it furthers the understanding of modern Chinese history by tracing the policies of the Chinese Communists (and the Nationalist/Guomindang government) related to Hong Kong and overseas Chinese.

"Hong Kong capitalists" refer in this book to the territory's (mostly Chinese) entrepreneurs, industrialists, and bankers, in short, the elites in the commercial, industrial, and financial sectors. The CCP was looking for people in these sectors who could be used to carry out various tasks at different times. Before the Second World War (1939–1945), the capitalists were seen as possible allies based on Lenin's perception of "national liberation movements" in backward areas.[87] Lenin argued that such movements "could not be truly proletarian because of the relative absence of industrial capitalism," and thus local Communists should work with the "native bourgeoisie" as the latter were also against foreign imperialism.[88] The CCP united front included the bourgeoisie who supported nationalist uprisings.[89]

In June 1949, Mao put an emphasis "On the People's Democratic Dictatorship," claiming that Chinese people comprised the working class, peasantry, urban petty bourgeoisie, and national bourgeoisie.[90] It was announced in the Common Program of September 1949 that China was forming a new democracy, and that all democratic classes should unite against imperialism and strive for the country's prosperity. The CCP sought a united front among the petty and national bourgeoisie, who were instrumental to China's reconstruction. In 1957, Premier Zhou Enlai recognized the significance of the leaders of the industrial and commercial sectors in Hong Kong. He said that Hong Kong entrepreneurs were mostly nationalistic, and targets of the Communist united front.[91] In 1991, the CCP believed that the national bourgeoisie including prominent industrialists, entrepreneurs, and professionals, would constitute the main body of the political system of the future Hong Kong SAR.[92]

This book comprises eight chapters. A part of Chapter 1 is a revised version of a published article, and chapters 2, 3, 4, 5, and 8 are updated, revised, and expanded versions of articles published in international refereed journals. The remaining part of Chapter 1 and chapters 6 and 7 are specially written for this volume. I have used newly published memoirs and recent research findings to update all of the articles, which after much revision and expansion have been increased by one-fourth to one-third of their original length. All of the previously published articles discuss the "united front" theory; hence, this book offers a coherent account of the history of the Chinese Communists in Hong Kong, with a central theme embraced throughout the chapters. Chapter 2 deals with the united front policy of the Chinese Communists in Hong Kong during the Sino-Japanese War. Their ultimate concern was to take advantage of Hong Kong's special position as an outpost that could link them to the outside world. They established united front organizations in the territory to seek and mobilize funds and materials for the war effort in mainland China. This chapter emphasizes that Hong Kong was a unique item on the Communist agenda, a convenient location for communication with Chinese worldwide. The objective was to create a solid united front against Japanese aggression even outside mainland China. This chapter describes the establishment and functions of the Office of the Eighth Route Army in Hong Kong, which was a leading united front organization under the resourceful leader Liao Chengzhi. In addition, it discusses the arrival and contribution of Madame Sun Yat-sen and the leftist writers and journalists in Hong Kong from the late 1930s to 1941. During this time, Liao Chengzhi and the Communists established working relations with Hong Kong businessmen. After the Second World War, the Communists created an industrial business club and invited local businessmen to various functions and talks.

Chapter 3 deals with the period from 1947 to 1984, when the Hong Kong Branch of the Xinhua News Agency carried out overt and covert operations in the territory. As "a question left over from history," Hong Kong was unique. On the one hand, the Chinese Communists refused to acknowledge the unequal treaties concerning Hong Kong, and thus refused to establish a consulate in the territory, which China considered its own. On the other hand, they understood that Hong Kong was an essential source of foreign currencies and continued to practice their previous policy of pragmatism toward the territory. The Chinese Communists were willing to adapt to Hong Kong's capitalist system, as they had during the Sino-Japanese War. Therefore, the Branch functioned as both a news agency and quasi-diplomatic organization for governmental communication. It succeeded in helping the Communists understand colonial capitalism and in clarifying Beijing's policies on the local authorities. More importantly, it followed Zhou Enlai's directives in moving ahead with its united work among the local business, commercial, industrial, and professional sectors. In the 1980s, the Branch became of great significance, and focused on united front work among the bourgeoisie, that is, penetrating the middle classes of Hong Kong society.

Chapter 4 traces the origins of the alliance of the Chinese Communists with Hong Kong's business elite and the establishment of the Basic Law committees in the period from 1979 to 1985. In this period, Beijing's prime concern was reunification, namely, Hong Kong's return to China in 1997. The central government was eager to facilitate a smooth transfer of rule, and thus made concerted efforts to form links with the conservative business sector of Hong Kong. In 1984, Deng Xiaoping asserted that the Chinese Communists were willing to work with Hong Kong capitalists so long as they were patriotic and supportive of reunification. Such efforts would ensure the future "stability and prosperity" of the Hong Kong SAR. Xu Jiatun (director of the Hong Kong Branch of the Xinhua News Agency, 1983–1990) was instrumental to the achievements of the united front among Hong Kong's business community. The Communists saw the "big bourgeoisie" continuing to be the main political force in Hong Kong. Hence, the Basic Law Drafting Committee included many "big capitalists" and tycoons, who represented the opinion of the rich and economically powerful elite of the territory. Very soon, the Business and Professional Group emerged from another body, the Basic Law Consultative Committee. The business elite and professionals were the main targets of Beijing's united front in Hong Kong.

Chapter 5 studies the involvement of the business sector in the drafting of the Basic Law, which would become the mini-constitution of the Hong Kong SAR, from 1985 to 1990. This sector had great influence in the drafting process after the formation of the Basic Law Drafting and Consultative Committees. During this period, the business elite competed among themselves to appease Beijing, which led to problems in the united front effort of the Communists. This chapter looks at the proposals of the Business and Professional Group, Louis Cha, and Cha Chi-ming. Throughout the process, the business elite failed to present themselves as a coordinated and united force in politics. In addition, middle-class professionals looked at the "big bourgeoisie" with distrust; hence, the Chinese Communists had difficulty reaching out to the middle class despite their efforts in working with the "big bourgeoisie." To penetrate into society through the top elite and then to befriend the middle stratum of professionals and businessmen had long been the objective of the united front in Hong Kong. This chapter also discusses the impact of the incident of June 4, 1989, on the Hong Kong elite and public. It examines the formation of the New Hong Kong Alliance, which caused controversy among members of the business elite, and the "Omelco consensus model," which was a response to the public mentality and emotions in Hong Kong.

In the years leading up to 1997, the Chinese Communists succeeded in consolidating big business support for the imminent transfer of rule. Chapter 6 analyzes in detail the formation of "a three-tier" united front in Hong Kong in preparation for the future Communist leadership of the SAR. It considers the lingering impact of the June 4 Incident and the problems of the "Omelco consensus model." It also looks at the eventual success of the Communist united front work in Hong Kong. The Chinese Communists announced several appointments of Hong Kong Affairs Advisers, who advised the State Council's Hong Kong and Macao Affairs Office and the Hong Kong Branch of the Xinhua News Agency. Local Hong Kong Affairs Advisers constituted the middle level of the united front in Hong Kong. To achieve its objectives, Beijing established the Preliminary Working Committee (PWC), which was the forerunner of the SAR Preparatory Committee. Local members of the PWC formed the top layer of the united front structure, and were the most trusted consultants of the Beijing leaders. In addition, this chapter introduces the District Affairs Advisers, who belonged to the bottom layer of the united front supporters. Finally, it describes the objectives and manifestation of Beijing's megaphone diplomacy, which was characteristic of the traditional practices of the united front, to criticize a common enemy to announce the Communist position and consolidate support.

Chapter 7 describes the process to select the future chief executive of the Hong Kong SAR from May to December 1996. It argues that there were issues that concerned both Beijing and Hong Kong people, and that both sides exhibited a great deal of pragmatism in their actions and responses during the selection process. This chapter traces the making of public opinion and the appearance of the "dream team" for the SAR government, namely, the partnership of Tung Chee-hwa and Anson Chan. In addition, it discusses the competition among several other candidates, stressing that public opinion greatly influenced the selection process, as a person low in popularity could not even secure a place in the competition. This chapter reveals that the united front in Hong Kong comprised mainly "big capitalists," whose priority was the maintenance of the status quo, meaning the continued domination of the business elite in local politics. Throughout the process, the united front took a conservative position, with the objective of facilitating the smooth transfer of rule in 1997.

Chapter 8 portrays the last colonial days from December 1996 to June 1997. This chapter shows that poll ratings changed in accordance with the confidence placed in the chief executive-designate, Tung Chee-hwa. His family had longstanding connections with Beijing, and Tung emphasized harmonious relations with the Chinese Communists. He belonged to the core of the Chinese Communist united front in Hong Kong. The front did not pose a threat to the public in general, as a cordial relationship existed between Tung and Beijing. The "pro-Beijing" supporters had proven their ability to work with the Communist leaders. In Hong Kong, people knew who these staunch supporters of the united front were. The only question was whether the united front, which aimed at maintaining Beijing's perception of the "status quo," would bring Hong Kong back to "the old colonial days" when democracy and various freedoms were not even issues of concern. The term "united front" and the practices of front members were not threatening to the people of Hong Kong.

Acknowledgment: A part of this chapter is a revised and updated version of the author's article: "Back to the Masses: The Historiography of Hong Kong's Recent Political Developments and the Prospects of Future Scholarship," *American Journal of Chinese Studies* 10, no. 1 (April 2003): 29–42. The author would like to thank *American Journal of Chinese Studies* for permission to publish this chapter.

The United Front Policy of the Chinese Communists in Hong Kong during the Sino-Japanese War, 1937–1945

1. Introduction

The 1997 handover issue began to trouble Hong Kong in the 1980s, during which time China became involved in the political debates in the territory. Beijing was anxious to keep itself informed about Hong Kong, and to make its views known to the people there. Throughout the decade, Deng Xiaoping announced China's latest policies, while communications of the Hong Kong and Macao Affairs Office of the State Council [HKMAO; Guowuyuan Gang Ao shiwu bangongshi] incited fear, raised hopes, and caused speculation. China also disseminated messages through local organizations in the territory. The Hong Kong Branch of the Xinhua News Agency [HK Xinhua; Xinhuashe Xianggang fenshe] functioned as a mouthpiece of Beijing, as did leftist newspapers, magazines, and companies. The CCP continued its united front work in Hong Kong, where its local branch was known as the Hong Kong and Macao Work Committee [HKMWC; Gang Ao gongzuo weiyuanhui].

Actually the CCP was involved in activities in Hong Kong during the Sino-Japanese War. The Chinese Communists aimed to use the territory as their link to the outside world to achieve their goals. In the late 1930s, they set up united front organizations in Hong Kong to channel resources for the war effort. After 1949, many people returned to mainland China with the hope of contributing to the construction of the new country. When China shut its doors to the world during the Cultural Revolution (1966–1976), Hong Kong was the only opening through which it could obtain foreign currency and material goods. As a borrowed place in a borrowed time, Hong Kong maintained its colonial status because of its utility value to China.[1] Many factors have contributed to Hong Kong's prosperity, the most often cited being the colonial administration in the prehandover period and hardworking character of the local people. Often overlooked is China's behavior: its tolerance of British rule and economic relations with the territory. Even Emily Lau, a journalist-turned-legislator who frequently speaks out against Beijing, acknowledged this in her article in the *Far Eastern Economic Review* in 1985, and seldom has it been so aptly put: "The role of the CCP in Hongkong, said a Hongkong Government source, has to be seen in the light of the territory's political reality. Hongkong's existence has always depended on China's acquiescence."[2]

This chapter focuses on Chinese Communist activities in Hong Kong during the Sino-Japanese War. It emphasizes that the territory was an outpost for the Chinese Communists, linking them to the outside world, and occupied a unique position in their agenda as its utility value was their primary consideration. During the Sino-Japanese War, the official position of the Chinese Communists was to forge an "anti-Japanese national united front" [*kang Ri minzu tongyi zhanxian*], based on the notion that society comprised three kinds of forces: progressive, middle, and conservative. Widely propagated, the united front policy at that time highlighted the need to both "struggle" (against enemies) and "unite" (all possible anti-Japanese forces). The Communists were to develop relations with the progressive forces (the most reliable allies), seek the support of the middle strata, and isolate the conservatives. The united front policy was most accommodating as it involved collaboration with Jiang Jieshi's (Chiang Kai-shek's) Guomindang to achieve the widest possible united front against the Japanese. So long as the party was anti-Japanese, it was regarded as supportive of the Communist war effort. In other words, the Chinese Communists were willing to work with people from different classes, political backgrounds, and communities. The united front policy aimed at creating an alliance with not only the population in mainland China but also Chinese societies overseas,[3] with Hong Kong as the base from which to coordinate anti-Japanese resources from these overseas communities.

This chapter addresses two shortcomings of traditional scholarship. First, there has been little study of early Communist activities in Hong Kong. Beijing tackled the 1997 question from the early 1980s, but this is not to say that the CCP had no prior involvement in Hong Kong, or that its early activities there were insignificant. Second, there has been an ungrounded and biased assumption that until the 1990s, the CCP had no understanding of Hong Kong's capitalist system. Such an assumption overlooks the contact between the Communists and local businessmen in the 1930s. The Chinese

Communists tried to adapt to Hong Kong's capitalist environment, and established a network of organizations and companies in the territory under local party control. They developed a different mentality, or culture, in dealing with Hong Kong matters. The Sino-Japanese War marked the resurgence of CCP activities in Hong Kong. Hence, the Communists had become accustomed to the foreign administration and capitalist system of the territory long before they addressed the 1997 question.

Chan Lau Kit-ching, one of the few scholars to address this topic, argues that the CCP had long been involved in Hong Kong matters even before its victory in 1949.[4] The territory is a special locality in the examination of the Chinese Communist movement in the south China region. Hence, in-depth research into the history of the movement in Hong Kong in the pre-1949 period is necessary: "It is crucial to look at it [this period] from different perspectives, at different levels, and in different localities."[5] This chapter fills in some of the gaps in the understanding of early twentieth-century Hong Kong history on the one hand, and of the regional dimension of the Chinese Communist movement on the other.

2. The Chinese Communist United Front Policy (The Second Guomindang-CCP United Front)

Lyman Van Slyke observes that at the beginning of the Sino-Japanese War, the Guomindang-CCP united front aimed at fighting against the Japanese.[6] During the war years, the CCP "increased its military strength from roughly 30,000 to nearly 1 million, and the people it governed from about 2 million to 96 million."[7] However, toward the end of the Sino-Japanese War, the Communists modified their united front policy, shifting from the original anti-Japanese emphasis to an anti-Guomindang one. Van Slyke points out that the "CCP did so because it had found that [the united front] policy to be valuable. During the years of war, the united front grew in strategic importance until it came to occupy a permanent place in Chinese Communist practice and ideology."[8]

After the outbreak of the Sino-Japanese War, the CCP divided Chinese society into three sectors—the left wing, intermediate section, and right wing of the anti-Japanese national united front.[9] The left wing comprised "the Communist-led masses": the proletariat, peasants, and urban petty bourgeoisie. The top priority of the Communists was to "extend and consolidate this wing" to form a "total resistance" against the Japanese.[10] The middle group was composed of "the national bourgeoisie and the upper stratum of the petty bourgeoisie."[11] According to the Communists, this sector was always wavering, and thus their task was to make it "move forward and change its stand."[12]

The right wing included the big landlords and big bourgeoisie, who were inclined toward "national capitulationism," namely, the surrender of Chinese interests to those of the Japanese and the subjugation of China to foreign imperialists, because they were afraid of "the destruction of their property in the war and the rise of the masses."[13] According to the CCP, "Many of them [the big landlords and big bourgeoisie] are already collaborators, many have become or are ready to become pro-Japanese, many are vacillating, and only a few, owing to special circumstances, are firmly anti-Japanese."[14] Some of them had joined the united front under pressure, and it was assumed that they would break away from it as soon as circumstances allowed. There were also those who tried to split the united front. Hence, the CCP had to "combat national capitulationism resolutely and, in the course of this struggle, to expand and consolidate the left wing and help the intermediate section to move forward and change its stand."[15]

In January 1940, Mao Zedong's tract "On New Democracy" appeared. Van Slyke observes that it was published at a time when the Guomindang-CCP collaboration had begun to crumble. Thus, Mao's intention was not only to situate the united front strategy within a theoretical construct but also to prepare the Communists for the imminent collapse of the alliance.[16] Most importantly, the "rational and moderate tone" of the article revealed the attempt of the Communists to seek a multiclass united front in its struggle for power against Guomindang.

In March of the same year, Mao put forward the CCP's three-thirds system in his essay "On the Question of Political Power in the Anti-Japanese Base Areas."[17] He proposed that, based on united front principles, the Communists should obtain one third of the seats in political organizations, the "non-Party left progressives" another third, and the intermediate sector the remaining third.[18] The united front strategy of the Chinese Communists during the Sino-Japanese War developed around these targets, and was modified based on changing circumstances with the ultimate objective of reaffirming the CCP.

3. Early United Front Organizations in Hong Kong and South China

In early 1937, Hong Kong was already preparing for war, with British authorities conducting a large-scale rehearsal in March involving the military, navy, and air force. Approximately 26,000 personnel participated in the event. This exhibit of warships and fighter planes was intended by the British to project the image that the colony was well equipped for at least self defense.[19] That same month, the Hong Kong government announced a blackout, initially during the early hours from 2 a.m. to 4 a.m.; a subsequent blackout lasted for the entire night. Not only were local Chinese being put on alert and their nationalistic sentiments aroused, they were also being given some idea of the impact that Japanese aggression would have on their livelihoods.

The outbreak of Sino-Japanese hostilities in the northeast of China in July 1937 and conflicts with the Japanese navy in Hong Kong waters further incited popular emotion. Different sectors of society staged anti-Japanese strikes and demonstrations, including printing industry workers and seamen's unions, among others. Seamen and workers on wharves refused to transport or deliver Japanese goods, while workers in foreign firms, metal industries, and coal companies took part in anti-Japanese rallies. In addition, students called for and organized donations for China.[20] In September 1937, university and secondary school students formed a patriotic alliance to solicit resources and promote support for the war effort.[21] With war raging in the interior of China, Japanese troops close to the Hong Kong-China border (they landed in Daya Bay, Shenzhen, in December), and the rising tide of nationalism among the Chinese population, Hong Kong was an open field for the united front work of the Communists to channel resources within the local society for the resistance in mainland China. In other words, the circumstances provided fertile ground for Communist activities in Hong Kong.

3.1. The Office of the Eighth Route Army in Hong Kong

After the outbreak of the Sino-Japanese War in July 1937, the Chinese Communists set up the Office of the Eighth Route Army in Hong Kong [Balujun zhu Xianggang banshichu] in January 1938 to take advantage of the territory's special position to advance their anti-Japanese course. The Office aimed to cultivate favorable foreign opinion and obtain support from Chinese communities in Hong Kong, Macao, and abroad.[22] According to the memoirs of a former Office member, it was established under the direction of the top CCP leadership. Zhou Enlai informed the British ambassador in China, Sir Archibald Clark-Kerr, of the need to have an office in Hong Kong to receive medical, material, and money donations from overseas Chinese [huaqiao]. Zhou said that the Eighth Route and New Fourth armies would dispatch representatives to Hong Kong to collect the donated money, medicine, and even vehicles, as such efforts had yet to be coordinated. On the one hand, the Office would facilitate united front work in Hong Kong, as well as the distribution of supplies to mainland China, and on the other hand, it would use Hong Kong as a base to channel information to Chinese communities overseas, to arouse their concern and solicit funding.

The colonial government knew about the intentions of the Chinese Communists. The Office was originally located at 18 Queen's Road Central, the site of Yuehua Company, which on the surface dealt with the tea trade. The reason for this semi-open position and the use of a company was to avoid infringing upon British "neutrality" in the Chinese resistance against Japan.[23] In 1939, the Office closed the company after some interference from the Hong Kong government, whose intention was to mollify the Japanese. The Office had been organizing anti-Japanese rallies and meetings, and some of its staff members were arrested and detained. The Office continued its work after the closure of Yuehua Company, with its members occupying different positions to conceal their real identities.[24]

The Office maintained only a semi-open profile, but its people were responsible for numerous activities, including correspondence, financial business, propaganda, work with overseas Chinese, donations, transportation, and covert work. The Office was anxious to promote communications with overseas Chinese communities, with a specific aim—to receive external material aid, and occasionally dispatched mail through seamen who had embarked in Hong Kong.[25] The Office's staff members were cautious and abided by stringent directives regarding underground work such as avoiding being photographed, staying away from relatives and friends, and being beware of possibilities of surveillance and interference in their work. From Hong Kong, the Chinese Communists sent people to Southeast Asian countries—Singapore, Vietnam, and the Philippines—to run newspapers to print and distribute propaganda material.[26] The territory was a meeting point or stopover for patriotic youth and professionals from overseas to begin their journey to the interior, to join the Communist movement. In 1938 and 1939, a few hundred patriots "returned to their mother country" through the arrangement of the Office.[27] Hong Kong was the center for the collection of donations, dissemination of information, and discharge of personnel.

The CCP sent Liao Chengzhi and Pan Hannian to Hong Kong to run the Office from its establishment in January 1938 until its closure in January 1942. Some Office members came from the CCP's central departments, and were in charge of local communication and confidential work. However, like the majority of the Office's staff, Liao and Pan had been transferred from Communist organizations in Hong Kong and Guangzhou. During their four-year tenure at the Office, they met with different people, including local and Macao residents, leaders of overseas Chinese communities, representatives of social groups, and foreigners in Hong Kong and Macao.[28] In the late 1970s, Liao became the HKMAO director, and was known among foreigners as "one of the few leaders of China who had an extensive experience of living abroad."[29]

Zhou Enlai sent Liao to Hong Kong because of the latter's ability to conduct united front work with the upper class and overseas Chinese.

Zhou urged Liao to expand the Communist influence in Hong Kong, "a territory the CCP could not lose," and to strengthen united front work there.[30] Also, Hong Kong occupied a geographical location where the Communists could facilitate communication with overseas Chinese in Southeast Asia and even the United States. According to Zhou, the united front work with the elite and prominent personalities in society was a "consistent long-term task."[31]

Having taken part in the Long March, Liao was trusted among the top CCP leadership. Before he took his new position with the Office, he was the director of the Eighth Route Army's Guangzhou office. Liao was appointed to conduct united front work in Hong Kong for a number of reasons. His parents and their families were overseas Chinese, and he had many relatives outside mainland China. Liao's father (Liao Zhongkai) had worked for Dr. Sun Yat-sen, his mother (He Xiangning) was a member of a rich Hong Kong family, and both were renowned Guomindang founders. Because of these various connections, Liao was knowledgeable about foreign matters and the affairs of Chinese in Hong Kong, Macao, and abroad. When overseas Chinese made donations to the Eighth Route and New Fourth armies, they sent money to Liao's Hong Kong bank account, for at that time only a few banks were willing to accept donations for the CCP.[32] Liao was also able to establish relations with the local businessmen, and to secure financial support for his Communist newspaper from banking friends.[33] In short, Liao was the most suitable person to carry out united front work with the upper and middle classes inside and outside China.[34]

Few would dispute the argument that, until his appointment, "Liao Chengzhi's career within the CCP had rested mainly on his personal talents coupled with his family background which had been rewarded by appointments in the field of propaganda and the media."[35] Liao had the ability, willingness, and necessary contacts to conduct united front work in Hong Kong. Upon arriving in the British colony, he followed his instructions to ask local Communists to further mobilize and solidify the united front.[36] Liao was to reach out to the largest possible number of people, from all sectors of society, so long as they did not uphold an anti-Communist stance. Such experience and networks would be valuable to Liao after the war, and in the 1980s in particular, when he became responsible for Hong Kong matters.

Like the anti-Japanese united front work of Mao Zedong in mainland China, that of the Office in Hong Kong covered many areas. Importantly, the Communists in Yan'an had little chance of obtaining external aid, and therefore they were willing to give much latitude to Liao and the Office to seek funding through various activities from Chinese communities in Hong Kong and overseas.[37] Together with the CCP Committee in

Hong Kong [Zhonggong Xianggang shiwei], the Office organized charity functions and encouraged donations. It opened the Hong Kong China News College [Xianggang Zhongguo xinwen xueyuan] and China News Agency [Zhongguo xinwen tongxunshe] in 1939, and trained a number of reporters.[38] The Office had the support of local leftist artists, and sponsored plays and films to promote the war effort. To spread anti-Japanese propaganda and promote an anti-Japanese national united front, it published the *Huaqiao tongxun* [Newsletter for overseas Chinese] for distribution in Southeast Asia.[39] In September 1940, the Office sent a telegram to Yan'an, in which Liao called for more consistent and coordinated propaganda work with overseas Chinese communities.[40]

The Office also worked with the Alliance for the Protection of China [Baowei Zhongguo tongmeng], which was formed by Madame Sun Yat-sen (Song Qingling). Liao, his sister (Liao Mengxing), and a comprador (a close friend of his) were executive committee members of the Alliance. Madame Sun stayed in Hong Kong from 1938 to 1941, and helped raise money for the war effort through such endeavors as the launching of the one-bowl-of-rice movement to provide for people in mainland China.[41] The Alliance printed an English-language newsletter that was distributed throughout Europe, the United States, and Southeast Asia.[42] Occasionally, *Dagongbao* reported on Madame Sun's and the Alliance's appeals for donations of food, medicine, and medical equipment to the interior.[43] Madame Sun also collaborated with cultural circles to organize fundraising performances, movies, and plays. British officials, members of the local Chinese elite, and Guomindang representatives attended the events to show their support for her relief efforts. The money raised was used in China for medical purposes, the Red Cross, the Eighth Route and New Fourth armies, workers, orphans, refugees, and so forth.[44] The Communists had earlier sent Zhou Enlai's wife—Deng Yingchao—to meet with Madame Sun in Hong Kong.[45] This signified that the Office and Communist leaders were well aware of the advantages of combining their efforts with those of Madame Sun and the Alliance.

3.2. Writers and Journalists

From 1939 to 1941, leftist writers and journalists arrived in Hong Kong after escaping from Chinese cities that had been invaded by the Japanese army. They became a force in the territory, and contributed significantly to the anti-Japanese campaigns.[46] In October 1939, they commemorated the late leftist intellectual Lu Xun.[47] Many of them (some of whom were CCP members) joined the Hong Kong branch of the Chinese National Literary Association for War Resistance [Zhonghua quanguo wenyijie kangdi xiehui Xianggang fenhui].[48] The Association had been founded in Hankou by leftist writers in 1938, to coordinate anti-Japanese resistance among literary and cultural circles in Chinese cities. The Hong Kong branch had the same objective—to facilitate local support for the war effort in mainland China. The Communists also reprinted Chongqing's weekly, *Qunzhong* [The people], in Hong Kong, and distributed the magazine abroad for propaganda purposes.[49]

Following the Wannan incident of January 1941, there was another influx of leftist writers into Hong Kong, which included such figures as Xia Yan and others who were familiar with the local cultural circles.[50] They were instrumental in the founding of the newspaper *Huashangbao* [Chinese merchants], which later would compare the Nationalist regime in Chongqing to fascism.[51] These leftist writers, journalists, and their newspaper were closely linked to Liao Chengzhi, who provided them with accommodation and work opportunities, and used *Huashangbao* as a platform to rally Chinese for the anti-Japanese war effort. Although a Communist newspaper, *Huashangbao* did not have a Communist name, to make it more acceptable to both local and overseas Chinese (another leftist publication at this time was *Dazhong shenghuo* [People's life]). Also, the name "*Huashangbao*" pointed to the financial support that the newspaper received from Chinese businessmen in Hong Kong and overseas.[52] It was registered under the name of Deng Wenzhao, who was Liao's cousin and a local businessman well connected in high circles. In April 1941, Liao reported to Zhou Enlai that *Huashangbao* had a circulation of over 5,500, making it the largest evening newspaper in Hong Kong. Nevertheless, it ran a deficit after paying for articles and public relations activities.[53] Publication of *Huashangbao* was suspended during the Japanese occupation of Hong Kong but resumed immediately after the conclusion of the Second World War.

The Communists were supportive of other publications, including famous writer Mao Dun's *Bitan* [To communicate], Yu Songhua's *Guangmingbao* [The light newspaper], the culturists' *Jiuguo yuekan* [Save the nation monthly], Zhang Tiesheng's *Qingnian zhishi* [The youth's knowledge], and Ma Guoliang's *Dadi huabao* [The earth pictorial], among others.[54] In addition, there were concerted efforts to cultivate ties with local newspapers, including *Xingdao ribao*, *Gongshang ribao*, *Huaqiao ribao*, and *Shishi wanbao*.[55] The united front work garnered positive attention from journalists. Mao Dun reported that Liao Chengzhi, the representative of the Chinese Communists in Hong Kong, held regular discussions with newcomers from mainland China on topics related to international politics.[56]

3.3. The CCP Committee in Hong Kong

An incident in 1940 demonstrates two features of Chinese Communist activities in Hong Kong: (1) conflicts existed among the Communists themselves, and (2) in the end, they were cautious of their own profile in the territory. At that time, the CCP Committee in Hong Kong promoted the slogan "Regain Hong Kong" and aimed to start open and regular publications.[57] However, whereas the Office maintained a semiopen position, the CCP Committee remained underground. Both organizations were subsumed under the Southern Bureau [*Nanfangju*], which was in charge of Communist activities in Guomindang-controlled areas and Japanese-occupied territories in south China, and of offices of the Eighth Route Army in Hong Kong and other mainland China cities. Zhou Enlai headed the Southern Bureau, and Liao was one of its thirteen committee members. Thus, the relationship between the Office and local CCP Committee became ambiguous. On the one hand, the former was neither under the direct guidance of nor in open communication with the latter. On the other hand, the two organizations were often supportive of each other. Also, because of his position in the Southern Bureau, Liao had a voice in the CCP Committee. On one occasion, the Office disagreed with the CCP Committee's decision to have open and regular publications, and reported the matter to the Southern Bureau. Zhou later sent a directive to the CCP Committee via Liao, which stated that Communist work in Hong Kong should be "covert but efficient, hiding for some time while gathering strength and waiting for opportunities."[58] It was harmful and reckless for the Chinese Communists to advocate regaining Hong Kong. At the same time, it was unnecessary for the CCP Committee to have open and regular publications. Such conflicts in objectives and authority between different Communist organizations in Hong Kong were characteristic of the relationship between HK Xinhua and the HKMWC in the 1980s.

3.4. The Southern Bureau

In fact, the different lines of authority accounted for many ambiguities and misunderstandings. The situation above is the norm in Chinese Communist history. Disputes among the Communists themselves caused difficulties of united front work. The Communists in Guangxi were also in conflict with each other. The following paragraphs highlight the similarity of problems of united front work in Hong Kong and on the mainland.

Conflicts were characteristic of relations between central and local party organizations, and of the Southern Bureau. During the Second World War, the Southern Bureau tried to dominate the local forces in south China, an example of which is its policy toward Guangxi province, which continues to arouse debate among historians of the Chinese Communist movement. In 1939, the Southern Bureau ended the activities of the Chinese Communist Work Committee in Guangxi [Zhonggong Guangxisheng gongwei]. According to mainland China sources, the decision resulted from the concern to establish united front work with Guomindang's Gui(lin) Faction.[59] The Guangxi Work Committee was formed in November 1936 and came under the Southern Work Committee [Zhonggong nanfang linshi gongwei], which had the authority to appoint its secretaries. For some time, the Communist organizations in Guangxi suffered from sabotage by the Gui Faction. In January 1939, the Southern Bureau established its Guilin Office [Guilin bangongshi], which took over the leadership of the Guangxi Work Committee. Six months later, in July, the Guilin Office ended the Guangxi Work Committee and the policy of cultivating local CCP members.

The main reason for this action was the failure of the Guangxi Work Committee to collaborate with the Gui Faction. In late 1938 and early 1939, Zhou Enlai and Ye Jianying, who headed the Southern Bureau, went to Guilin several times to conduct united front work with the Gui leaders. The Communist leaders believed that the Guangxi Work Committee posed a psychological threat to the Gui Faction, arousing unnecessary suspicions and antagonisms.[60] The lack of effective leadership handicapped the Guangxi Work Committee. Because the group was secretive by nature, rectification of the problem was difficult. Factionalism also burdened its work. Therefore, the Southern Bureau decided to terminate the Guangxi Work Committee.[61]

The Southern Bureau was well equipped for united front work among the masses. Zhou Enlai listed five guidelines for forming grassroots alliances. First, cadres must maintain close connections with the masses. Second, they should organize sub-branches in regional areas and develop all possible resources. Third, local Communist parties should solidify and strengthen their ideological basis and structure, to become truly underground parties of the masses. Fourth, they should infiltrate the masses, and live and work with them. Fifth, they must coordinate both public and private work and communications inside and outside the party. These five points made clear that connections with the masses were fundamental to the party's underground work.[62] In Hong Kong, as noted, the Communists collaborated with labor unions, such as those of tram workers and seamen, in organizing strikes and anti-Japanese rallies.[63]

The Southern Bureau's mass strategy included running its own newspapers, propaganda work, and campaigns.[64] *Xinhua ribao* [The new China daily] is the most obvious example. While *Xinhua ribao* was under the direct control of the Southern Bureau, it obtained legal status even in Guomindang-controlled areas. Its target was the working class, and it reported on their living conditions and demands, acting as a counterforce against Guomindang. In addition, the newspaper promulgated the Communist party line, principles, policies, and fundamental political views, and published many CCP documents. In January 1940, it compiled the commentaries of the Yan'an newspapers and published booklets for distribution, even in Guomindang-controlled areas. The material included the CCP rectification documents and Mao Zedong's essays on a coalition government. In addition to workers, the publications were aimed at young people, and more importantly, intellectuals and progressive elites. *Xinhua ribao* published articles from democratic organizations and the upper and middle classes, to appeal to the largest possible number of people and reduce the support for Guomindang. Zhou Enlai not only headed the Southern Bureau but also wrote for the newspaper and was involved in editorial work.

Celebrating the second anniversary of *Xinhua ribao* in January 1941, Ye Jianying emphasized the importance of gaining popular support. Like Zhou Enlai, he believed that the Communists should secure the sympathy of the greatest number of people to gain the widest possible support. In March 1942, in response to this issue, Mao Zedong asked that the newspaper be made an anti-fascist platform.[65] In the Sino-Japanese War, the Communists were involved in their second united front with Guomindang (at least in theory, after 1940). Thus, they carried out both legal and underground activities. After 1940, their united front was mainly an alliance with the masses to consolidate and expand Communist power. Even the top CCP leadership made an effort to promote the cause. In the Chinese Communist history, local united front activities had always received directives and guidance from the central leadership.

In addition, the CCP made sure that local united front work used proper slogans. An editorial of *Xinhua ribao* in September 1939 entitled "It is Necessary to Implement Democratic Politics" said, "The Chinese Communist Party basically advocated the steady and consistent progression of national political life to that of democratic politics."[66] It asserted that "democratic politics, which the CCP called for in the historical period of the Sino-Japanese War, represented neither the bourgeois democracy in bourgeois countries nor the complete Socialist democracy of the Soviet Union, but the more manageable democracy of the situation."[67] The central leadership paid close attention to local Communist organizations, and was ready to intervene in any aspect of their work.

3.5. Difficulties of the Communist United Front Work

The different lines of command accounted for many of the conflicts among the Communists in their local united front work. In addition, their underground activities became difficult as they tried to avoid antagonizing the local ruling authorities. The desire to expand united front work, together with the need to maintain a certain degree of obscurity, led to different platforms and policies among the Communists. Some favored a moderate approach for fear of arousing unnecessary suspicions, whereas others believed that radicalism was the means to increase their influence in opposition territories. Policy differences could only be resolved by referring them to the highest command. Hence, the central leadership intervened in times of deadlock, conflicts, and power struggles, which often made the situation more confusing and complex.

In addition, the Communists acknowledged shortcomings in leading the local labor movement. They reported that they were involved in strikes of workers at wharves in 1937 and 1938, in which some three thousand workers participated. Publishing company and newspaper workers protested against Japanese aggression.[68] Nevertheless, the Communists admitted that they lacked planning and coordination regarding the labor movement. No consistent attempts were made to organize workers after strikes, and thus momentum was lost. Moreover, the Communists did not offer concrete relief measures to improve the livelihood of workers. In summary, united front work among the working class was piecemeal and uncoordinated.[69]

4. The Counterforce: The Guomindang Presence in Hong Kong

The Communists in Hong Kong not only dealt with the local British administration and later the Japanese occupation forces but also the Guomindang media and counter-united front efforts. Like the Communists, the Nationalists had a long history of activity in the territory. The most obvious form of the Guomindang presence was its newspapers, which received various kinds of patronage and operated under different persons. While the expression "united front" had always been Communist terminology, the publicity work of Guomindang actually represented the same principle, with the objective of rallying support for their own cause.

The origins of Guomindang newspapers in Hong Kong date back to the time of the Guangdong warlord Chen Jiongming, who sponsored *Zhongguo xinwenbao* [China news]. The newspaper was run by Chen Qiulin, who later revolted against his leader and was appointed to Guomindang's supervisory committee. In August 1925, he was shot in Guangzhou. The rise and fall of these figures affected the duration of Guomindang newspapers. In 1930, Wang Jingwei (who later established a puppet government in Nanjing during the Sino-Japanese War) paid for *Nanhua ribao* [South China daily]. In 1932, Hu Hanmin supported *Zhongxingbao* [Restoration], and in 1934, Chen Mingshu founded *Dazhongbao* [The masses].[70]

The first Hong Kong newspaper to be financed by the central authorities of Guomindang was *Guomin ribao* [The Nationalists]. After the outbreak of the Sino-Japanese War, Hong Kong became a base for not only the Communists but also the Nationalists from which to disseminate anti-Japanese propaganda, secure foreign aid, and boost the morale of overseas Chinese. General Tao Baichuan went from Chongqing to Hong Kong to establish *Guomin ribao*, which received the endorsement of Jiang Jieshi, who had earlier discussed its possibility with the General. Its office was in Central district, and in June 1939, the first issue appeared. In December 1941, when Hong Kong fell under Japanese rule, its publication was suspended, as Tao, who was the director of the newspaper, and other Guomindang members returned to Chongqing. After the Japanese surrendered in August 1945, the publication of *Guomin ribao* resumed.[71]

Hong Kong has always attracted both foreign sympathy and criticism. Thus, the Communists and Nationalists alike regarded the territory as an important outpost for propaganda work and obtaining material and financial aid. Hong Kong was also a place where the two parties could gather and make use of the expertise of overseas Chinese. United front work in Hong Kong received attention from leaders of both sides. Hence, local party work was not only a regional matter but also of concern at high party levels.

5. The Japanese Occupation (1941–1945) and the Communist Guerillas

Between October and December of 1941, the British approached Liao Chengzhi and the Office of the Eighth Route Army to see if the Communists could be of assistance in the face of the Japanese threat.[72] The British were willing to collaborate with the Communists in an attack against the Japanese airport in Hainan: the former would send explosives to Guangzhouwan, and in turn, the Office would transfer the supplies to Hainan for the launching of guerila warfare. Liao considered the plan beneficial to the Communists, who would accept armaments, medicine, money, and other material support from the British but avoid taking orders only from the British in any intelligence activities. Liao replied that an office for the guerilas and a radio station were essential in Hong Kong.[73] The negotiations seemed to be progressing well; Liao reported to Yan'an, and received endorsement from Mao Zedong to bomb Hainan's airport.[74] Mao even warned Liao to avoid making excessive demands of the British.[75] On December 7, 1941, Liao sent a telegram to Mao detailing the plans; however, the next day, the Japanese invaded Hong Kong and ended any possibility for the operation.

The Japanese invasion affected the activities of the Communists. The British surrendered to the Japanese in December 1941, and the Office closed in January 1942, at which time, under Liao's command, a number of Communists escaped from Hong Kong together with over eight hundred local sympathizers and families, who were mainly from cultural circles.[76] The Communists had been instructed by Zhou Enlai to carry out the escape, and in February 1942, they reported to him that Liao Chengzhi and others including Mao Dun and Xia Yan had escaped safely to the interior.[77]

During the Japanese occupation, Hong Kong guerillas were active in resistance efforts. In February 1942, they became a subsidiary of the Guangdong People's Anti-Japanese Guerilla Force [Guangdong renmin kang Ri youji zongdui]. Later, the guerillas were known as the East River Column [Dongjiang zongdui].[78] Their headquarters were in Saikung in the New Territories, and they recouped their strength along the Hong Kong-mainland China border. Working among grassroots groups and villages, the Communist guerillas amassed support through self-protection teams, women's groups, youth groups, and so forth. While they gathered information of the enemy, they also provided education for villagers.[79] A local Chinese who joined the guerillas was Huang Zuomei, who was born in Hong Kong and graduated from the famous Queen's College. When the guerillas established their liaison office in 1944, Huang served as a translator and worked closely with the Allies (the Americans and the British). In 1946, Huang received an invitation from the British Crown to represent the guerrillas, and to attend a parade celebrating war victories in London. He was awarded an MBE (Member of British Empire), illustrative of the war alliance between the Communist guerillas and British military.[80] Huang and the guerillas made possible the escape of foreigners (the best known of whom is Lindsay Ride) from Hong Kong during the Japanese occupation.[81]

6. The Establishment of the Hong Kong Branch of the Xinhua News Agency in 1947

Before 1947, the Communists did not have a representative organization in Hong Kong. It was only in the midst of the Chinese Civil War (1945–1949) that the CCP Central Committee set up the Hong Kong Central Branch Bureau [Zhonggong zhongyang Xianggang fenju]. It was established directly under the guidance of Zhou Enlai to coordinate the Communist struggle against Guomindang in south China, and to facilitate communication as the Communists advanced southward.[82] The Bureau had specific objectives: (1) cultivate a base for propaganda through creating networks among cultural circles and sponsoring publications and newspapers; (2) carry out united front work with prominent persons in society; (3) arrange for the return of patriots to mainland China to establish new political authorities; (4) open Ta Teh Institute [Dade xueyuan] for local youths and students from Southeast Asia; and (5) seek opportunities among the grassroots.[83]

Shortly afterward, the CCP also established the Hong Kong Branch of the Xinhua News Agency (HK Xinhua), which began news releases in May 1947. The Agency was established in Yan'an in April 1937 and quickly set up branch offices in many Communist areas to advocate CCP policies and report on local situations. For propaganda reasons, the Agency started English-language broadcasts in 1944. It ran newspapers, publications, and organizations in Guomindang-controlled areas, transmitting news in China and overseas. However, the Civil War resulted in the termination of its operations and publications in Guomindang territories. Thereafter, the Communists relied on Hong Kong as a base for united work with local and overseas Chinese communities, to continue broadcasts through news agencies and connect with outsiders.[84] The British colony had long been a principal site for Communist overseas liaison work. The establishment of the Hong Kong Branch after the Xinhua News Agency could no longer function in Guomindang areas suggests the tolerance of the British of the Communists' presence.

HK Xinhua's director was Qiao Guanhua, whose appointment demonstrated the significance of the Agency.[85] During the Sino-Japanese War, Qiao Guanhua spent some time in Hong Kong and paid close attention to international developments. He wrote the editorial for *Xingbao* [Star], which was well received by local and visiting scholars. Interestingly, the paper belonged to the son of Jiang Jieshi's brother-in-law Kong Xiangxi.[86] When Qiao's criticism of Roosevelt's diplomacy resulted in complaints from Americans, Jiang Jieshi asked for "strict investigation" into the matter.[87] Qiao also wrote for *Shishi wanbao* [Evening news], mainly on international politics. His articles include "New International Development: Discussion about the Growing Intimacy between the British and Russians," and, on the Spanish Civil War, "Mysterious Madrid" and "The Mediterranean Tide."[88] In his article "From the West Front to the East Front," Qiao expressed the usual Communist suspicions, pointing to a Western conspiracy to use the Soviet-Finnish War against the Soviet Union.[89] After Qiao returned to Chongqing, he continued to comment on world affairs, and his articles appeared in the local paper, *Xinhua ribao*.[90] With his background, Qiao's appointment as director of HK Xinhua revealed the significance and perceived difficulties of this Communist front in the territory, the outpost for foreign observers. When HK Xinhua came into being in early 1947, its address was 174 Nathan Road, which had long been the location of Communist organizations; according to some sources, it was the living quarters for the Communists until the Japanese invasion of the territory.[91]

Qiao Guanhua was instrumental in the establishment of contact between the Chinese Communists and foreign authorities. In 1948, Qiao told the British that the CCP would not take Hong Kong by force as the territory was essentially a diplomatic matter.[92] In fact, the Chinese Communists seemed to support Hong Kong capitalism. They set up an industrial business club [*gongshang julebu*], and invited local businessmen to banquets and talks.[93] Zhou Enlai's aims illustrate the Communist position. According to a former party secretary of HK Xinhua, Zhou's goals in 1949 were to recognize the importance of Hong Kong's capitalist system and encourage local nationalist sentiments. The Communists had specific objectives: (1) adjust to Hong Kong's historical situation and reality; (2) understand the mutually beneficial relationship between Hong Kong and China; (3) aim at unification with Taiwan and improved relations with overseas Chinese; (4) fight against the containment policy of Western imperialist countries; and (5) solve the historical problem of Hong Kong in the very long run.[94]

With the founding of the People's Republic of China (PRC) in October 1949, HK Xinhua became the agent of the Beijing government, speaking on behalf of the latter in Hong Kong while continuing as a news agency. On the one hand, the British objected to the establishment of an office of the Beijing government in Hong Kong, to preclude the emergence of two centers of authority locally, the existing one being the colonial administration. On the other hand, Beijing could not tolerate the idea of establishing a consulate in Hong Kong, as the PRC government asserted that Hong Kong was a part of China, and claimed sovereignty over the territory.[95]

7. Conclusion

During the Sino-Japanese War, the Chinese Communists took advantage of Hong Kong's situation. They recognized the utility value of Hong Kong in securing material assistance and cultivating favorable foreign opinion. They tried to adapt to the local environment and establish their own stronghold in the territory. Hong Kong matters demanded special consideration, and required caution, patience, and endurance on the part of the Chinese Communists. As Zhou Enlai repeatedly emphasized, the Chinese Communists recognized the special position and utility value of the territory, and tried to avoid addressing the Hong Kong question in their own political debates. Hong Kong was a unique item among the Communist agendas.

At the same time, the Communists became accustomed to the capitalist environment in Hong Kong. They acquired a different culture in dealing with the local matters of the territory. Whereas mainland China was engaged in ideological revolution, the Communists in Hong Kong were practical and flexible. Long before the emergence of the 1997 issue, the

CCP had experience with and an understanding of Hong Kong affairs. The traditional assumption that the Communists were ignorant about Hong Kong before the 1980s is simply untrue. As this chapter has shown, the CCP was active in the territory during the Sino-Japanese War, and their involvement there requires closer examination.

Acknowledgment: This chapter is an expanded and updated version of the author's article, "The Chinese Communists, Hong Kong, and the Sino-Japanese War," *American Journal of Chinese Studies* 7, no. 2 (October 2000): 131–45. The author is appreciative of the journal's permission for the publication of this chapter.

3

Overt and Covert Functions of the Hong Kong Branch of the Xinhua News Agency, 1947–1984

1. Introduction

Hong Kong, as a British colony, had been unable to conduct independent diplomatic relations. All of its external relations were handled by London. However, since the inception in 1949 of the People's Republic of China (PRC), Beijing had staunchly maintained that Hong Kong by rights was Chinese territory, and publicly refused to acknowledge the original Treaty of Nanjing that had ceded Hong Kong Island to the British. Beijing, therefore, refused to establish a consulate in this territory that it considered its own. At the same time, it recognized that Hong Kong was an indispensable source of foreign currencies and adopted a pragmatic policy toward capitalism.

As it had no direct relations with Hong Kong for thirty-three years (1949–1982), the Beijing government dealt with the British Hong Kong government in a roundabout fashion through London or the Hong Kong Branch of the Communist-controlled Xinhua News Agency (HK Xinhua), which provided a clandestine but also more direct link. Thus, HK Xinhua became an important conduit of relations between Beijing and Hong Kong in two ways: overtly, it functioned as a news agency, bringing information from the outside world to China and news of activities inside China to Hong Kong; covertly, it operated as a quasi-diplomatic channel for government exchange. HK Xinhua aided the Communists in understanding the local capitalist society while helping accustom local society to some of the central government's policies and personnel. Thus, it acted as a kind of lubricant to familiarize capitalist Hong Kong with Communist ways and accustomed the Communists on the other side of the border to capitalism.

HK Xinhua facilitated the unofficial relations between the British colonial government and Beijing—for the former, it was a source of information about Beijing's positions; for the latter, it was the mouthpiece of the CCP. Although HK Xinhua did not have the official status of a representative organization, it assumed virtually equivalent responsibilities. As one indicator of its significance, high-ranking Chinese officials were usually appointed to the news agency, including its former director Xu Jiatun, who was a member of the CCP's Central Committee, the highest decision-making body of the Chinese Communists.

Although formally never more than a news organization, HK Xinhua coordinated many leftist activities inside the colony; on the other side, within the CCP itself, it encouraged a mutually acceptable working relationship with the local Hong Kong capitalists. Beijing benefited from the successful adaptation of HK Xinhua to the capitalist environment.[1] HK Xinhua's many years of covert activities enabled close relations between Beijing and Hong Kong's business elite, who dominated local politics. By the 1980s, Beijing had come to rely on this group to support unification. This strategy guided the activities of HK Xinhua, which also helped strengthen such thinking.

This chapter examines the activities of HK Xinhua in its dual function as a diplomatic liaison and collaborator with Hong Kong capitalists. Britain was able to hold on to Hong Kong without interference for so long because of the colony's usefulness to China. The larger Communist regime could have engulfed the tiny capitalist city at any time; instead, Hong Kong grew and prospered with the Communist regime just on its doorstep for almost half a century. By tracing the activities of HK Xinhua, this chapter argues that the CCP took a practical view of Hong Kong and the local capitalists long before Beijing openly advocated the "one country, two systems" concept.

In a meeting in September 1982, Deng Xiaoping discussed the issues at hand with the British prime minister Margaret Thatcher, and both sides agreed on the joint objective of maintaining Hong Kong's "stability and prosperity."[2] Negotiations over the sovereignty of Hong Kong continued until September 1984, and three months later Beijing and London signed the Sino-British Joint Declaration announcing the return of Hong Kong to China in 1997. The two sides then established formal channels of intergovernmental communication that superseded the informal functions of HK Xinhua.

2. The Early Years of HK Xinhua, 1947–1958

The Xinhua News Agency was established as an official party mouthpiece in April 1937 at the Chinese Communist headquarters in Yan'an, a town in the northwestern province of Shaanxi where the Communist government had its headquarters during the Sino-Japanese War and the Civil War. The agency later opened various branch offices to spread Communist propaganda and local news. In 1944 it instituted English-language broadcasts to appeal to foreign observers. Subsequently, Zhou Enlai decided to start the Hong Kong branch to redirect much work in Guomindang areas to the colony.[3]

Taking advantage of the opportunity to reach an outside audience, its Hong Kong branch began news releases in May 1947 under the leadership of Qiao Guanhua, who in 1971 became China's delegate to the United Nations.[4] As a British colony, Hong Kong was officially neutral during the Chinese Civil War, but both the Communists and the Nationalists tried to win the colony's sympathy and support. HK Xinhua promoted the Communist effort and competed with the Guomindang news agency in reporting the military situation to overseas spectators. The CCP promised that it would honor Hong Kong's neutrality, emphasizing the colony's unique position, and swore never to attempt to take Hong Kong by force.[5]

Immediately after its establishment in 1947, HK Xinhua launched united front work in the commercial and industrial sectors of Hong Kong. It was following the directives of Zhou Enlai, who had stressed that capitalists were the chief targets of the local united front effort.[6] It was to open up this field of work that had been temporarily halted during the Japanese occupation following the escape from Hong Kong of Chinese Communists and intellectuals led by Liao Chengzhi. With the Communist front of HK Xinhua in Hong Kong, the work with local capitalists moved into high gear. The progression of the Civil War in 1947 also witnessed the relocation from mainland China to Hong Kong of the leaders of democratic parties and intellectuals, some of whom provided links between HK Xinhua and the local businessmen.[7] The Communists also established a college known as Ta Teh Institute [Dade xueyuan], which lasted for only a short time, from 1946 to 1949, with the motive of soliciting the expertise of intellectuals and culturalists who had moved to Hong Kong because of the ongoing Civil War in mainland China.[8]

The Communists came to understand the Hong Kong situation, and categorized the local capitalists according to their place of origin: the "Guangzhou (Canton) clique," which ran the biggest businesses in Hong Kong, the "Xiamen clique," which had close ties with overseas Chinese in Southeast Asia, the "Sichuan clique," and the "Jiangsu-Zhejiang clique."[9] HK Xinhua established a target force for the united front work, and members included people with positions in local enterprises, which gave them access to chambers of commerce and clubs. This target force had a Chaozhou member who participated in activities of the Chaozhou club, and a Kejia (Hakka) member who worked with the Kejia businessmen. Thus, through kinship ties, business connections, and dealings with local social groups, the Communists infiltrated Hong Kong society and developed networks. United front work was most successful through personal contacts, not political propaganda.

Through these activities, the CCP seemed tacitly to support the capitalist economy in Hong Kong, if only for political purposes. The Communists set up an industrial business club in Hong Kong and invited businessmen to banquets and talks.[10] The club was registered with the Hong Kong government in 1948 and located on Connaught Road West. At the club's weekly dinners, prominent intellectuals held discussions with local businessmen on current issues. United front work was conducted by not only the Communists but also those recently arrived leaders of democratic parties and intellectuals. Until its closure in spring 1949, the club functioned as a rallying point for the Communists, their sympathizers, neutrals, patriots, culturalists, capitalists, and others to confer on the war situation and economic conditions in mainland China.

During the Civil War, HK Xinhua did not cover local Hong Kong events for the Chinese press. Instead, its primary task was to record telegraphic dispatches from the mainland and then send out news releases to local and overseas newspapers. At that time, it distributed the *Xinhua News Agency Daily News Release* in both Chinese and English, and in Hong Kong, leftist newspapers such as *Wenhuibao* carried the Xinhua News Agency's mainland releases.[11] The Communists also published their English-language journal—*China Digest*—for distribution overseas.[12]

Zhou Enlai was in charge of the Communists in Hong Kong. As recollected by a former party secretary of HK Xinhua, Zhou recognized the importance of Hong Kong's capitalist system and at the same time encouraged patriotic sentiment. In 1949, he outlined these principles: to adapt to Hong Kong's situation and reality; to recognize the mutually beneficial relationship between Hong Kong and China; to foster the long-term goals of unification with Taiwan and improvement of relations with overseas Chinese; to take advantage of Hong Kong as an opening to foreign trade to fight against America's containment policy; and in due course to solve the historical question of Hong Kong.[13] The ultimate goal was the reunification of Hong Kong with China proper.

The Communists in Hong Kong sometimes advocated radical action, but Beijing warned against overt violence. After the Korean War broke out in June 1950 and the United States sent the Seventh Fleet to the Taiwan Strait to protect the Nationalist government from invasion, CCP members in Hong Kong saw the colony as a symbol of national humiliation. They had doubts about the continuance of British rule in Hong Kong and of such insult.[14] In response, Zhou emphasized the advantages of maintaining Hong Kong's present situation. First, the territory was useful for Beijing's united front effort in rallying all possible forces; second, Hong Kong served as a "window" for China to the outside world, a "watch tower, a weather station and a bridge tower" through which to break the Western embargoes against China. According to Zhou, the Communists should even "protect the present Hong Kong situation and status, including its British colonial economy and capitalist system."[15]

When Beijing wanted to establish "an official representative" in Hong Kong, the British objected to the idea for fear of two centers of authority, and counterproposed establishing a PRC consulate in the colony. To the central government, however, this would implicitly acknowledge Hong Kong as a part of British territory, and since it in principle claimed sovereignty over Hong Kong, a consulate was unacceptable. The compromise was that HK Xinhua would serve as Beijing's unofficial representative while outwardly maintaining the status of a news organization.[16] On many occasions, when China's Ministry of Foreign Affairs wished to file a protest with the British, HK Xinhua contacted the Hong Kong government. However, whereas foreign consulates communicated with the British governor's political adviser, HK Xinhua was allowed to contact only the police's special branch that dealt with local political activities. The single exception was an incident in March 1968 when the police detained several HK Xinhua reporters. In response to this incident, HK Xinhua for the first time reached the governor's political adviser.[17]

If included geographically in China proper, Hong Kong would be situated in the southern portion of Guangdong province, and Guangdong therefore claimed authority over matters involving Hong Kong. From 1949 to 1957, HK Xinhua was mainly subordinate to the Guangdong provincial government. The State Council's Foreign Affairs Office was under the leadership of its first deputy head, Liao Chengzhi, and supervised the Hong Kong and Macao group and propaganda group that handled Hong Kong matters.[18] Directives sent out by the State Council's Foreign Affairs Office passed through Guangdong officials before being forwarded to Hong Kong. Huang Zuomei, a local Chinese from Hong Kong, succeeded Liao as HK Xinhua's director and led the branch until 1955, when he was on the way to Bandung Conference and died in a plane explosion engineered by Guomindang. At this point, HK Xinhua did in fact function as a news agency, although it occasionally served as Beijing's representative in communicating to the Hong Kong government.[19]

At the end of the central government's First Five-Year Plan in 1957, local Hong Kong Communists, who were increasingly familiar with the principles of the CCP, questioned whether they should continue to work hand in glove with the local capitalists while Beijing was eliminating private ownership in mainland China. Again, Zhou Enlai said that Hong Kong's situation was different from that of Shanghai, for example, where the industrial and business communities followed CCP policies. Hong Kong, he maintained, could survive only under its present capitalist system. Its continued survival was advantageous to China, which used Hong Kong as a base to maintain economic relations with the outside world and to obtain foreign currencies. Even after the Great Leap Forward (1958–1960), when many Guangdong residents fled to Hong Kong to escape economic difficulties, Zhou assured the people of Hong Kong that it would be business as usual for the colony.[20]

More importantly, Zhou emphasized, Mao Zedong and others in the top CCP leadership had agreed to cooperate with the local business elite. The CCP supported a united front policy favorable toward Hong Kong capitalists, with whom its leaders hoped to work in the future. The term "united front" stemmed from the days when the CCP and Guomindang had joined forces in opposition to the warlords in the 1920s and the Japanese invasion of China in the 1930s. In practice, the strategy called for forming alliances with supporters of all kinds; winning the hearts of neutrals; and isolating and eventually destroying Chinese enemies. In their own words, the Communists would "make friends with" [*jiao pengyou*] all those who did not explicitly oppose them. In Hong Kong, the united front policy referred to an accommodation reached between Socialist principles and capitalist practices. As Zhou pointed out, the Communist position was to help maintain the status quo in Hong Kong, and to acknowledge the patriotic sentiment and friendship of local capitalists. The Communists in Hong Kong, according to this policy, would concentrate on propaganda work while still cooperating with the local capitalists. Thus, local party members needed to be flexible in handling the existing situation. Slow and gradual infiltration and continuous propaganda were crucial.[21]

The CCP also wanted to work with Hong Kong capitalists to use the colony as a base to circumvent the economic blockade on China that many anti-Communist Western nations had established after l949. Zhou stressed two points: first, the capitalist system of Hong Kong should be preserved; second, Hong Kong entrepreneurs were patriotic and friends of the Communists.[22] These points became the guidelines of Communist infiltration into Hong Kong. Western embargoes made Hong Kong "an all-important middle ground" for material goods for China; therefore, the support of local businessmen was critical.[23]

3. HK Xinhua, 1958–1966

HK Xinhua was originally established in the colony as a news agency that dealt with political matters only in times of need. After the death of Huang

Zuomei in 1955, HK Xinhua did not have a new director until 1958. During the interim, HK Xinhua was headed by its chief editor.[24] However, under the branch's third director, Liang Weilin, who held the position from 1958 to 1978, the agenda changed, and HK Xinhua became involved in political work while retaining its news reporting function as a cover. It was responsible for coordinating Communist work in the territory and uniting leftist organizations, truly becoming a Communist front. To deal with the shift in priorities, it was divided into two branches. The chief bureau, which was engaged in the promotion of political activities and major tasks, was the "bigger branch" [da fenshe]; a subordinate office, which reported and disseminated news, became the "smaller branch" [xiao fenshe]. The two sections were under separate authority, although those personnel who were not involved in journalism were still known as reporters. HK Xinhua also moved from Kowloon to a new address on Hong Kong Island.

The Xinhua News Agency's Beijing headquarters continued to supervise the news section, but the authority over the bigger branch is unclear. Some observers argue that, as in the past, the political branch was under the control of Guangdong provincial officials, whereas others maintain that it was directly administered from Beijing. An issue of a Hong Kong magazine run by former employees of a leftist newspaper argues that HK Xinhua was directly supervised by the State Council's Foreign Affairs Office, while Guangdong was in effect the home front.[25] The Foreign Affairs Office assumed overall responsibility over HK Xinhua, and Guangdong no longer ensured contact between Beijing and the Chinese Communists in Hong Kong.

HK Xinhua continued to grow during the 1960s, when Hong Kong's importance as a base from which China could conduct indirect diplomatic activities with foreign consulates became clear.[26] Two new deputy directors—Liang Shangyuan and Zhu Manping—were appointed at the behest of the PRC's Ministry of Foreign Affairs and the State Council's Overseas Chinese Affairs Committee, respectively. Liang was responsible for managing HK Xinhua's external matters, while Zhu was to establish links with Chinese abroad. Their appointment consolidated the role and image of HK Xinhua as China's representative in the colony. Liang was familiar with the local situation, having worked in Liao Chengzhi's Office of the Eighth Route Army in Hong Kong. It is important to note that Liang was the first high-ranking official assigned from the Ministry of Foreign Affairs to Hong Kong, which indicates that the Communists recognized that the colony was a favorable meeting point of foreign diplomats. The British acknowledged the Communist move; nevertheless, Liang did not enjoy the status of a diplomat in Hong Kong. Following the established practice, he could only contact the police's special branch for political activities, not the governor's political adviser.

To the Chinese Communists, Hong Kong was the south door of China through which Beijing carried out a Hong Kong policy of "long-term utilization."[27] Business conducted through Hong Kong provided much-needed foreign currencies to China, and in return China allowed water and other necessities to be supplied from the mainland. Trade from Hong Kong between 1961 and 1972 earned five billion U.S. dollars for China—a significant source of foreign-exchange income.[28]

4. The Cultural Revolution, 1966–1976

In 1966, Mao Zedong launched the Cultural Revolution, ushering in a decade of leftist extremism and turmoil that devastated Chinese society until his death in 1976. Young recruits called Red Guards were encouraged to struggle against the so-called four olds: old thoughts, old culture, old customs, and old habits. During this period, the Revolutionary Leading Small Group established within the Foreign Affairs Office (of the State Council) superseded the original Foreign Affairs Office, and Foreign Affairs Office officials were forced to leave their original positions. Those who dealt with Hong Kong were assigned to the Ministry of Foreign Affairs' Western Europe desk, which until 1977 was responsible for chaperoning visitors from Hong Kong.[29]

HK Xinhua itself became a victim of the Cultural Revolution when two of its deputy directors, Liang Shangyuan and Zhu Manping, who had earlier been appointed by the Ministry of Foreign Affairs and the State Council respectively, were indicted. Liang, whose previous assignment had involved overseas Chinese communities during the Sino-Japanese War, was accused of having connections with Taiwan. Both Liang and Zhu were dismissed. Beijing did not find replacements until 1973, by which time communication between Beijing and the CCP in Hong Kong had broken down, jeopardizing HK Xinhua's dual mission.[30] As the Ministry of Foreign Affairs in Beijing paid little attention to Hong Kong, the Guangdong Military Committee assumed responsibility for sending directives to HK Xinhua. The Second Military Small Group in Guangdong provided assistance to Communists in Hong Kong, and chaperoned visitors from Hong Kong and Macao, who were usually from their local unions, schools, and the film industry. These people were responding to the Cultural Revolution, and were the "patriotic masses" and "revolutionary masses" infected with revolutionary fervor. At this time, Guangdong rather than Beijing monitored Hong Kong matters. Social unrest attributed to local Communists in the colony further damaged HK Xinhua's image as it was known to have a hand in party affairs. Although the British Hong Kong government arrested the owners and editors of some local leftist newspapers, it left HK Xinhua alone.[31]

Communist supporters in Hong Kong, emulating the Red Guards, incited several disturbances that came to the attention of radical authorities in Beijing and Guangdong, who were themselves commanding Hong Kong union leaders to confront the colonial government through the instigation of labor crises detrimental to the legitimacy of the administration. In June 1967, the leftist newspaper *Dagongbao* announced that over 50,000 Red Guards, radicals, and people in Guangdong had set up a committee to support rebels in Hong Kong. There was mention of rallies of these people in Guangdong for the cause in Hong Kong and the 1925 Guangdong-Hong Kong Strike, to illustrate the historical bonding of radicals in both places.[32] *Dagongbao* also called attention to the local "Hongkong and Kowloon Struggle Committee's" denunciation of the "atrocities" committed by the colonial authorities against the workers.[33] It reported demonstrations of a People's Liberation Army unit stationed at Shataukok on the mainland side of the border. The army men held Mao's red book and shouted slogans against British rule in Hong Kong.[34]

However, Mao Zedong virtually disregarded the 1967 Hong Kong riots. Richard Evans, British ambassador to China from 1984 to 1988, points out that Mao did not "play any part in promoting the destruction of the British mission in Peking [Beijing] by a mob after the British government had rejected an ultimatum about the treatment of demonstrators in Hong Kong."[35] Nor did Mao attempt to exploit the unrest to gain control of Hong Kong or Macao.[36] According to Evans, Mao was not as troubled about the reunification issue as were some local Communists, and was willing to live with the "'stinking privy' of Hong Kong at the bottom of its garden."[37] Whereas radicals in mainland China protested against the British imperialist presence in Hong Kong and urged Communists there to take matters into their own hands, the supreme leader did not appear to be concerned about the colony. By September 1967, however, even the mainland radicals had lost interest, and the Hong Kong Communists were left on their own.[38]

The Hong Kong government was aware that local Communists were disillusioned by "the continued lack of support" from Beijing.[39] Leftist publishers, editors, and reporters had become targets of the colonial authorities. Communist premises on Connaught Road Central and out in Taipo in the New Territories were searched by police.[40] Also, from September 1967 onward, the local Communist press continued to have trouble with the government. In September, a *Dagongbao* reporter took matters into his own hands, forcing his way into the Court, and caused a disturbance. Inside the Court, his counterparts from *Jingbao* and *Wenhuibao* shouted protests and were arrested. Demonstrators often submitted HK Xinhua's head office as their address to the police's special branch.[41] At the same time, the colonial government was concerned about the so-called mosquito broadsheets, which it described as either from "enthusiastic amateurs" or a "planned attempt to encourage and guide activities of a terrorist nature."[42] It believed that the existing regulations against inflammatory posters and actions against the "sensitive" Communist quarters, where these leaflets were printed, were possible solutions to the problem. To forestall further incitement of such activities, the government considered passing emergency regulations against Communist broadcasters and press.[43] It had earlier sentenced Communist reporters to imprisonment. Even proprietors of leftist printers were sent to jail, and their companies were fined or ordered to close down.[44] There were many such incidents, which became matters of discussion between the Hong Kong government and London's Commonwealth Office.

Despite their anti-British feelings, the Hong Kong rioters never publicly called for the return of the territory to China. The Cultural Revolution sputtered to an end some ten years later and had little further effect on Hong Kong save for the thousands of refugees who crossed the border into the colony to seek refuge. Some of these were repatriated, but others were tacitly allowed to stay to provide Hong Kong's famously cheap labor.[45]

5. Post-Cultural Revolution, 1976–1984

When a semblance of peace had returned to mainland China, Hong Kong resumed its role in China's economic and diplomatic relations. Wang Kuang replaced Liang Weilin as director of HK Xinhua in the summer of 1978, signifying the beginning of a new era. In the same year, the supervision of HK Xinhua was transferred from Guangdong authorities back to Beijing, where a new bureau was established—the Hong Kong and Macao Affairs Office (HKMAO) under the directorship of Liao Chengzhi. The bureau assumed the status of a State Council department.[46] Nevertheless, conflicts soon developed between Beijing and HK Xinhua.

According to a mainland publication on China's united front, the new HKMAO received directives from the State Council and formulated guidelines and policies for Hong Kong and Macao. Although the HKMAO was a regular bureau located in Beijing, it supervised the Hong Kong and Macao Work Committee (HKMWC), which was actually the local CCP organization. The HKMAO reported economic conditions in Hong Kong and Macao to the State Council. More importantly, it handled all political, cultural, and economic activities in Hong Kong and Macao, and conducted united front work with both grassroots and upper-class organizations.[47] This Chinese source explains that the HKMAO "coordinated and administered the various types of work on Hong Kong and Macao, helped the Central [government] lead the Hong Kong and Macao Work Committee

[HKMWC] in united front work with the grassroots and the upper class, nationalistic cultural propaganda and education, party, and cadre work."[48] In addition, the HKMAO supported the economic activities, organizations, and personnel of mainland authorities in Hong Kong, and looked after cultural, sports, academic, and scientific exchanges between mainland China and Hong Kong. For some time, the HKMAO also tackled Hong Kong matters related to foreign governments, Taiwan, and overseas Chinese communities.

The establishment of the HKMAO was actually a conciliatory move toward resolving the Hong Kong problem, which had preoccupied both the British and Chinese from the late 1970s onward. Because the issue of Hong Kong's return to mainland China in 1997 was highly sensitive, the HKMAO remained covert for some time to avoid unnecessary speculation from the British and the Hong Kong government. Beijing did not reveal the existence of the HKMAO until 1983. After focusing on the Sino-British negotiations that resulted in the 1984 Joint Declaration, the HKMAO proceeded to the business of the Basic Law. It was separate from the Hong Kong and Macao Affairs Office of the Ministry of Foreign Affairs, which was formed in 1985 and lower in rank. The HKMAO dealt with the internal affairs of Hong Kong and Macao, while its counterpart in the Ministry of Foreign Affairs handled diplomatic matters related to the two colonies.[49]

HK Xinhua served as an umbrella for local leftist organizations and a conduit for the HKMAO. While Wang Kuang was HK Xinhua's director, it operated under the direction of the HKMAO, which was headed by Liao Chengzhi. Liao was very familiar with Hong Kong matters and outranked Wang. When Liao died suddenly in 1983, Ji Pengfei was appointed from Beijing to succeed him. Ji, in contrast, was unfamiliar with the situation in Hong Kong, and therefore relied heavily on his HKMAO staff for advice. At that time, Li Hou and Lu Ping were among the HKMAO personnel, and well acquainted with everyday matters related to Hong Kong. In 1983, Xu Jiatun, an official senior to Wang Kuang, Li Hou, and Lu Ping, was appointed to head up HK Xinhua. Although Ji was senior to the HK Xinhua chief in the governmental hierarchy, he and Xu were CCP members of equal status. Under such circumstances, the HKMAO under Ji in Beijing found it difficult to control HK Xinhua, now under Xu in Hong Kong.[50]

6. Xu Jiatun: Director of HK Xinhua

When Xu Jiatun was appointed director of HK Xinhua in 1983, he was the first secretary of Jiangsu province, and had been among the leadership there for twenty-seven years. According to Xu's memoirs published in Taiwan in 1993 and in Hong Kong in 1994, Deng Xiaoping personally agreed to his appointment to the Hong Kong post. Xu recalled meeting Deng alone and reporting directly to him for the first time in Suzhou. Although the interview had been scheduled for only twenty minutes, Deng was so impressed with Xu's leadership and the progress of reform in Jiangsu that the conversation lasted for more than two hours. Deng had the ultimate say on Hong Kong matters, and definitely on the assignment of someone to the important position of director of HK Xinhua. With Deng's blessing, Xu assumed a status higher than that of his predecessors and could communicate directly to Deng on Hong Kong affairs.[51] As the new chief of HK Xinhua, Xu's official title was director, but his real occupation was to be secretary of the local CCP, namely, the HKMWC, and overall supervisor for the Beijing government in Hong Kong. The HKMWC was given provincial status after Xu's appointment, implying that the status of HK Xinhua would rise correspondingly.[52]

At first glance, Xu's appointment seems an anomaly. HK Xinhua's previous directors had been Cantonese, whereas Xu, who came from Jiangsu, could not even speak the Cantonese dialect. Further, he had no experience in Hong Kong, no diplomatic experience, and was already sixty-seven when he took the post. Former directors including Wang Kuang and Liang Weilin were from Guangdong, whereas Xu's experience in Jiangsu was unrelated to Hong Kong. At the time of the Sino-British negotiations, the media had doubts about his ability to cope with the complicated issues.[53] In his memoirs, Xu admitted the difficulties of the job: he had lived most of his life in mainland China and had to start a new career at retirement age. However, as a member of the CCP Central Committee, he could communicate directly with Beijing. He had a high profile politically, and his appointment reflected the importance of the Hong Kong question to the Chinese government. Observers in Hong Kong were surprised by Xu's appointment but noted that his qualifications (provincial first secretary) exceeded those of his predecessors.[54] As HK Xinhua had been directly under the State Council, its status was already equivalent to that of a top-ranking, centrally controlled city organization in mainland China. Xu's rank (as a Central Committee member and provincial leader) guaranteed him respect even among top party officials; undoubtedly, HK Xinhua's position and significance would rise.[55]

Xu proved to be a skillful practitioner of united front policies. In an interview published in the leftist magazine *Guangjiaojing yuekan* [*Wide Angle* monthly] shortly before his appointment, Xu stated that he hoped to create a bridge between the State Council and local community to ensure mutual communication, and to match the policies of the Beijing government with Hong Kong's practical situation. He was aware that the retention of old departments, titles, and personnel from the Cultural Revolution had caused problems in the organization and confused political activities with journalism.[56] Within his first year, Xu had decisively restructured the organization. He announced four transformations, revolution, rejuvenation, specialization, and intellectualization, and appointed new and younger personnel so that the average age of HK Xinhua officers dropped from 65 to 55. He streamlined the branch's internal structure and reduced the number of deputy directors. Another innovation was to employ younger Hong Kong residents, one of whom was Chung Shui-ming, a chartered accountant, University of Hong Kong graduate, and Sino-British Land Commission member.[57]

Most important was Xu's decision to move HK Xinhua's news section from its headquarters in Wanchai to a new location, thus clearly separating the political and journalism spheres. He announced that HK Xinhua was in fact more than a news agency: it was China's representative in Hong Kong. By 1987, its structure, comprising departments, divisions, and district offices, had become public knowledge. Under the director there were now four deputy directors. The titles of the departments—including research, propaganda, culture and education, arts and sports, economics, social work, coordination, external affairs, administration and management, and personnel—finally represented their actual functions. In addition, HK Xinhua established branch offices in Central and other localities.[58]

As a CCP Central Committee member, Xu Jiatun was the most senior party official ever to have worked in Hong Kong. He had impressive credentials stretching back to 1956, when as a top official in Jiangsu he had been praised as the youngest provincial leader in the nation. However, during the Cultural Revolution, he was labeled "a capitalist roader," and like a great many of the more moderate party officials, disappeared from view. Xu did not reappear in politics until the 1970s, when he was appointed to the prestigious position of first secretary of Jiangsu, which he held until 1983.[59]

Under Xu's leadership, HK Xinhua changed from being a covert to an open organization. Talking to reporters, Xu said that he hoped to satisfy local concerns while contributing to the ultimate unification of Hong Kong with China.[60] Immediately upon arriving in Hong Kong, he spoke with the leftist media, including the newspapers *Wenhuibao* and *Dagongbao*, offices, schools, trading firms, and banks. In appearance he changed from looking like a typically remote Chinese official with sunglasses, untidy hair, and ill-fitting clothes to an approachable and energetic public figure. In his memoirs, Xu mentioned that he bought new glasses and suits.[61] He showed up at various public events, including banquets, sport competitions, and theatrical performances. Instead of closing HK Xinhua's doors to the outside, Xu made the unusual move of inviting guests to its headquarters.

He spoke to many groups, such as University of Hong Kong students, the Lions Club, university alumni, and the Hong Kong General Chamber of Commerce. The media formed an impression of Xu as an official who was always willing to cooperate, and who even sent gifts of fruit baskets to journalists critical of Beijing.[62]

7. The United Front Strategy

HK Xinhua was connected with major PRC commercial organizations in Hong Kong including the China Merchants Steam Navigation Company and China Resources, and local trade unions and leftist bodies. It was also affiliated with the Bank of China's Hong Kong branch, whose new skyscraper designed by the Chinese-born American architect I. M. Pei soon towered over other tall buildings in the territory. The chief executives of these commercial organizations had long been represented in the local CCP—the HKMWC—and had direct access to their superiors in Beijing. They acted with a certain degree of autonomy in economic matters.[63] Leftist enterprises came to play an increasingly important role in the local economy and had close connections with the top Hong Kong business elite in the 1980s.

As some Hong Kong journalists observed, Xu's united front policy aimed to create an alliance with the upper-class capitalists and thus secure upper-middle-class support for the future takeover of Hong Kong.[64] With the commencement of Sino-British talks in July 1983, Beijing realized that there would be a long period of diplomatic negotiation prior to the final retrocession of Hong Kong. To ensure a smooth transition to Chinese rule, it sought to ally itself with the traditional pillars of Hong Kong society, namely, the business establishment. Zhou Enlai had emphasized the importance of developing a working relationship with Hong Kong capitalists, and now the CCP finally put his guidelines into effect. As Xu noted in his memoirs: "I therefore raised in the Hong Kong and Macao Work Committee [in 1983] that we should employ our 'resources' to cultivate a group of pro-China capitalists in Hong Kong and Macao. China's enterprises in Hong Kong needed not be afraid of criticisms, and should contribute toward this directive. Moreover, [they] had to make use of the 'resources' from the mainland—these were even larger 'resources'—in order to secure the hearts of the people and contribute toward the prosperity and stability of Hong Kong."[65] On another occasion, Xu insisted that "the middle class was the chief target of the struggle for the united front work." He hoped to use the united front strategy to achieve the support of the "big bourgeoisie."[66] Once such capitalists were willing to work with the CCP, he concluded, the middle stratum would follow. The local business leaders were therefore the top priority of the Chinese Communists in Hong Kong.

Hence, Beijing deliberately cultivated pro-China capitalists in Hong Kong. Xu believed that the political orientation of Hong Kong capitalists was often connected with their business concerns. Whereas some businessmen were pro-China, others were pro-Britain, and still others often changed sides. Xu explained that this depended on their different channels of making money. For years, HK Xinhua promoted relations between Beijing and Hong Kong Communists and local businessmen. It nominated prominent Hong Kong businessmen, industrialists, personalities such as Li Ka-shing (tycoon and chairman of Cheung Kong Holdings), professionals, and academics to meet with Deng Xiaoping. During the two years of Sino-British negotiations, Xu helped Hong Kong representatives from the Trade Development Council, Federation of Hong Kong Industries, Hong Kong General Chamber of Commerce, Factory Owners Association, Chinese Manufacturers Association, Legislative Council, and Urban Council make frequent visits to Beijing to meet with top CCP leaders.[67]

The emphasis on Hong Kong capitalists corresponded with growing PRC investment in the territory. The construction of the China Resources Building in Wanchai, the land reclamation of China Merchants in the Western District, the China Cement Company, and I. M. Pei's new Bank of China building aroused local and in some cases international interest. In addition, the State Council and central government financed the Ever Bright Company, a distinguished mainland enterprise managed by the late Liu Shaoqi's brother-in-law Wang Guangying, in Hong Kong. Meanwhile, the Bank of China became the second largest banking group in the territory in the 1980s.[68]

After the signing of the Sino-British Joint Declaration, Beijing and London were soon at odds as the latter tried to carry out representative government reforms in Hong Kong. The British aimed to introduce significant changes to Hong Kong's political structure, and issued the Green Paper and White Paper on representative government. At a press conference, Xu complained that "somebody had not been following the book in handling affairs," implying that the British had betrayed the Joint Declaration through the suggested reforms.[69] He responded rather emotionally to questions, and the incident provoked debate and criticism among Hong Kong people.

8. Post-1984 Era

The Hong Kong Basic Law Drafting Committee, formed in 1985, had the task of drafting a mini-constitution for the future Hong Kong SAR. The drafting of the Basic Law was an important episode in Hong Kong history in the latter part of the 1980s. The committee's 59 members, among whom 23 were from Hong Kong, were selected by HK Xinhua authorities.[70] As Xu explained, Beijing tried to incorporate the elite from all sectors into the committee, most prominently the business elite, bankers, and industrialists, and to respect the interests of different groups in society. Thus, in a policy that would have been startling to old-time Communists, Beijing relied on the conservative and entrenched business establishment, especially tycoons and those in the upper-most echelons of society.

Xu also facilitated the localization process of HK Xinhua. In September 1987, he removed certain staff members and promoted local Hong Kong Chinese to important positions in the branch. This step had the dual purpose of eliminating opposition and strengthening his position in the organization. Xu supported the more conservative proposals for the future democratization process of Hong Kong of the Basic Law Drafting Committee. While he had mobilized the support of pro-Beijing groups, he had also rallied the support of local neutral forces for the conservative proposals. The local media regarded his moves as characteristic of the united front work of the Communists.[71]

Xu's political career came to an abrupt end early in 1990. He had found it increasingly difficult to work with the central government regarding policies on Hong Kong after the Tiananmen Incident, which took place in Beijing on June 4, 1989. Xu had allowed his subordinates to participate in local demonstrations to support Beijing's student movement (though he subsequently advised them to avoid slogans against CCP leaders including Deng Xiaoping), and the leftist newspapers to report truthfully on the incident.[72] In December 1989, Beijing decided to replace Xu, and in February 1990 appointed Zhou Nan as the new director of HK Xinhua. In May, Xu secretly went to Los Angeles, where he had friends, to escape from possible political indictment. He had heard that leaders in Beijing would soon cancel his Party membership.[73]

In an interview with Hong Kong's *South China Morning Post* many years later, in July 2007, Xu revealed that shortly after the 1989 incident, a group of more than ten tycoons proposed to pay HK$10 billion for ten years after 1997 for "self-rule" in Hong Kong. They were "a group of business and community leaders," and were "all upper class elites."[74] The son-in-law of the late shipping magnate Sir Pao Yue-kong, worried about the confidence crisis in Hong Kong related to the 1997 issue, approached Xu with the proposal after the crackdown. Xu recounted that he replied that the central government would not agree to it but agreed to forward it to Beijing. He mentioned the proposal to then CCP general secretary Jiang Zemin and filed a report to Beijing leaders, including Deng Xiaoping. A month later, Xu met with the HKMAO director, Ji Pengfei, and the deputies Li Hou and Lu Ping in

Beijing; the latter, he said, considered the proposal "an act of treason." It was also mentioned in the memoirs of Xu's successor, Zhou Nan, which were published around the same time in 2007.[75]

9. Conclusion

In both its covert and overt activities, HK Xinhua grew in importance during the years between 1947 and 1990. Its task at the beginning of this period was to promote the Communist effort in the Chinese Civil War, mainly through propaganda and news reporting. After the establishment of the PRC in October 1949, the complicated diplomatic status of Hong Kong demanded that HK Xinhua perform covert functions not intended at the time of its creation. Gradually, the news agency adapted to the local capitalist environment. When negotiations over the return of Hong Kong began, HK Xinhua assumed greater significance, becoming directly accountable to Beijing. Xu Jiatun, its director from 1983 to 1990 and the highest-ranking Communist official stationed in Hong Kong, acted as a spokesman for Beijing and brought HK Xinhua out of the closet, making its diplomatic functions manifest and following the well-regarded united front principles established by Zhou Enlai. The branch's many years of activities paved the way for the implementation of the "one country, two systems" policy under which Hong Kong could continue to operate in a capitalist environment while being under a larger Socialist entity.

Despite all of the pre- and posthandover speculation about the future of the territory, Hong Kong could not have survived the years between 1949 and 1997 had Beijing not tolerated its colonial status. As the history of HK Xinhua shows, the CCP's policy was always pragmatic. On the local scene, HK Xinhua nourished a culture of collaboration with and support of Hong Kong capitalism. The ostensible news agency aimed to secure the good will of local businessmen, while the Chinese Communists actively courted local leaders. Thus, the capitalist system in Hong Kong was slowly integrated into the Communist consciousness even before the territory joined China politically. Since the handover, the fundamentally capitalist system that long supported business interests in Hong Kong has found solid support in the Hong Kong SAR government, based at least in part on the decades of HK Xinhua activities that strove to bring the two systems into relationship.

Acknowledgment: This chapter is an expanded and updated version of the author's article: "Overt and Covert Functions of the Hong Kong Branch of the Xinhua News Agency, 1947–1984," *Historian* 62, no. 1 (Fall 1999): 31–46. The author would like to thank Wiley-Blackwell for permission to publish this chapter.

4

The Origins of the Chinese Communist Alliance with the Hong Kong Business Elite, the 1997 Question, and the Basic Law Committees, 1979–1985

1. Introduction

With the establishment of the Hong Kong SAR, its chief executive Tung Chee-hwa became the focus of attention. The appointment of Tung, a shipping tycoon, signified the dominance of business interests in the government. There were many reports of the close relations between Beijing and the Hong Kong business establishment, which dated back to the late 1970s and early 1980s when the Chinese Communists adopted a united front policy toward the local business leaders. Hong Kong's reversion to sovereignty of the PRC "created an urgent need" for HK Xinhua "to expand its working agenda to include achieving its direct political participation and expanding its influence in the transitional period."[1] This chapter traces the history of the Chinese Communist alliance with the Hong Kong business elite from 1979 to 1985.

In the early 1980s, China's presence in Hong Kong was becoming increasingly obvious, and arousing considerable attention and speculation.[2] In 1983, Xu Jiatun, a high-ranking Chinese Communist, became the director of HK Xinhua. That year also witnessed the beginning of the Sino-British talks that would lead to the signing of the 1984 Sino-British Joint Declaration on Hong Kong's future, and a long period of diplomatic struggle between Beijing and London. China's recovery of sovereignty over Hong Kong would be one of the most important episodes in the country's history since it had opened its doors to the world in 1978. The world was watching to see whether the Chinese Communist system could maintain and promote Hong Kong's capitalist economy and prosperity. While Hong Kong's future depended very much on China, the credibility of the Communist reform effort rested on developments in the territory after 1997. To ensure a smooth transition to Chinese rule, Beijing sought to ally itself with the traditional pillars of Hong Kong society, namely, the conservative business leaders. For Beijing and the Chinese Communists in Hong Kong, the ultimate target of the united front effort was the local business elite.

Reunification was China's prime concern, and to facilitate the return of Hong Kong to Chinese rule, the Chinese Communists were eager to collaborate with the local business elite, regarding them as "patriots" so long as they were supportive of the Beijing government and were of use in the transition period from the signing of the Sino-British Joint Declaration in 1984 to the handover in 1997. Deng Xiaoping commented in 1984 that it did not matter whether they were capitalists as they were patriots and hence instrumental to China's recovery of sovereignty over Hong Kong and the stability and prosperity of the place.[3] Jamie Allen noted, "Deng set the tone by stating that since the [Chinese Communist] Party's policy on Hong Kong was different from the mainland—that is, the maintenance of capitalism not the creation of socialism—the targets of the united front would have to be different too"[4] while Xu Jiatun was "extremely productive in winning over the colony's business elite to the united front."[5]

2. The Controversies

Beijing had long been reluctant to tackle the Hong Kong question for fear that its recovery of the territory would lead to drastic political and administrative changes, which might create unwanted difficulties in dealing with Western countries. In 1979, Governor Sir Murray MacLehose visited Beijing, and on his return to Hong Kong relayed Deng Xiaoping's assurance that investors could "set their hearts at ease."[6] Apparently the two leaders had discussed China's sovereignty over Hong Kong, although this conversation was not reported.[7] According to Xu Jiatun, Sino-British negotiations would not have started so early had MacLehose not asked about the territory.[8] This raises the question of whether the negotiations would have been the same had the Communist leadership had more time to think about Hong Kong.[9] In his memoirs, published in 2001, Sir Chung Sze-yuen, who had been a senior member of both the Executive and Legislative Councils, adds an epilogue to the story.[10] He remembers asking MacLehose in 1983 who initiated the Hong Kong question; the latter replied it was Deng who had done so because "prior to his trip he [MacLehose] did relay to the Chinese Authorities that he would mention to Deng his proposal of selling land in the leased territories with 15-year lease as if there were no 1997 deadline."[11] Deng was quick to assert the Chinese position in the meeting before MacLehose could raise the 1997 issue.

China's position on sovereignty accounted for its intransigence on many occasions. At the beginning of the Sino-British negotiations, it was the main source of tension. The British prime minister Margaret Thatcher, who was well known for her iron will and lack of diplomacy, visited Hong Kong on her return from her trip to Beijing in September 1982 and spoke against the Chinese government. She had probably not consulted her Foreign Office before she asserted that the treaties on Hong Kong were valid under international law. She said that any government that did not adhere to them was untrustworthy, and that Britain had a "moral responsibility and duty" to the Hong Kong people.[12] Thatcher was well aware of China's position on the sovereignty question before she visited Beijing, and her statement regarding the unequal treaties could not have resulted from misunderstanding or misjudgment. Coming soon after the 1981 British Nationality Act, which denied Hong Kong people the right of abode in Britain, her arrogant assertion reminded China of its past experience with imperialist condescension, and Beijing became defensive in the face of perceived foreign pressure.

Whereas Britain's control over the New Territories would end with the expiration of the lease in 1997, it had obtained Hong Kong Island through the 1842 Treaty of Nanjing and the Kowloon Peninsula through the 1860 Beijing Convention. In her memoirs, Thatcher claims that her aim was to "exchange sovereignty over the island of Hong Kong in return for continued British administration of the entire Colony well into the future."[13] In her meeting with Deng, she raised the possibility "that after 1997 British administration would continue with the same system of law, the same political system, and the same independent currency."[14] In brief, Thatcher went to China with the purpose of trading sovereignty for administration. This could well explain why she insisted on the legality of the unequal treaties after her Beijing trip: it was not that she was ignorant of China's position but rather wishful thinking that Beijing would yield to the demands of the British. In her memoirs, she talks about the rising status of Britain: "By the time I visited the Far East in September 1982 Britain's standing in the world, and my own, had been transformed as a result of victory in the Falklands."[15] Thatcher was in the prime of her career, and naturally thought that she could attain further success in foreign matters.

After Thatcher's September visit, London hoped to maintain its administration of Hong Kong after 1997. This would become the source of a deadlock in future discussions. In August and September 1983, HK Xinhua, pro-Beijing newspapers, and leftist unions initiated a number of events and actions, commonly known as "megaphone diplomacy," to assert China's position on sovereignty and condemn Britain's intention to continue its administration after 1997.[16] Beijing maintained that sovereignty and administration could not be separated. It wanted to eliminate the British administrative and political influence in Hong Kong, and thus was highly distrustful of liberal politicians, some of whom were outspoken critics of Beijing or appeared to have Western backing.

While China wanted to end the British colonial influence in Hong Kong, it realized that it needed to preserve the territory's capitalist system to ensure its continued economic success. Hong Kong's stability and prosperity would enhance China's image abroad and be favorable to its economic reforms. The successful handling of the Hong Kong question would be a major stroke of diplomacy on China's part, demonstrating the viability of the notion of "one country, two systems" and serving as great propaganda for its reunification policy toward Taiwan. This notion was first formulated for Taiwan. In September 1981, Ye Jianying, chairman of the NPC Standing Committee, mentioned the establishment of Taiwan as a special administrative region in his nine-point proposal to Guomindang. At that time, however, observers speculated on the application of the concept to Hong Kong, as China restated its determination to regain sovereignty over the territory.[17]

Hong Kong was a historical problem that was complicated by international considerations. China was concerned with how to implement changes while preserving the territory's stability. In November 1982, Beijing's spokesman on Hong Kong and Macao Affairs, Liao Chengzhi, told a group of Hong Kong industrialists that China would be able to recover sovereignty over Hong Kong without the capitalist system and lifestyle of the territory being affected. Striking a balance between change and continuity, Beijing sought to ally itself with the established elite in Hong Kong.

3. Pre-1984

In July 1983, the first and second rounds of the Sino-British talks took place, which official announcements described as "useful and constructive" and "useful," respectively. Conflicts arose in August in the third round, when Britain sought to trade its recognition of Chinese sovereignty (after Thatcher's insistence on the validity of the unequal treaties in September 1982) for the continuation of British administration after 1997. It then seemed to reverse its position—in September, members of the Executive Council (Exco) and Legislative Council (Legco) criticized the former British prime minister, Edward Heath, for accepting China's insistence on sovereignty over Hong Kong. When the fifth round of negotiations began in October, some observers believed that the British had given up their claim to sovereignty over Hong Kong after 1997.[18]

Early in March 1983 Thatcher had sent a "private letter" to the Chinese premier, Zhao Ziyang. In her memoirs, the first volume of which was published in 1993, she discloses its content: "Provided that agreement could be reached between the British and Chinese Government on administrative arrangements for Hong Kong which would guarantee the future prosperity and stability of Hong Kong, and would be acceptable to the British Parliament and to the people of Hong Kong as well as to the Chinese Government, I *would be prepared to recommend* to Parliament that sovereignty over the whole of Hong Kong should revert to China."[19] In October, she sent another letter to Zhao, saying that the British were willing to handle the Hong Kong question along Beijing's lines.[20] Not only did Thatcher abandon Britain's sovereignty claim, she also acknowledged that the British administration in Hong Kong had to end in 1997. She later instructed the British ambassador to China, Sir Percy Cradock, to explain to Beijing the meaning of her October letter. She said that there would be "no link of authority or accountability between Britain and Hong Kong after 1997."[21] In December 1983, China reiterated its twofold policy of regaining sovereignty and maintaining the territory's stability and prosperity.[22]

4. Phase 1: The Beginning of Multitarget United Front Work, January–March 1984

In the last stages of the negotiations, Beijing sought the cooperation of Hong Kong's "unofficial ruling elite," namely, the unofficial members of Exco and Legco. Responding to questions after her speech at the Foreign Correspondents' Club on January 6, 1984, Executive and Legislative Councilor Lydia Dunn said that she supported calls for Legco and perhaps even Exco elections, but believed that the British administrative presence might not be required to ensure Hong Kong's stability after 1997.[23] This was the first time an Exco member openly supported elections. Only a few days later, speaking at the University of Hong Kong, Xu Jiatun reaffirmed Beijing's pledge to retain Hong Kong's capitalist system, ensuring the territory a high degree of autonomy for fifty years after 1997. He also reiterated China's decision to establish Hong Kong as a special administrative region, which would be run by local officials.

The timing of the two events is significant. It seems likely that Dunn had consulted the Hong Kong government before commenting on the British administration. Her statement suggested that the British no longer insisted on retaining administrative power after 1997, and Xu was quick to support the notion of Hong Kong people governing themselves. Dunn's remark also indicated that China would be capable of preserving Hong Kong's stability and prosperity, and Xu followed up by stressing Beijing's promise to maintain the capitalist system.

Dunn probably spoke for Britain, and China wanted to appear to be on good terms with Exco and Legco members, whose confidence in the future would enhance its image. More importantly, any signs of mistrust on their part would be damaging to the public morale. Sir Chung Sze-yuen, then senior Exco member, told reporters that Hong Kong people would soon know about their future.[24] His remark was immediately confirmed by pro-Beijing circles in Hong Kong, which leaked messages that China and Britain would issue a joint statement in June. This was three months ahead of the September deadline that Beijing had announced earlier, at which time, it added, it would declare a unilateral statement if both sides failed to reach an agreement. When Roger Lobo, a senior Legco member, introduced a motion that Legco hold an open debate on the Sino-British negotiations before an agreement was reached, Xu only expressed his hope that Britain would "handle this matter properly."[25] Lobo called for the motion shortly before British Foreign Office Minister of State Richard Luce and British Ambassador to Beijing Sir Richard Evans were to meet with Governor Sir Edward Youde, the Exco, and the senior civil service. Although Beijing had opposed the "three-legged stool" approach, which would allow Hong Kong to participate in the negotiations, Xu avoided being openly seen to suppress local demands.

Arousing considerable attention at this time was Beijing's impressive investment in Hong Kong, which included property lending by some leftist banks, the building of the Bank of China Tower in Central and the China Resources Building in Wanchai, the Western District land reclamation carried out by the China Merchants Steam Navigation Company, and the China Cement Company.[26] Most prominent among the ventures was Ever Bright, a Beijing-backed enterprise created with the support of the State Council and a loan from the Chinese government.[27] Its head, Wang Guangying, was the vice chairman of the Chinese People's Political Consultative Conference (CPPCC), former vice mayor of Tianjin, brother-in-law of Liu Shaoqi (chairman of the PRC, 1959–1968), and a self-confessed "big capitalist." Having taken a number of bold steps, including the purchase of Hong Kong's largest electronics manufacturer and Bank of East Asia shares and the creation of seven subsidiary companies, Wang appeared to have outdone many local entrepreneurs, and gained much publicity.[28]

China Resources had long been established in Hong Kong but registered as a limited company only in July 1983. It reorganized and soon grew to incorporate more than thirty affiliated companies, signifying its determination to develop business in the territory. In addition to selling mainland goods in Hong Kong, it expanded its local investment to approximately HK\$3 billion by November 1983. More importantly, it started a localization process, employing local professionals and focusing on advertising and research into the consumer market. With the placement of Hong Kong personnel in major areas including management, personnel, public relations, and research, China Resources was set to become a prominent player in the local economy.[29]

Another important investor was the China Merchants Steam Navigation Company, which was responsible for a large share of the import of goods from mainland China to Hong Kong by sea. A resourceful mainland enterprise, China Merchants was worth almost HK\$80 billion, and owned warehouses, wharves, ocean liners, and repair services. Steps in localization and expansion were also taken by the Bank of China, which demonstrated its ambition through the formation of a banking group of thirteen mainland banks (including itself) in Hong Kong. The Bank of China adopted a high profile and spent a great deal on advertising to enhance its corporate image. Its new building was to herald a new era for the Bank of China in Hong Kong.[30] Throughout the 1980s, mainland companies ventured into various sectors of the economy, and were in the spotlight with their bold attempts to increase their influence in Hong Kong. The impact of mainland China was starting to be felt locally.

HK Xinhua together with China Resources, a trading company, the China Merchants Steam Navigation Company, a shipping service, and the Bank of China, with its group of affiliated banks, formed a united front rallying industrial and business allies to China's side. In 1985, the Hong Kong-based magazine *Far Eastern Economic Review*, which attracts a worldwide readership, commented on the representation of personalities from these mainland companies on the HKMWC, which was in fact the CCP in Hong Kong. The magazine elaborated on the lines of command—China Resources was under China's Ministry of Foreign Economic Relations and Trade, and China Merchants answered to the Ministry of Communications.[31] Through trade and investment, the Beijing government was forging a united front with Hong Kong capitalists. The united front work was multi-faceted, and economic activities played a significant role in the Chinese Communist strategy in Hong Kong.

5. April–July 1984

In April, unofficial members of Exco met with Secretary of State for Foreign and Commonwealth Affairs Sir Geoffrey Howe in London before his visit to Beijing to try to persuade him to obtain specific guarantees from China regarding the maintenance of important economic and social institutions in Hong Kong. Their efforts were futile because Howe did not make any assurances, and even avoided using the word "guarantees" in his press conference in Hong Kong after the trip.[32] He said only that Britain would make sure the territory enjoyed "a high degree of autonomy" with regard to administration, law making, the enforcement of public order, and the maintenance of existing freedoms after 1997.

Howe's reply reinforced existing public doubts, and China was not slow to realize this. Aiming at winning back good will, Beijing welcomed visits from some Hong Kong interest groups.[33] The director of the HKMAO, Ji Pengfei, met with delegations from the Heung Yee Kuk (a representative body for the New Territories), the Urban Council, district boards, and neighborhood associations. He made a number of promises, which included the following:

(1) Hong Kong people could hold both British and Chinese passports in the future;
(2) Chinese troops, which might be sent to the territory, would not interfere with the local administration;
(3) New Territories land leases would extend beyond 1997;
(4) Hong Kong would enjoy separate export quotas, membership in international organizations, and ship registry;
(5) it would have its own central bank to issue money;
(6) its commercial relations with Taiwan would not be affected;
(7) the future chief executive would be appointed or elected; and
(8) Hong Kong people would enjoy freedom of speech, travel, publication, and strike, and exemption from military draft.[34]

China was interested in securing support from the business, industrial, and professional sectors in Hong Kong. Frequent "pilgrimages" to Beijing to gauge the latest opinion of mainland officials were made by visitors who included representatives from the Trade Development Council, Factory Owners Association, Chinese Manufacturers' Association, and the Urban and Legislative Councils, and prominent businessmen, industrialists, professionals, and academics.[35] In June, Deng met with a group of Hong Kong business leaders, including the chairmen of the Federation of Hong Kong Industries, Hong Kong General Chamber of Commerce, and Chinese Manufacturers' Association. He also met with Lydia Dunn and Sir Chung Sze-yuen, and stressed, "Reunification of the country is the aspiration of the whole nation" and "new problems must be solved by new means."[36] He said that the successful management of the Hong Kong question would serve as a precedent for dealing with other international problems. Deng also implied that if China could effectively implement the "one country, two systems" policy in Hong Kong, then the Taiwan problem could also be solved. With regard to the notion of *"Gangren zhi Gang"* [Hong Kong people governing Hong Kong], he said that future leaders of the territory must be "patriots,"[37] "love the motherland and Hongkong," support China's resumption of sovereignty over the territory, and protect Hong Kong's stability and prosperity. Foreign countries had looked down on China in the past, Deng said, but mainland China had changed, and Hong Kong people should share in the national pride and have confidence in their ability to govern themselves.[38] He emphasized that Hong Kong people should believe in their future. The meetings with these delegations served as a means for Beijing to convey the message that it was concerned about the preservation of Hong Kong's capitalist economy and lifestyle.[39]

Regarding the issue of sovereignty, China held firm. Deng had earlier insisted on the stationing of troops in the territory after 1997, and called this "a symbol of safeguarding the territory of the People's Republic of China and a symbol of safeguarding our state sovereignty, as well as a guarantee of Hongkong's stability and prosperity."[40] He even questioned whether Hong Kong could be considered a part of China should Beijing give up the right to send troops there.

6. August–December 1984

Sir Geoffrey Howe's second visit to Beijing (July 27–31) and his stopover afterward in Hong Kong marked the final stage of the negotiations, as the British agreed to China's demand for the establishment of a joint liaison group, to exchange information, and to discuss the implementation of the agreement. At the same time, local leaders were preparing for future leadership contests, to fill the power vacuum after the British departure in 1997. Different groups were expected to appear before the 1985 District Board Election, which would produce an electoral college to select at least six Legco members. These groups fell into three main categories: the left wing (pro-Beijing), right wing (pro-Guomindang), and pro-Hong Kong faction.[41]

On September 26, the Sino-British Joint Declaration was initialed. In his October meeting with Hong Kong's Chief Secretary Sir Philip Haddoncave, Premier Zhao Ziyang emphasized that Beijing was "much concerned about Hongkong's stability and prosperity," which were beneficial to China's reunification and the Four Modernizations. He said that "a turbulent and economically depressed Hongkong" was not to China's long-term advantage.[42] Zhao was confident that the agreement would promote Hong Kong's prosperity and create further opportunities for Sino-British negotiations. The *Beijing Review* stated that the Joint Declaration had brought economic stability to Hong Kong, and cited many examples in support of this assertion.

It pointed out that the Hang Seng Index had risen, land sales had increased, American, Japanese, and South-East Asian investment had grown, and Hong Kong had increased in importance as a world financial, shipping, and trading center.[43] It quoted a Hong Kong labor leader, L. K. Ding, who said that his people should now feel more secure and have more faith than before.[44] In December, Thatcher and Zhao signed the Joint Declaration in Beijing.

7. January–May 1985

Hong Kong's economic strength provided the best guarantee for its future. From 1978 to 1984, its domestic exports and re-exports to China increased more than one hundredfold. Big enterprises including Jardine, Matheson & Company and Hutchison Whampoa established China desks.[45] Meanwhile, China stepped up its investment in Hong Kong. The Bank of China cooperated with local China-controlled and Chinese banks to form a "syndication club" to muster resources.[46] It had the support of local banker David Li, who was general manager of the Bank of East Asia and chairman of the Chinese Banks' Association, and would soon be involved in the drafting of the Basic Law. Together with its sister banks, the Bank of China established a joint automatic teller service to compete with that of the Hongkong Bank/ Hang Seng Bank collaboration.

With the ascendance of China and the foreseeable retreat of Britain, local politicians struggled to make their way up and adjust to the new situation. Having played an advisory role in the past, unofficial members of Exco and Legco were in a good position to compete for political power. By forming alliances and parties, some of them were already jockeying for position in the future government.[47] China was ready to work with these potential government policymakers, as it had already made efforts to be on good terms with them. A London newspaper called Lydia Dunn "the most powerful woman in Hongkong."[48] Another unofficial member of Exco and Legco, Maria Tam, attracted attention when she formed the Progressive Hongkong Society (PHS) with Urban Councilor Philip Kwok. The PHS was supported by powerful families in Hong Kong, including the Tungs of Orient Overseas Holdings, the Fungs of Fung Ping Fan & Company, the Lees of Lee Hysan Estate Company, the Chars of China Dyeing Works, and the Los of Great Eagle Company. It was difficult to draw a line between these local politicians and Hong Kong's wealthiest business establishment. Unofficial members of Legco Allen Lee, Selina Chow, and Stephen Cheong also planned to form their own political party, and were eager to secure local support.[49] They too were members of the business and professional elite. Political power in Hong Kong in the future seemed to be in the hands of the big capitalists.

8. Phase 2: Collaboration with the Local Business Establishment

In his memoirs, Xu Jiatun devotes an entire chapter to united front work in Hong Kong.[50] Even before his arrival in Hong Kong, he understood that his task was to rally the support of the local business establishment. He revealed: "Deng Xiaoping has said many times that Hong Kong will not implement the 'Four Cardinal Principles,' one of which was the leadership of the CCP. With such understanding, '*Gangren zhi Gang*' means 'Hong Kong people governing Hong Kong' with the capitalist system remaining intact. It was to be 'Hong Kong people governing Hong Kong' chiefly under the political leadership of the bourgeoisie, and was not to be 'Hong Kong people governing Hong Kong' chiefly under the political leadership of the proletariat. Thus, Beijing cannot send its people to have 'Beijing people governing Hong Kong.'"[51] Xu said matter-of-factly that in future, "Hong Kong people governing Hong Kong" would be a coalition government of all classes, but with the bourgeoisie as the main body. In his meeting with Zhao Ziyang and Ji Pengfei, he boldly claimed that the first Hong Kong SAR chief executive would most probably be of "pro-British" background. According to Xu, they did not deny such a possibility.[52]

Such ideas formed not only the basis of his united front work, Xu asserted, but also the major consideration in planning the future political system of the SAR. He stated: "At present, the united front work in Hong Kong involves having more friends, winning the hearts of the local people, and searching for and cultivating talents for the administration of the territory after 1997."[53] His task was to unite all people who "were patriotic and loved Hong Kong," whether or not they supported Socialism and the leadership of the CCP. Xu recalled Deng saying at a meeting of the CCP Central Standing Committee that one "must be willing to do the work of a great rightist, a great spy," and be "willing to communicate with them [the united front targets] and befriended with them."[54] The HKMWC and HK Xinhua divided society into three groups, namely, the left, the right, and the middle. According to the Communists, the great rightists were the "pro-British," "pro-U.S.," and "pro-Taiwan" elites within the big bourgeoisie.[55] To do great rightist work, one had to gain the support of these elites. Xu kept this in mind when he started his united front work in Hong Kong.

Later, Xu would invite Exco and Legco members to banquets that celebrated the Chinese New Year and commemorated the establishment of the PRC. As the Exco and Legco were part of the British colonial government in Hong Kong, Xu was cautious, saying that he "respected" but did not "recognize" the status of the Exco and Legco members.[56] He said that the greatest concern of Beijing was to secure the goodwill of the big capitalists in Hong Kong.[57] Thus, HK Xinhua was responsible for nominating local people to meet with Deng. Xu provided Beijing with the names of tycoons with whom he was in regular contact, including Pao Yue-kong, Li Ka-shing, Run Run Shaw, Henry Fok, and Cha Chi-ming. His aim was to cultivate a group of "pro-China" capitalists in Hong Kong, as he believed that the political orientation of businessmen was directly related to their economic interests.[58]

Several years later, the Hong Kong magazine *Contemporary* reproduced an excerpt from a mainland China article titled "The Social Class Structure of Hong Kong under the Conditions of One Country, Two Systems."[59] After the June 4 Incident in 1989, the editor and some employees of a local leftist newspaper had resigned and established *Contemporary*. The magazine provided inside information about local Communist activities, and ran until 1995. *Contemporary* did not offer the original date of the appearance of the above mentioned article, saying only that it had been published recently. Its content was similar to that which Xu had discussed in his memoirs; that is, it indicated that both Beijing and HK Xinhua emphasized the importance of the local business elite in united front work in Hong Kong.

The Communists saw Hong Kong society as comprising three distinct strata, the big capitalists, the middle class, and workers. Each group wanted to protect its position and promote its own interests after 1997. The big capitalists were concerned about their stake in the original social system, the middle class expected more opportunities for advancement through political reform and changes, and the workers aimed at improving their working and living conditions. The Communists had their own idea of the future political system in Hong Kong. The article said: "The top political echelon of Hong Kong must adapt to its capitalist economic structure and class structure, *so Hong Kong's future political system will have the local patriotic capitalists as the main body, and [they will] ally with other classes to form a non-Socialist political system* .... At present, Hong Kong has already witnessed many prominent industrialists, businessmen, professionals, and their organizations actively participating in local political activities, reflecting this trend."[60]

How did the Communists view the contribution of this capitalist leadership under the principle of "one country, two systems"? They said that because Hong Kong occupied only a small land area and had a tiny population compared to that of China, its capitalist system would not have much effect on the Socialist national polity. China would regain its sovereignty over Hong Kong, which would become an SAR, and the handover of the territory in 1997 would only strengthen Beijing's alliance with the local patriotic capitalists.[61] Like Xu, this source described the future SAR government as being led by Hong Kong's top business leaders, and talked about the benefits of their being China's allies. This scenario—capitalist leadership and alliance with the Communists after 1997—seemed advantageous to the Chinese Communists.

9. June–July 1985

The establishment of the Basic Law Drafting Committee (BLDC) and Basic Law Consultative Committee (BLCC) signaled China's growing interest in Hong Kong's business elite, who appeared to enjoy great attention from Beijing leaders and to have access to them. The creation of the Basic Law was meant to be a step toward the implementation of the concepts of "*Gangren zhi Gang*" and "a high degree of autonomy" after 1997. In 1982, Liao Chengzhi, Beijing's spokesman on Hong Kong and Macao Affairs, frequently met with local delegations, and discussed Hong Kong issues with his advisers. He came to the conclusion that China's rule of Hong Kong would be successful only if the local people ran their own government.[62] The drafting of and consultations on the Basic Law provided Hong Kong people with opportunities to participate in their own political development. In his meeting with representatives of the Hong Kong Factory Owners Association in November 1982, Liao was the first high-ranking cadre to use the term "*Gangren zhi Gang*."[63]

Although Beijing agreed that Hong Kong people should be involved in the making of the Basic Law, it had to decide how this should be done.[64] In April 1984, Ji Pengfei promised that the BLDC would include Hong Kong members and listen to the opinion of different classes in society. He said that the drafting of the Basic Law would follow a "two ups and two downs" procedure, meaning that the BLDC would extensively solicit opinions before making the first draft, and this draft would then be available for public discussion before being amended. However, Ji was uncertain about the selection of the Hong Kong members and said that this still needed to be thought out.

In May 1984, Xu Jiatun stated that anyone who supported the return of the territory to China could offer suggestions about the Basic Law, and Hong Kong people should organize the BLCC. Beijing seemed to recognize that the BLDC was too small to appear representative, and wanted the BLCC to include different sectors of society. In August of the same year, Ye Feng, HK Xinhua's deputy director, promised that the BLCC would incorporate many Hong Kong members, including representatives from the legal sector and major associations and those who had received university education.

On June 18, 1985, the Eleventh Plenary Session of the Standing Committee of the Sixth NPC approved the draft membership list of the BLDC, which had 59 members, 23 of whom came from Hong Kong.[65] The BLDC would have to decide on its working procedures and the organization of subgroups to handle specific issues. Its members from mainland China included important figures who had long been involved in dealings with Hong Kong, such as Ji Pengfei, Xu Jiatun, Mao Junnian (deputy secretary-general of HK Xinhua), Li Hou (deputy director of the HKMAO), and Lu Ping (deputy director and secretary-general of the HKMAO).

HK Xinhua was responsible for selecting the Hong Kong members of the BLDC.[66] Xu said that when choosing committee members, Beijing tried to incorporate the elite from all sectors, and to take care of the interests of different groups in society. In fact, many Hong Kong members who were finally appointed had very strong connections with the mainland. Four were already insiders in the Beijing government or the CCP: Ann Tse-kai, a member of the CPPCC Standing Committee; Fei Yimin, the Hong Kong and Macao representative to the NPC; Henry Fok, who held both of the above positions; and Sanford Yung, a member of the Guangdong Provincial People's Political Consultative Conference.[67] Ann and Fei were also named vice chairmen of the BLDC. When asked about being selected, Ann stressed the importance of Hong Kong's manufacturing industries and its stability and prosperity.[68] Fei, the local publisher of *Dagongbao* (*Ta Kung Pao*), said that the Joint Declaration had been well received and should be the guideline for the future Basic Law. Fok, president of the Hong Kong Chinese General Chamber of Commerce, considered the 40 percent Hong Kong membership sufficient indication that China highly respected local opinion. A chartered accountant, Yung said he would work for the prosperity of Hong Kong. Yung and Lu Ping, then secretary-general of the HKMAO, had been schoolmates at St. John's College in Shanghai, and Yung's grandfather (whose name in Pinyin is Rong Hong) was the first Chinese student to receive government support to study abroad.[69] These Hong Kong members of the BLDC shared a similar background and all saw economic affairs as a priority.

The BLDC had many Hong Kong "big capitalists," including eight in addition to the four mentioned above. Also named a vice chairman of the BLDC, Sir Pao Yue-kong was a world famous shipping magnate and former chairman of the Worldwide Shipping Group and Kowloon Wharf. He said he would pay particular attention to Hong Kong's free economic system, its position as an international financial center and free port, and the people's right to travel.[70] David Li was another vice chairman of the drafting committee, and the director and chief manager of the Bank of East Asia, which had close China connections and backing. Cha Chi-ming, a renowned industrialist and permanent adviser to the board of directors of Yan Chai Hospital, said that the Basic Law would be advantageous to both Hong Kong and China, and that he would be particularly interested in the development of the industrial, business, and banking sectors. *Ming Pao*'s publisher, Louis Cha, promised to work for Hong Kong's stability and prosperity, and the maintenance of its social and economic system and lifestyle for fifty years after 1997. Cheng Ching-fun, director of the Chinese Manufacturers' Association and managing director of Daqing Petroleum, stated that he hoped that the Joint Declaration would gain the confidence of the world and be a guarantee of the continuation of the prosperity of Hong Kong. Lau Wong-fat was chairman of the Heung Yee Kuk, an advisory body to the government representing a small New Territories population whose ancestry could be traced back to the time of the British takeover. Like the others, he stressed the importance of Hong Kong's socioeconomic structure and its continuation after 1997. Li Ka-shing, chairman of Cheung Kong Holdings and probably the most prominent tycoon in Hong Kong, said that he believed that the Basic Law was instrumental in preserving Hong Kong as a free, orderly, and law-abiding society, which was crucial to its industrial and business development. Wong Po-yan, chairman and managing director of United Oversea Enterprises and honorary president of the Chinese Manufacturers' Association, promised to work for the implementation of the "one country, two systems" policy in Hong Kong.

The composition of the BLDC demonstrates the focus of China's united front policy on the business elite, the bankers and industrialists comprising the conservative and entrenched business establishment—tycoons and those in the uppermost echelons of society. The members listed above were in their fifties, sixties, or seventies, with an average age of sixty-two.[71] There was little concern for the grassroots population or younger political leaders and groups.[72] Some participants in the plenary session of the NPC Standing Committee felt that the BLDC members were a bit too old.[73] When questioned about the lack of representation of the younger and lower class populations, Xu Jiatun replied that such a concern was not unreasonable, but since the drafting committee could not be too large and Hong Kong members made up only 40 percent of the seats, there must be limited participation.[74] He said that the selection of the local members had taken many factors into consideration: Hong Kong's historical background and reality, the concern for its prosperity, and different opinions in society.

Others on the BLDC whose interests were closely aligned with those of Beijing were Liu Yiu-chu, a lawyer, and Tam Yiu-chung, a trade unionist, who would soon be busy defending the Beijing government against harsh attacks. Liu was the legal adviser of many Beijing-owned companies, and Tam was the vice chairman of the leftist Hong Kong Federation of Trade Unions. Among the remaining Hong Kong members, three were from the education sector, one was from the medical field, three came from the legal profession, and two were religious leaders. The BLDC had reserved two seats for pro-Taiwan people, but they refused to participate.[75] Interestingly, Hong Kong's *Dagongbao* raised the concern that the BLDC did not have members who could represent the Taiwan perspective.[76]

A prominent local scholar, Ambrose Y. C. King, characterized the composition of the BLDC as "the political absorption of economics," a deliberate Communist strategy,[77] and observed that most of the Hong Kong members were from the upper-middle and upper classes—"the leaders of the economic market or the reputable personalities of various professions."[78] He stated: "This carefully-thought-out membership list by the PRC Government was clearly intended to please the strategic elites of the Hong Kong economy, and it is indeed with a purpose to augment the capitalist system in Hong Kong."[79] He continued, "China is interested in maintaining the status quo; it shows no sign of discontinuing the elitist politics which has been the dominant mode of politics in the colony for years."[80] Paralleling his famous statement about the "administrative absorption of politics" of the British Hong Kong government, King said that "what China seemed to adopt is a model which could be called the 'political absorption of economics.'"[81] Traditionally, the Hong Kong government had acted as an "absorber," trying to minimize political conflicts through the granting of special positions to the business elite. Now, Beijing was trying to make use of the political arrangement to consolidate the support of those in Hong Kong who were the most economically powerful.

The BLDC first met in Beijing from July 1–5. On the first day, Ji Pengfei, who was now the BLDC chairman, announced that the drafting of the Basic Law would take about four to five years, and the committee would hand in the final draft to the NPC for approval in 1990.[82] The first draft would be available for public discussion in late 1988 before being further revised and submitted to the NPC. This corresponded with his earlier comment that the drafting process would involve "two ups and downs." The first meeting mainly concerned the workings of the BLDC and drafting procedures, and provided its members with opportunities to exchange their opinion on the Basic Law. Another item, which was not listed on the agenda, was how to establish the BLCC, and this attracted the most attention.

10. August–December 1985

Upon returning from their first meeting in Beijing, the Hong Kong BLDC members held a preparatory meeting to discuss matters concerning the BLCC, and established a six-member subgroup to set up this new committee. In late August, the BLDC subgroup put forth a draft constitution for the

BLCC, and called for the use of "democratic consultation" to solicit opinions on the Basic Law.[83] In addition, the subgroup outlined three methods for the selection of BLCC members:

(1) certain associations, registered groups, or other Basic Law interest groups could "recommend" their people to the consultative committee;

(2) the Hong Kong BLDC members would make a number of appointments; and

(3) individuals and group representatives could also apply for posts.

From the beginning, the BLDC was to play a more decisive role than the BLCC.[84]

The BLCC members were to come from ten categories: the industrial and business sector, the financial sector, the legal profession, professionals, the media, labor and grassroots associations, religious persons, foreigners, BLDC members, and others. In December 1985, the BLCC was established with a membership of 180. The Business and Professional Group (BPG) later emerged within the BLCC, and became an "important connecting link between the legislature and businessmen, industrialists and financiers."[85] Its members included tycoons and the upper-class business elite, some of whom were also Legco members.

The appointment of united front targets to the Basic Law bodies helped Beijing consolidate its support in Hong Kong before 1997. In turn, these local elites seized the opportunity to play a greater political role in the future of the territory. Beijing also placed Hong Kong representatives in its NPC and CPPCC. In 1985, it announced the new batch of appointees, who were known to be staunch loyalists of the central government and came from the business, commercial, industrial, education, and professional sectors, trade unions, and the media.[86] Among the delegates to the NPC were Hong Kong's *Dagongbao* publisher Fei Yimin and leftist school principal Ng Hong-mun, while those to the CPPCC included industrialist Ann Tse-kai, the tycoon Henry Fok, and *Mirror* publisher Xu Simin. It was obvious to the Hong Kong public that these people belonged to the pro-Beijing group.

With Beijing spearheading united front work, HK Xinhua rose in status to become a State Council department. Its reorganization in late 1985 led to the formation of ten new departments: administration and management, research, propaganda, external affairs, economics, culture and education, arts and sports, coordination, social work, and personnel.[87] The coordination department was responsible for networking with Hong Kong's business and professional elites. The new structure of HK Xinhua reflected the growing importance of the Hong Kong issue and China's willingness to support the local pro-Beijing camp.

11. Conclusion

China's "one nation, two systems" policy was based on conservative and realistic considerations. On the one hand, Beijing was determined to end the British colonial influence and highly skeptical of local political demands. On the other hand, it understood that it must preserve Hong Kong's capitalist system and lifestyle, and to some extent maintain the territory's status quo. In 1984 and the first few months of 1985, it pursued an open strategy and tried to secure the good will of the largest number of people. During the process, it realized that the territory's business elite would be its major source of support. By mid-1985, Beijing was prepared to work with local business leaders to decide the future political institutions of Hong Kong. Even HK Xinhua supported Beijing's policy of collaboration with the business elite. The establishment of the BLDC and BLCC signified the implementation of such a policy. From the very beginning of the transitional period, Beijing exhibited a behavioral pattern that could be termed "the political absorption of economics." By the end of 1985 it was obvious that China favored the local business elite, who provided Beijing with the most solid support. These business leaders were the most economically powerful among Hong Kong society, and their contribution was important to the prosperity of Hong Kong and mainland China. They considered the territory's return to China to be inevitable, and became a "pro-Beijing" group to protect their vested interests. At the same time, Beijing was intent on making its voice heard in the territory. The alliance between the Chinese Communists and Hong Kong's business elite was thus the result of mutual interests. The policy of collaboration carried over into the 1990s, and will continue in the future.

Acknowledgment: This chapter is an expanded and updated version of the author's article: "The Origins of the Chinese Communists' Alliance with the Business Elite in Hong Kong: The 1997 Question and the Basic Law Committees, 1979–1985," *Modern Chinese History Society of Hong Kong Bulletin*, nos. 9–10 (October 1999): 51–67. The author would like to thank the Modern Chinese History Society of Hong Kong for permission to publish this chapter.

5

The Involvement of the Business Elite in the Drafting of Hong Kong's Basic Law and the Problems of the United Front Policy, 1985–1990

1. Introduction

From 1985 to 1990, a number of groups participated in the drafting of the Basic Law, which would be the "mini-constitution" of the SAR after Hong Kong's reversion to Chinese sovereignty. During this period, the Hong Kong people engaged in fierce debates as the different groups put forth their proposals for the most suitable political institutions of the future SAR. The most heated arguments were centered on the constitutional structure of the SAR, namely, the election of its chief executive and legislature.[1] These five years, crucial in Hong Kong's history, witnessed the implementation of China's united front policy toward the territory. Beijing adopted characteristic united front tactics to secure allies, win over those who were neutral, and fight opponents, with the ultimate aim to increase the number of China's supporters. This chapter argues that Beijing had considerable difficulty in achieving this objective.

2. Hong Kong's Transition to Chinese Sovereignty

Various groups were involved from 1985 to 1990 in the drafting of the Basic Law for the SAR. The Hong Kong people participated in intense debates regarding which of the proposals for the political institutions of the SAR would be the most suitable. The Basic Law would determine the pace of democratization for the territory, and the representatives of Hong Kong and Beijing wanted to ensure that its content satisfied their respective demands. In the BLDC, these representatives struggled tirelessly to wield maximum influence. In the BLCC, the business, industrial, and professional elite became the dominant voice representing Hong Kong.

During this five-year period, China implemented a united front policy to secure allies, win over those who were neutral, and fight opponents. While the business leaders of Hong Kong were supporters of the united front policy, the middle class was skeptical of China's intentions, and the pro-democracy faction held opposite views. This chapter argues that China encountered great difficulty in its united front work in two respects. First, a split emerged within the business elite of Hong Kong, who competed among themselves to curry favor with Beijing. It was observed that "instead of a unified elite under the control of the colonial regime, different elite competed with one another for political spoils and status."[2] Second, the confidence of the middle stratum of the local population reached its nadir during this period. The breakdown in communications between Beijing and the local business elite indicated that the united front policy had produced chaos, mistrust, and disillusionment. At the same time, Beijing had failed to expand its influence among the middle class in Hong Kong. This chapter elaborates on the various rivalries between business leaders and the conflicts between Beijing and its local representatives.

3. China's United Front Policy

Hong Kong's business leaders constituted the primary target of Beijing's united front work in the territory.[3] According to a local account of the Basic Law drafting process, which was published in 1991, Hong Kong journalists stated that Beijing placed a heavy emphasis on the "big capitalists" in its Hong Kong policy. This focus corresponds with Xu Jiatun's united fronttactics in aiming for an alliance with the big capitalists to secure upper-middle-class support and consolidate China's position in Hong Kong.[4] From 1983 to 1990, Xu was director of HK Xinhua. In his memoirs, Xu writes: "I therefore raised in the Hong Kong and Macao Work Committee [in 1983] that we should employ our 'resources' to cultivate a group of pro-China capitalists in Hong Kong and Macao. China's enterprises in Hong Kong needed not be afraid of criticisms, and should contribute toward this directive."[5] At a meeting of the Shenzhen Work Committee in 1983, Xu reported that the middle class "was the chief target of the struggle for the united front work. In order to open the situation for a united front in Hong Kong, [the Chinese Communists] must achieve a breakthrough with the big bourgeoisie."[6] Furthermore, he stated, "once the representatives of the big bourgeoisie are willing to contact us, the middle stratum will find it easier to communicate with us."[7]

The emphasis on Hong Kong's business elite in China's united front policy had historical roots. In the 1960s, a widely held view was as follows: "Power in Hong Kong, it has been said, resides in the Jockey Club, Jardine and Matheson, the Hong Kong and Shanghai Bank, and the Governor—in that order."[8] In the past, the Hong Kong government had invited business leaders into the Exco and Legco, resulting in what was called the "administrative absorption of politics." Alluding to this practice, Ambrose Y. C. King described China's handling of the BLDC and the BLCC in the late 1980s as the "political absorption of economics."[9] Accordingly, the involvement of business in the Basic Law committees was China's expression and elaboration of its united front policy.[10]

4. The Formation of the BLDC and BLCC

Within the BLDC, which first met in July 1985, local business and industrial elites constituted a majority, and together with upper-middle-class professionals became the dominant voice among the Hong Kong representatives in the drafting process. This committee consisted of fifty-nine members, twenty-three of whom were from Hong Kong. Among the latter, twelve were so-called big capitalists.[11] Traditionally, China's spokespersons in Hong Kong were leftists and leftist trade unionists. With Hong Kong's impending return to Chinese sovereignty in 1997, however, business leaders and some of the professional elite, who had been the most fearful of Communism, came to support the Beijing government. They did so for the same reason they had previously supported the British Hong Kong government, namely, the desire to maintain local stability and secure reliable political backing for their investment interests. By the 1980s, those who sided with Beijing were labeled "pro-China," a term that applied not only to the leftists but eventually to all of China's united front allies and friends.

The business establishment exerted further influence on the drafting of the Basic Law with the formation of the BLCC in December 1985, which included 180 Hong Kong members acting as an advisory body to the BLDC. According to Hong Kong's *South China Morning Post*, the BLCC had a "wide-ranging membership" that fell "broadly into the category of moderates, ranging from artists to lawyers, businessmen, community workers, civil servants and media representatives."[12]

Conflicts arose, however, when the business and professional groups of the BLCC put forth their proposals for the political system that they deemed suitable for the future SAR. The early praise for the BLCC gave way to accusations that its Standing Committee had a strong pro-China bias.

The *Hong Kong Standard* reported, "The newly elected Standing Committee of the Basic Law Consultative Committee includes people from different strata and ideologies, but the centre of power is obviously swayed to the Chinese side."[13] In addition, the upper-class elite appeared to have had a better chance of getting elected. Of the fifteen elected Standing Committee members, six were from the commercial and industrial sectors, seven were from the professional and academic sectors, and two were "grassroots" representatives.[14]

It was surprising to local journalists that among the candidates running for a position on the Standing Committee, Lo Tak-shing, executive partner of Lo & Lo Solicitors, obtained the greatest number of votes, with a total of 132. The *Hong Kong Standard* reported, "The highest number of votes was obtained by Mr Lo Tak-shing, a past executive and legislative councillor who resigned from the post in protest of Britain's failure to meet its obligation to the people of Hong Kong last year."[15] Lo had argued for full British citizenship for the people of Hong Kong who held British passports. According to *The Standard*, Lo was "the big surprise of the day," as he had been "in protest against the terms of the Sino-British agreement," and subsequently had even opened a company to help locals to emigrate.[16] The newspaper said: "Mr Lo told THE STANDARD that he might have been chosen because of the need for balance."[17] Although Lo maintained that his election provided for more diverse representation, later events revealed that he helped to tilt the balance in favor of China.

5. The Business and Professional Group (BPG) of the BLCC and Its Proposals

In November 1986, a local magazine, *Pai Shing Semi-monthly*, raised the question of whether "Hong Kong [was] on the Road toward 'Business Monopoly of Politics?'" Before the three special groups of the BLDC met in Xiamen in late August 1986, fifty-seven BLCC members from the industrial and business sectors released a proposal for the government structure of the future SAR, which called for the creation of an electoral college of 600 people responsible for choosing the chief executive and some members of the legislature after 1997.[18] Their support for indirect elections triggered a series of debates on the subject. The BLCC expanded its membership in November to include seventy-one industrialists, businessmen, and professionals, who named themselves the Business and Professional Group (BPG) of the BLCC. In the BPG proposal, the electoral college would select the chief executive from among three candidates proposed by a nomination committee. This committee would consist of twenty people who would come from, and be elected by, the 600 members of the electoral college. These twenty people would neither have the voting power reserved for the other 580 members nor be able to stand for election for the position of chief executive.[19]

In a paper entitled "How to Elect the Chief Executive of the Future Hong Kong SAR Government,"[20] the BPG explained that the objective of its proposed election procedure was to make sure that Hong Kong and its people enjoyed stability and prosperity.[21] The paper asserted that the plan would create a government system beneficial to "the welfare of all Hong Kong people."[22] More importantly, it stated: "We believe that an environment conducive to business operating efficiently is a vital element in the overall well being of all Hong Kong people in future."[23] The mentality of the business establishment differed little from that in the past; to wit, economic concerns dictated the direction and rate of political development.

The paper provided details about the nomination and election procedures. The twenty-member nomination committee would serve as "a search team, a body to receive recommendations and applications and to vet candidates."[24] However, these members could neither vote for nor becandidates. The other 580 members of the electoral college would vote for the chief executive, who would be "eligible for re-nomination and election to a second term" but "subject to a two-term limit."[25] A candidate had to obtain an absolute majority of votes to be elected chief executive.

According to the BPG, its proposal was "most likely to preserve the separation of the Powers [sic] of the Executive from the powers of the Legislature."[26] It offered the following grounds to justify this claim. First, under the proposal, the electoral college would be broadly based, and less than 15 percent of the members would come from the legislature; second, the chief executive would be accountable to the legislature; and third, "the Electoral College system minimises the tendency for confrontational politics which would be more likely to result from other systems of election."[27] The BPG emphasized its belief that confrontational party politics would be counterproductive to Hong Kong's interests.[28] It then modified the proposed composition of the electoral college: statutory and permanent nonstatutory bodies lost seats to labor and professionals, which each gained twenty more seats, and to the education sector, which received ten more seats.[29]

However, public concern emerged regarding the dominance of big business in the electoral college. If the BPG's proposal was adopted, then industrial, commercial, and financial representatives together would comprise approximately one third of the committee (180 seats). Another third would be made up of the professional sector (80 seats) together with representatives from labor unions (80 seats) and religious (10 seats) and educational representatives (30 seats), and the remaining third would include Legco (80 seats), the Urban and Regional Councils and District Boards (50 seats), social, charitable, and sports organizations (60 seats), and the Civil Service (30 seats).[30]

The professional members were loosely affiliated and came from various sources—the Hong Kong Bar Association, Dental Association, Medical Association, Nurses Association, Hong Kong Institute of Architects, Institute of Engineers, Institute of Surveyors, Institute of Bankers, Hong Kong Society of Accountants, Hong Kong Law Society, and Chartered Institute of Builders, among others.[31] Labor unions were divided. Some people feared that the system of functional constituencies might enable the business elite to have a dominant voice in the legislative and local bodies, especially as social groups always sought the support of the business sector.

In response to such concerns, members of the BPG defended their proposal, including Lo Tak-shing, Vincent Lo, owner of Shui On Group Ltd., and Stephen Cheong, an industrialist and a banker. Representing the stance of the local business elite, Cheong, who was also a Legco member, "expressed grave doubts over the desirability of introducing direct elections."[32] Because Hong Kong had "survived and thrived economically without having to undertake political experimentation," Cheong did not "see any pragmatic reason why Hong Kong must be that impatient to establish beyond any doubt the desirability of direct elections."[33] Hong Kong's business leaders were very cautious about political reform, and wanted to delay the introduction of direct elections.

6. The Business and Professional Elites as Targets of the United Front Policy

The business elite in Hong Kong were supportive of the traditional and current government policy toward Hong Kong, namely, to ensure an independent bureaucratic structure and extensive consultative system.[34] From their perspective, experimentation with Western democracy in Hong Kong was very risky. They considered naïve the advocacy of the adoption of democratic institutions to counter and resist Communism, as nothing could prevent China from reestablishing ontrol over Hong Kong. Only by maintaining its prosperity and demonstrating its value to China could Hong Kong avoid direct interference from the central government. According to the BPG, changing the existing system in Hong Kong would put off foreign investors. It also argued that Western democratic traditions had taken hundreds of years to establish, and that Hong Kong could not achieve complete democracy within ten years, even if such was desired.

In reality, the BPG was promoting elitist politics while trying to argue that the share of the different sectors in the electoral college was based on their relative social status and economic power. It was evident that the BPG's purpose was to appoint the elite to the administration.[35] Historically, businessmen in Hong Kong were an important class as they possessed the most wealth and provided the government with crucial support. The "proposal of the seventy-one" intended to continue this tradition of elitist politics to avoid unwanted changes. In Exco and Legco, the business elite had occupied a large proportion of the unofficial representation.[36] Commentators criticized this phenomenon, arguing that the "emerging socioeconomic elites were being coopted into an administration-dominated polity."[37]

The proposal of the BPG elites aimed at counteracting the pro-democracy faction, which called for direct elections of the chief executive and the legislature after 1997, and for more electoral seats in the legislative body. The original fifty-seven business and professional members sought support for their proposal from other BLDC and BLCC members prior to the BLDC meeting held in late August. The timing of the BPG's proposal had caught the pro-democracy faction by surprise, but it responded by putting forward its own proposal, which was drafted by nineteen BLCC members. On the one hand, the BPG had expanded to seventy-one members, taking up nearly 40 percent of the BLCC, and obtained the backing of factory owners, land and property owners, construction companies, and the engineers' association.[38] On the other hand, the pro-democracy faction had modified the "proposal of the nineteen," and its newly revised "190 model" garnered a wide range of support from BLCC members, Executive and Legislative Councilors, district board members, lawyers, doctors, religious leaders, and university professors.

In proposing an electoral college system of voting, the BPG was aiming to avoid the emergence of political parties and confrontational politics.[39] Regarding the composition of the legislature after 1997, the seventy-one members of the BPG suggested that 50 percent be chosen by functional constituencies, 25 percent by the electoral college, and the remaining 25 percent by direct election. They were vehemently opposed to the proposal put forward by the pro-democracy faction, which called for the direct election of the chief executive and 50 percent of the seats in the SAR legislature.

The BPG's distrust of direct elections and party politics was strikingly similar to that of Beijing. In July 1986, shortly before the fifty-seven BLCC members put forth their proposal, Lu Ping commented that party politics was harmful to the stability of Hong Kong, and that democracy was not contingent upon the practice of direct elections.[40] As secretary-general of the HKMAO, he "received directives from the State Council and formulated guidelines and policies for Hong Kong and Macao."[41]

The preference of Hong Kong's business and professional elites to preserve the status quo and their disregard of the rising political consciousness of the local population were reminiscent of Beijing's attitude toward the political reforms that the governments of London and Hong Kong had pushed for ever since the signing of the Joint Declaration in 1984. China was suspicious of England's intentions, and accused the British government of trying to retain influence in the SAR after 1997 and internationalize the Hong Kong issue. At the same time, it had no patience for the pro-democracy faction. China stuck to the lines stipulated by the Joint Declaration: "The Hong Kong Special Administrative Region shall maintain the capitalist economic and trade systems previously practised in Hong Kong."[42]

7. The Drafting of the Basic Law

In February 1987, the BLDC's Beijing-Hong Kong relations committee passed a draft of the preamble to the Basic Law. The document stated that the Basic Law followed Article 31 of the Chinese Constitution, to safeguard China's fundamental guidelines for policy implementation toward Hong Kong after 1997.[43] It emphasized the "one country, two systems" concept, which allowed Hong Kong to maintain its capitalist system. In addition to the preamble, the committee outlined the general principles of Chapter One of the Basic Law.

The drafting of the Basic Law enabled the conservative business and professional elites to exercise political influence.[44] After further expanding its membership, the BPG became known as the Group of Eighty-Nine, and its proposal for Hong Kong's future political system came to be known as the "Model of Eighty-Nine." In this model of the composition of the electoral college, business and professional persons would occupy the majority of the seats, which aroused charges that they wanted to control the elections. Responding to this criticism, the Group of Eighty-Nine argued that the people of Hong Kong did not understand democracy well enough to participate in general elections. Therefore, the elite could serve as their representatives.[45]

In 1988, recognizing the need to obtain extensive support for its plan, the Group of Eighty-Nine modified its proposed method of electing the chief executive. The electoral college would still choose the chief executive in 1997, but the method of "one man-one vote" would be adopted after 1997 if one half of the registered voters participated in the legislative elections. In this event, the consent of two thirds of the legislature and the chief executive would be required to introduce general elections.

Throughout the drafting process, the business establishment failed to present itself as a coordinated or united force in politics. Although it shared the general concern for maintaining Hong Kong's prosperity and controlling the rate of political reform, it lacked experience in forming political groups or parties. More importantly, business leaders were reluctant to get involved in "open" or "grassroots" political activities, and instead exerted influence on government policies through informal channels. Sociologist Wong Siu-lun recognized the local businessmen's weakness and predicted that they would perform poorly in direct elections.[46] Wong explained that there was "the undercurrent of distrust and ambivalence towards business ... among the educated elite and the public."[47] His argument was that business leaders had insufficient political expertise to be successful in open politics.

A general distrust of the business establishment was prevalent in Hong Kong, with middle-class professionals suspicious of the upper-class business elite. More specifically, the former were "quite skeptical of the integrity of the parties engaged in the economic competition."[48] The results of a local public opinion survey reflected this generally negative attitude towards business leaders. In the "Hong Kong Professionals and Attitudes Survey" of 1988–1989, among slightly more than 2,200 respondents of university or polytechnic educational backgrounds, nearly 45 percent felt that business leaders were neither honest nor dependable, approximately 42 percent did not have confidence in the business elite, and almost 60 percent thought that business leaders had too much political power.[49]

8. The Split in the Business Establishment

The business elite was not a cohesive force and suffered from internal disputes. Therefore, it is not surprising that a split emerged in the Group of Eighty-Nine over the future political system of Hong Kong. Group members, including Lo Tak-shing, formed the New Hong Kong Alliance in May 1989, before the June 4, 1989, Tiananmen crackdown. The Alliance proposed a bicameral legislature for the future SAR, and seemed to have the support of HK Xinhua and Beijing. The remaining members of the Group of Eighty-Nine, led by Vincent Lo, appeared to be on the losing end. The split revealed the characteristics and inherent weaknesses of the local business establishment, especially in regard to their relations with Beijing.

8.1. The Cha-Cha Model

The Group of Eighty-Nine had originally formed to oppose the proposal of the pro-democracy faction, which China also found unacceptable. By late 1988, however, the publisher of the newspaper *Ming Pao*, Louis Cha, had moved to establish a compromise between pro-democracy faction and Beijing. Controversy immediately resulted from this action, and business circles subsequently suffered from internal strife. As a result, the Louis Cha model was not accepted.

On November 17, 1988, Cha put forth what he called a reform model of "three stages in order and gradation."[50] A co-sponsor of the BLDC subgroup on political structure, he distributed his proposal to its members two days before their Guangzhou meeting. In Cha's model, Hong Kong's political reform was to proceed through three stages after 1997. Each stage would last for fifteen years, and a referendum would be called to decide whether or not to proceed to the next stage. At the center of the three-stage model was the establishment of an election committee composed of one thousand people, which would be responsible for choosing the chief executive.

During the first stage, election committee members would be equally divided among (1) those from the industrial/business/financial sectors, (2) professionals, (3) labor/religious/social service representatives, and (4) members of Legco, District Boards, and the Civil Service. During the second stage, the representatives from each sector would be reduced by half, and the other half of the election committee would be chosen by popular election. During the third stage, the election committee would become a nomination committee, choosing three candidates to run for the post of the chief executive. At that point, the Hong Kong electorate would vote for the chief executive. As for the legislature, Cha proposed that during the first stage, 25 percent of the eighty seats would be decided by popular election while the remaining seats would come from the functional constituencies, including (1) the industrial/business/financial sectors, (2) professionals, and (3) labor/religious/social service representatives. During the second stage, the proportion would change to one half chosen by popular vote, increasing to 100 percent in the third and final stage.

Cha's model, which represented a much more conservative stance than that taken by the majority of the Group of Eighty-Nine, shocked the local community and was severely criticized. In contrast to the Group's proposal, in which popular elections for the chief executive were to be held twenty years after 1997, Cha's model advocated a longer waiting period of thirty to forty-five years. In a conciliatory gesture, Cha revised his proposal before the Guangzhou meeting convened, reducing the original three stages to two. This meant that the chief executive would be directly elected fifteen years after Hong Kong's return to China, with direct elections for the entire legislature sixteen years after 1997.

When Cha's model became public, the Hong Kong media accused him of serving China's interests. According to local journalists, Cha had met with Li Hou (BLDC secretary-general), Lu Ping (BLDC deputy secretary), Mao Junnian (BLDC deputy secretary), and Xiao Weiyun (the other co-sponsor and BLDC member) before revealing his revised plan. The mainland China drafters had been worried that his proposed reform plan was too conservative for the people of Hong Kong to accept; hence, Cha modified his plan. In response, Li Hou supported Cha's model as the basis for discussion at the Guangzhou meeting.

When the BLDC general meeting assembled in January 1989, it had to vote on the revised drafts of Cha's model. Hong Kong drafter Cha Chi-ming was one of those who advocated adding four restrictions to the implementation of future referendums. He proposed that any referendum must first obtain prior approval from the majority of the legislature, the chief executive, and China's NPC Standing Committee before it could be carried out, and be considered legitimate only if 30 percent of the electorate voted for it. The "democrats" criticized Cha Chi-ming's revision, saying it made a referendum nearly impossible and removed the only democratic element in the Louis Cha proposal.[51] However, the Cha-Cha compromise model received a two-thirds majority vote (thirty-eight votes) and was passed, and the second draft of the Basic Law appeared for public consultation in February.

The emergence of the Cha-Cha model revealed certain characteristics and inherent weaknesses of China's united front efforts. When the mainland China drafters opposed the proposals of the pro-democracy faction, Louis Cha introduced his conservative model, and hoped that pro-democracy leaders Martin Lee and Szeto Wah would speak against it at the BLDC meeting.[52] Thus, putting forward another government model was a deliberate ploy by Cha to broaden support for China's intentions, and he aimed to reach a point at which a compromise might be made. Such a compromise was important in China's united front work to gain supporters and sympathizers. The local media attacked Louis Cha for paying court to China, but he defended himself, saying that his proposal was acceptable to Beijing, unlikely to be defeated, and thus instrumental in striking a balance between opposing views. By postponing popular elections for so many years after 1997, Cha argued, democracy would still have a chance to develop in the SAR. He apparently believed that this was more practical than insisting upon the rapid political reform advocated by the pro-democracy faction, which in his view had little chance of success. Whether Louis Cha was serving local interests or those of China, the question here is how he learned about Beijing's intentions—an important issue in relation to the perceived weakness within the united front effort.

8.2. Difficulties of the United Front Policy

China's united front work suffered from a lack of policy coordination and differences of opinion between Xu Jiatun and Beijing. According to local journalists, Louis Cha had consulted with Xu to get a better understanding of China's intentions. Cha then proposed his model, which required a waiting period of forty-five years before the introduction of popular elections into Hong Kong, but suggested the implementation of a referendum process to allow for an element of democracy. What Cha did not realize was that Xu's ideas had been too conservative for Beijing; China had already developed its own version of what the future political structure of Hong Kong should be.[53] The HKMAO had won in the debates held among mainland leaders by proposing faster reform than that advocated by Xu. Nevertheless, neither the HKMAO nor any mainland authority would agree to the idea of a referendum. At the BLDC subgroup meeting in November 1988, Lu Ping objected to the use of referendums in Louis Cha's model.[54] The later Cha Chi-ming revision gained the support of the Beijing drafters and won the majority of votes because of its imposition of restrictions on referendums.[55] As HKMAO officials, Lu Ping and Li Hou were more sensitive to public opinion in Hong Kong, but were caught off-guard when their mainland colleagues upheld the Cha-Cha model. Although Louis Cha had extensive access to China and was not afraid to stand up for his views, he found that he was misinformed. Local politicians who were not necessarily well informed about mainland politics and governmental affairs were also misled. This demonstrates that the mainland leaders lacked a clear vision and were unable to coordinate their efforts with Xu on the Hong Kong policy.

Local parties were poorly prepared and incapable of making compromises, a critically important factor in the united front effort. Because Louis Cha's model was more conservative than the business group had hoped for, concessions were not necessary. In addition, the group itself was divided, and some of its members would soon form their own political parties; thus, it did not have the will to engage in complex debates and bargains. The leaders of the pro-democracy faction, Martin Lee and Szeto Wah, chose a strategy of silent opposition in both the subgroup and BLDC meetings, although they explained their position at the very beginning of the first meeting.[56] This tactic was not what Louis Cha had predicted. Subsequently, however, Lee and Wah did harshly criticize the mainstream model, and the pro-democracy faction reiterated its fundamental position of direct election of the chief executive. The *South China Morning Post* reported that while other "political proposals on the composition of the Hongkong SAR legislature allowed for 25 to 50 per cent of the seats to be directly elected with 40 per cent a possible compromise," the pro-democracy faction paid little attention "to the issue and concentrated largely on the electoral system [for the selection of the chief executive]."[57] As the pro-democracy faction had no chance of attaining its main objective, it decided not to compromise on the pace of political reform for the SAR.[58]

Meanwhile, the local media criticized Beijing's manipulations—its promotion of elitism and backdoor politics.[59] Xu hoped that China would shift its focus from the big capitalists to the middle class. Regarding the Louis Cha incident, China failed in its united front effort; it was unable to facilitate a compromise because of its conservative position and inability to expand its influence to the middle class.

8.3. The New Hong Kong Alliance and Further Controversies

In March 1989, the New Hong Kong Alliance was formed. It consisted of over twenty members, including Legislative Councilors, District Board members, civil servants, and core members of the Group of Eighty-Nine.[60] Lo Tak-shing, a former Exco and Legco member and subsequent vice chair of the BLCC Standing Committee, was the Alliance's organizer and spokesperson.

The June 4 Incident at Tiananmen Square shocked the world and led to widespread condemnation of China. It terrified the people of Hong Kong, whose confidence in the future very much depended on their perception of China. In Hong Kong, the stock market tumbled, sales fell, public confidence declined, and emigration rose. Uncertain about Beijing politics and the effect of the June 4 Incident on Hong Kong's economy, many people, including politicians, worried about the prospects of political reform. For a short time following June 4, political groups sought to achieve a compromise while fighting for faster democratization than that proposed in the Cha-Cha model.

Exco and Legco members had introduced the Omelco consensus model on May 24 after the central government had declared martial law in Beijing (May 20). According to the proposal, 50 percent of the seats in the first Hong Kong SAR legislature would come from direct election, with 100 percent in the third legislature in 2003. Lydia Dunn, a senior Legco member, acknowledged that the two councils were able to reach a consensus as a result of the events in Beijing and because of the Hong Kong people's support of the student movement there.[61] Legco members of the Group of Eighty-Nine, including Stephen Cheong and James Tien, also agreed to faster democratization. In the other camp, Szeto Wah promised to persuade other pro-democracy faction members to accept the Omelco consensus model.

Nevertheless, this spirit of cooperation proved to be short-lived. Two months later, the Group of Eighty-Nine and the pro-democracy faction were again at odds with each other. While all Exco and Legco members agreed that at least 50 percent of the legislature should be directly elected in the 1995 elections, Martin Lee argued that the number should be "no less than" two thirds, and both Cheong and Tien immediately voiced their opposition. The June 4 Incident strengthened the resolve of the pro-democracy faction to insist on greater democratization, and it revised its 190 model. While continuing to call for the direct election of the chief executive, some members of the pro-democracy faction also called for the direct election of one half of the legislature in 1991 and the entire body in 1995. The Group of Eighty-Nine accused the pro-democracy faction of demanding too much.[62] Thus, although the student movement in Beijing appeared initially to have brought the two sides of the political spectrum together in Hong Kong, the crackdown that followed set them apart again.

While images from the June 4 Incident were still fresh in the minds of the people of Hong Kong, the second draft of the Basic Law followed the Cha-Cha model, which allowed for fifteen of fifty-five Legco seats to be directly elected in 1997. In August, the Alliance put forth its revised proposal, which was even more conservative. Although the Alliance had earlier emphasized its concern for the welfare of all classes, its new proposal for the Basic Law marked a definite split within the Group of Eighty-Nine. In essence, the Alliance asked for a bicameral legislature for the SAR. In its proposal, one council would be elected by the people and District Boards while the other council would be chosen by functional groups representing different occupational backgrounds. The two councils would have the same rights and responsibilities, and at least 50 percent of the vote of each council would be needed to pass a new law. The media was quick to criticize the proposal, suggesting that the business/industrial and professional sectors would be able to dominate among the functional groups without the need for their members to participate in popular elections. Business and professional representatives could then pose a significant threat to the pro-democracy forces in the legislature.[63] Furthermore, only one fourth of the legislature would be directly elected under the terms of this proposal, even less than the 27 percent that was originally scheduled for 1997 in the second draft of the Basic Law. More importantly, the percentage would remain the same in the future, so that the legislature could not progress toward greater democracy.

8.4. Competition among the Business Elite

Lo Tak-shing's meeting with leaders in Beijing led to speculation that some Alliance members had good relations with China. While the Alliance denied the China factor behind its proposal, the HKMAO, HK Xinhua, Joint Liaison Group, and Basic Law mainland drafters said that the plan deserved special consideration. In addition, the Alliance did not seek support from other business leaders, as there was dissent among the business representatives of the BLCC. James Tien argued that the Alliance's proposal would reduce the means of communication between the councilors from different groups, making conflicts within the legislature irreconcilable. Allen Lee, an independent businessman and senior Legco member, warned that a bicameral structure was unsuitable for Hong Kong because of internal divisions and impediments to political reform if the proposal was ratified.[64] Even Basic Law drafter Li Ka-shing, one of the wealthiest business tycoons in Asia, openly stated that he would not support a bicameral legislature.[65] Apparently, the Alliance's proposal was supported by China but not the local community. Many believed that it was aimed against the pro-democracy faction and Omelco consensus model.[66] The latter was true, as China regarded Exco and Legco to be part of the Hong Kong British government. Whether the idea of a bicameral legislature came from the Alliance or Beijing, it certainly had China's support.

By the second time the notion was raised, the proposal for a bicameral legislature had already motivated diverse forces to work together to produce a compromise model for the Basic Law. Their goal was to develop a plan that would allow for a greater degree of democracy than that proposed by the Alliance, yet be acceptable to China. Responding to worldwide condemnation after the June 4 Incident, Beijing said that Hong Kong was being used as a base of subversion against China. Beijing was referring to the action of pro-democracy leaders Martin Lee and Szeto Wah, who had resigned from their positions in the BLDC as a protest against Beijing's suppression of the student movement. Subsequently, *Renmin ribao* [*People's Daily*, Beijing] charged Lee and Wah with engaging in subversive activities against China. Furthermore, Sino-British relations had reached a low point. Responding to international pressure, London felt it necessary to appear to be fighting on behalf of the people of Hong Kong for greater democracy after 1997. However, when the Alliance put forth an ultraconservative model that appeared to have China's support, the opposition parties realized that they had to cooperate with each other. Meanwhile, Exco and Legco members were still promoting their Omelco consensus model, which was regarded by China as a product of the Hong Kong British government, and, therefore, had no chance of succeeding.[67]

In another effort to reach a compromise, a new model was presented during the second consultation period, which was extended as a result of the June 4 Incident. The proposal appeared in July when the middle forces, namely, the "Educationalists" and Vincent Lo's Group of Eighty-Nine, called for a new proportion of representation in the Hong Kong SAR legislature in 1997, with 40 percent of the seats to come from direct election, 40 percent from functional constituencies, and 20 percent from the electoral college. Within the Group of Eighty-Nine, twelve voted for this "four: four: two" model, whereas Lo Tak-shing and three others opposed it.[68]

8.5. The United Front's Manipulations

China's decision to support the proposal for a bicameral legislature was a well-calculated move to gain an ally, namely, the Alliance, in the midst of criticism after the June 4 Incident. In this way, the united front effort returned to the original objective of securing China's dominance and collaboration with the business establishment. Nevertheless, Beijing was unable to foresee the split among the business elite and the dramatic rivalries this engendered. Furthermore, it had not expected that the Alliance would provoke such widespread negative feelings and attacks from every party. Hence, it began to back away from its position of total support for the Alliance. According to a local news source, China was searching for alternatives to a bicameral legislature.[69] Because the Alliance was isolated from the rest of Hong Kong society, even the business community, China was inclined to offer the impression that more options were available.

In the end, the final draft of the Basic Law was the result of Sino-British negotiations behind closed doors. Although local parties had been promoting their own models throughout the drafting process, the articles of the Basic Law were settled through high-level bargaining between the governments of Beijing and London. Before the BLDC met in Beijing in February 1990, "an ultimate 'compromise'" was reached as a result of "behind-the-scenes" diplomatic negotiations.[70] The public knew only of the visits to Beijing by the British Prime Minister's personal adviser, Sir Percy Cradock, and Governor David Wilson, and the visit to Hong Kong by Foreign Secretary Douglas Hurd in the first two months of 1990. China and Britain were able to reach a deal after seven secret dialogues between January 18 and February 12, although the content of these talks did not become public knowledge for some time.[71] During the seventh dialogue on February 12, one day before the BLDC meeting convened in Beijing, Hurd informed Foreign Minister Qian Qichen that the Basic Law would specify that the number of directly elected seats in the Hong Kong SAR legislature be twenty in 1997, twenty-four in 1999, and thirty in 2003.[72]

In many ways, China's initial support for the Alliance resembled the Louis Cha case. Both Cha and the Alliance introduced a model that was hoped to be acceptable to China and those in Hong Kong. The business class provided fundamental support for the united front policy. While China intended to dominate in the debates over what model was most suitable for Hong Kong, it sought to ally itself with a certain minority of the business community. After the June 4 Incident, however, the united front effort targeted only a select few of the upper-class business leaders. This setback was obviously a direct consequence of the decline in China's world image and prestige after June 4, 1989. The well-being of the people of Hong Kong depended on the local economy, which was greatly affected by the performance of mainland China. The projection of a gloomy outlook and an uncertain future by China would lead to lower levels of confidence among Hong Kong people and an unfavorable attitude toward the united front effort.

9. The Basic Law

The Basic Law was adopted on April 4, 1990. According to Article 45, "The Chief Executive of the Hong Kong Special Administrative Region shall be selected by election or through consultations held locally and be appointed by the Central People's Government."[73] It holds that the selection method is suitable for conditions in Hong Kong and "in accordance with the principle of gradual and orderly progress."[74]

The Basic Law specified that in 1997, the first chief executive would be chosen in accordance with the "Decision of the National People's Congress on the Method for the Formation of the First Government and the First Legislative Council of the Hong Kong Special Administrative Region." Adopted by the Seventh NPC in April 1990, this Decision stated that a Selection Committee of four hundred members should "recommend the candidate for the first Chief Executive through local consultations or through nomination and election after consultations, and report the recommended candidate to the Central People's Government for appointment."[75]

In its first term, the legislative body was to be composed in accordance with the above-mentioned Decision, which stated that it should "be composed of 60 members, with 20 members returned by geographical constituencies through direct elections, 10 members returned by an election committee, and 30 members returned by functional constituencies."[76] In its second term, thirty of the legislative members would come from functional constituencies, six from the election committee, and twenty-four from geographical constituencies through direct election. In the third term, thirty members would come from functional constituencies and the other thirty from geographical constituencies through direct election. Amendments to alter the legislature's formation would be possible after 2007, but would require the consent of the chief executive and a two-thirds majority of the legislature.[77]

10. Conclusion

The discord within the Hong Kong business community, as evidenced by the split within the Group of Eighty-Nine, had not been anticipated by Beijing. Initially, Beijing supported the proposal for a bicameral legislature to get breathing space in the midst of the hostile response to its suppression of the student movement in June 1989. It was unable to foresee that the business community would launch harsh attacks against the Alliance, its primary working partner at the time. Beijing was baffled by the local business community, whose members changed their position as they saw fit.

For their part, Hong Kong's business leaders fought to win acceptance for their proposals as they had political ambitions and were competing with each other to gain favor with China. This competition revealed the business elite's determination to protect its own interests and the decisive role that Beijing played in the drafting process. Thus, it is evident that although the original united front policy aimed at attaining a breakthrough with the big capitalists and securing the good will of the larger Hong Kong society, China abandoned this approach and chose to deal directly with the British government to finalize the articles of the Basic Law.

Acknowledgment: This chapter is an expanded and updated version of the author's article: "The Failure of the United Front Policy: The Involvement of Business in the Drafting of Hong Kong's Basic Law, 1985–1990," *Asian Perspective* 24, no. 2 (2000): 173–98. The author gratefully acknowledges permission from *Asian Perspective* to publish this chapter.

The Chinese Communists' United Front with Big Business and Their Collaboration on the Handover, 1990–1997

1. Introduction

Although the united front effort had limitations, the Chinese Communists were successful in soliciting the support of big business in the years preceding 1997 in preparation for the handover. Beijing did not hesitate to announce those who were its staunch supporters and those whom it considered troublemakers. The ultimate objective was to ensure the smooth transfer of the administration of Hong Kong in 1997. In forming the Preliminary Work Committee (PWC) and appointing the Hong Kong Affairs Advisers and District Affairs Advisers, the Chinese Communists created a three-tier united front to consolidate their position regarding the future leadership of the Hong Kong SAR. Thus, the united front work of this period was more restricted than the effort made in the 1980s, as Beijing did not select members of the United Democrats of Hong Kong, who had opposing opinions and were critical of the Communist strategy. In contrast to earlier times, the Chinese Communists openly declared the enemy of the united front—the last governor of Hong Kong, Christopher (Chris) Patten.

2. The Impact of the Tiananmen Incident of June 4, 1989

The student movement in Beijing in 1989 caught the world's attention. People in Hong Kong vigilantly monitored the events in mainland China, which dominated the media. The pro-democracy faction was quick to respond to the calls of the demonstrators in Beijing. In May 1989, pro-democracy leaders Martin Lee and Szeto Wah, among others, formed the Hong Kong Alliance in Support of the Patriotic Democratic Movement in China, which sent local donations—money and material resources—to the mainland. Lee and Wah also resigned from the BLDC in protest against the Beijing government.[1] On May 21, more than one million Hong Kong people took to the streets in the first major rally in support of the Beijing protesters.[2] The students' fervor touched the hearts of many in Hong Kong, regardless of their political stand. Even Louis Cha, who had advocated a conservative model for the political institutions of the future Hong Kong SAR government, joined the list of BLDC members who resigned.[3]

The unofficial members of the Exco and Legco took the initiative and called for direct elections for one half of the seats of the legislature in 1995 and all of the seats in 2003.[4] This was the Omelco consensus model, which came from the Office of the Members of the Executive and Legislative Councils. According to Sir Chung Sze-yuen, a senior member of Exco from 1980 to 1988, the June 4 Incident provoked the Hong Kong British government and unofficial members of Exco and Legco to depart from their traditional "historic neutrality" toward domestic developments in mainland China.[5] Sir Sze-yuen had tried to persuade Lydia Dunn and Allen Lee, senior unofficial members, to refrain from approving the consensus model, which asked for a faster rate of democratization than the Basic Law allowed, but he was unsuccessful. In his memoirs, he writes that the local colonial administration had always prohibited activities that would appear hostile to the Beijing government and provoke a reaction.[6] Therefore, he was alarmed to see the arrival in Hong Kong of a mainland Chinese dissident, who had been issued a visa by the British embassy in the United States, because such a scenario had not happened before. Moreover, Exco and Legco unofficial members were urging London to grant "the three million Hong Kong-born British nationals" the right of residence in the United Kingdom.[7] Sir Sze-yuen recollected that he cautioned both Dunn and Lee against making a strong request, and asked them to appeal to the public to be less emotional and agitated.[8] After the June 4 Incident, the political climate in Hong Kong shifted, with increased demand for democracy after 1997. On the one hand, this allowed for cooperation among different parties that otherwise would not have met for media-tion and dialogue. On the other hand, relations between the Hong Kong government and Beijing underwent periods of squabbles, disputes, and rivalries in the remaining years before 1997.

As the 1990s unfolded, Hong Kong witnessed the first direct election of eighteen seats (representing nine geographical constituencies) of the Legco. Academics Alvin Y. So and Reginald Y. Kwok observed that with many of the democrats (previously identified as members or advocates of the pro-democracy movement) entering Legco, "a nascent democracy movement" had developed to ask for the direct election of all members of the legislature and guarantees for an independent legislature and judicial freedom to forestall interference from Beijing after 1997.[9] So and Kwok added that the "democrats began to campaign on an anti-Beijing line in the early 1990s."[10] Emerging in the 1990s as a political force was Hong Kong's middle class, which comprised, as it does elsewhere, professionals, the well educated, and the economically better off. They were locally born and, unlike their parents, who had escaped from turmoil in mainland China, emotionally attached to Hong Kong, and demanded greater political opportunities for themselves. Similar to the efforts of the Chinese Communists and Xu Jiatun in the 1980s, the objective of the united front work in the 1990s was to secure the support of the upper class to obtain a breakthrough in relations with the middle class, whom the democrats and liberals sought to represent.

In the remaining years of the transition period, disagreement arose about "Hong Kong's status quo," which China vowed to maintain for fifty years after 1997. Beijing believed that the colonial administration and democrats aimed at a face lift of the local political institutions within the few years before 1997, to force upon the Communists a fait accompli. According to the CCP leaders, the British had not given Hong Kong democracy for 150 years, but all at once had become enthused about political reform. China agreed not to make significant changes for fifty years after 1997 with the understanding that the status quo referred to those circumstances in 1984 when the Beijing government signed the Joint Declaration.[11] Thus, when the Hong Kong government and local politicians called for a faster rate of democratization to provide more guarantees for the freedoms of the people after 1997, China thought that such moves were directed against Beijing itself. The arrival of Chris Patten to replace David Wilson as governor of Hong Kong in 1992 caused further controversy, as the latter, who was a Sinologist, had seemed complacent about China. With issues related to elections and political reform occupying news headlines, a heated rivalry developed between the Hong Kong government and Beijing, which led to various accusations and conspiracies that haunted the territory up to 1997.

3. The United Front Work of the Communists and the Hong Kong Affairs Advisers

In 1991, the Chinese Communists assessed Hong Kong's social structure and identified three classes—the bourgeoisie, the middle class, and workers—each having its own interests to safeguard and objectives to pursue.[12] According to the Communists, the bourgeoisie wanted the social structure to remain intact, to protect their business interests; the middle class sought more advancement opportunities through political change; and workers aimed at improving their working and living conditions. A CCP article described Hong Kong's status quo: a local political superstructure closely related to the existing capitalist economy and class structure. Therefore, the bourgeoisie would continue to dominate in future political institutions and unite with other classes of society.[13] The Communists believed that during the transition period, prominent industrialists, business leaders, professionals, and political groups already played an active role in politics, reflecting bourgeoisie domination in government institutions. The main issues under discussion then were the future political structure of Hong Kong, the Basic Law, and relations between Hong Kong and China.[14]

The Communists identified the status quo as public consultation and participation in social matters, judicial independence, basic freedoms, and the rule of law, which would be beneficial to the implementation of the "one country, two systems" policy. The CCP article elaborated that Hong Kong's basic freedoms, free trade, and economy were fundamental to the "democratic system" under the "one country, two systems" principle.[15] As noted, the Chinese Communists saw the status quo under British rule as including the practice of consultation.[16] Therefore, when the democrats demanded direct elections, Beijing naturally saw this as a deviation from the status quo in the territory and an attempt to counteract the possibility of interference by Beijing in Hong Kong affairs after 1997.

With the impending return of Hong Kong to China, Beijing was anxious to consolidate support for its final takeover of the territory, and thus appointed in 1992 local advisers who were on its side.[17] In his memoirs, Sir Chung Sze-yuen recalls a dinner arranged by Vincent Lo of the Business and Professionals Federation (BPF). Lu Ping, then Director of the HKMAO, invited Sir Sze-yuen to join a group of Hong Kong Affairs Advisers, whom China would soon announce to the public. In March 1992, Beijing appointed forty-four Hong Kong Affairs Advisers, who would serve two years with the HKMAO and HK Xinhua. The purpose was "to co-opt eminent community figures into the pro-China camp," and the advisers "were supposed to render advice to Beijing on matters with respect to Hong Kong."[18] HK Xinhua, with about 500 to 600 employees,[19] centered on united front work which meant "identifying credible locals to speak out on China's behalf on critical issues."[20]

Subsequently, three more batches of advisers were appointed, bringing the total number to 186. Sir Sze-yuen accepted the offer to serve as an adviser but then faced charges that he was switching over to China's side.

He explained that his aim was to serve the people of Hong Kong rather than the Beijing government, as his loyalty had always rested with the local population and not with any government. He said that the advisers did not constitute an organization; rather, they operated in an "individual capacity" and could express their views freely. He regularly sent in "written submissions" on his views on Hong Kong politics to the HKMAO and HK Xinhua.[21]

Responding to queries about whether China was establishing another power center in Hong Kong, the Ministry of Foreign Affairs said that Beijing had no such intention, and was only gathering public opinion for the HKMAO and HK Xinhua during the transition period.[22] HKMAO director Lu Ping claimed that China wanted to improve its assessment of public opinion in this period.[23] There were reports that the Hong Kong government was concerned about the role of the advisers, and that the governor, Sir David Wilson, had sought clarification from China. However, local Communist sources said that the advisers would "not be a formal group with constitution" in an attempt to end speculation about "another nucleus of power" in Hong Kong,[24] while the Ministry of Foreign Affairs stated that the appointment of Hong Kong Affairs Advisers would not interfere with the local administration.[25]

The appointment of forty-four advisers in March 1992 is representative of the Chinese Communist united front effort after the June 4 Incident. Beijing was seeking united front allies only among its staunch supporters or conservatives—those who had served in the Basic Law drafting and consultative committees, representatives of China's NPC and CPPCC, industrial/business/professional elites, former and incumbent Legco members, and so forth. Most importantly, none of those appointed was a democrat, and would not raise controversy within the group. A local academic observed that the Chinese Communists assumed a more conservative posture, and that the appointments did not represent an attempt to rally people with opposite views, namely, those calling for faster democratization and political reform. The membership of united front allies became more restricted, especially compared with the 1985 selection of BLCC members, which was a move to solicit local supporters, as even pro-democracy advocates were invited to join.[26] China was on the defensive, facing charges and demands after the June 4 Incident. For the time being, the Chinese Communists retreated from the more encompassing united front strategy of the 1980s. They were prepared to listen only to close allies in Hong Kong. Conciliation had given way to struggles, allegations, and news headlines.

The Communists identified their close allies in a high-profile manner. The *South China Morning Post* reported the "high-powered turnout" of

Communist leaders in an appointment ceremony in Beijing's Great Hall of the People in March 1992.[27] On that occasion, President Yang Shangkun, Premier Li Peng, vice premiers Wu Xueqian, Zou Jiahua, and Zhu Rongji, HKMAO director Lu Ping, and HK Xinhua director Zhou Nan showed their support for the Hong Kong Affairs Advisers. The Communist leaders were eager to publicize their close allies in Hong Kong. The *South China Morning Post* provided detailed coverage of the new appointees, one half of whom came from the business elite, with many having served on the Basic Law committees and some in the NPC and CPPCC. Eight advisers were listed as professionals, and had similar experience in the Basic Law committees, NPC, and CPPCC. Of those remaining, ten were political appointees, two were religious leaders, and two were representatives from the New Territories.

Some of the advisers were tycoons, including Cha Chi-ming, who sponsored the "go-slow political model during Basic Law discussions," Henry Fok, who had "extensive business interests" in mainland China, and Li Ka-shing, whose words carried "great weight."[28] Also among those appointed was Tung Chee-hwa, who would become the first chief executive of the Hong Kong SAR in 1997. The *South China Morning Post* called him a "low profile pro-China businessman," whom Beijing had chosen as "counsel for its considerable interests in Hongkong."[29] Wong Po-yan, David Li, Vincent Lo, Ann Tse-kai, Gordon Wu, and Sir Run Run Shaw were among the business group. Sir Chung Sze-yuen and New Hong Kong Alliance founder Lo Tak-shing were also on the advisory panel.

The day after their appointment, the forty-four advisers listened to General Secretary Jiang Zemin, who emphasized that the British should cooperate with Beijing on Hong Kong matters, and that China's domestic affairs were not the business of Hong Kong people. Also present were former HKMAO director Ji Pengfei, United Front Department head Ding Guangen, Lu Ping, and Zhou Nan.[30] The success of the united front depended on the shared cultural traditions of mainland China and Hong Kong, the mutual desire for closer ties, and the need for the advisers to comment on the Hong Kong situation.[31] Jiang Zemin talked about the background of the collaboration, the motive behind the appointments, and the tasks ahead. Whereas some advisers had political ambitions, others had no wish to run for election, such as real estate tycoon Gordon Wu, who claimed that he did not represent any constituency, and would not be tied down in political matters.

Beijing did not appoint any democrats in the first batch of advisers. The conservative outlook of the appointees made it clear to the Hong Kong public that the Communists were excluding those with views different from their own, especially members of the United Democrats of Hong Kong.[32] The leaders of the United Democrats, including Martin Lee, also constituted the leadership of the Hong Kong Alliance in Support of the Patriotic Democratic Movement in China, and had called for the overthrow of the Beijing government responsible for the June 4 Incident. On the one hand, the appointment of the forty-four advisers drew the line between close friends and others. On the other hand, Lu Ping used the same "divide and rule" tactic with the democrats and liberals on a visit to Hong Kong.[33] On that occasion, he met with the liberals (moderates) of the Meeting Point and the Association for Democracy and People's Livelihood, but avoided the United Democrats, who won twelve of the eighteen directly elected Legco seats in September 1991. Lu chose to meet with "less confrontational" people—the liberals of political parties, academics, and intellectuals—and business leaders.[34] As local analyst Frank Ching observed, Beijing rejected opinions on Hong Kong opposite to its own, and Lu Ping refused to meet with people with diverse and contrasting views.[35]

In their choice of the first group of advisers, the Communists showed the outside world their close allies, and what kind of advice they were seeking. These advisers were the core of the united front allies, as some of them had been serving in the NPC and CPPCC. It was said that Beijing was gathering and nurturing pro-China leaders for Hong Kong: "There's a feeling among Chinese officials that if China doesn't start grooming its own leaders now then it will be left at the mercy of the Hongkong Government."[36] Later, other advisory groups were named, and appointees included those from the outer layers of united front targets—moderates or liberals from the Meeting Point and the Association for Democracy and People's Livelihood. The second and third groups of advisers comprised "a small number of 'soft' democrats and academics," but did not include members of the United Democrats.[37]

4. The United Front Strategy and Megaphone Politics

The united front work not only rallied allies but also singled out enemies. During the transition period leading up to 1997, the Chinese Communists were at odds with the British over a number of issues, and many times, the former made known their stance in public circles before negotiations. Lu Ping visited Guangzhou in March 1992, and on this and many other occasions lashed out at the Hong Kong administration and London.[38] He criticized the Hong Kong government budget on the grounds that its basic principles deviated from those of the Basic Law. He asked why the Hong Kong Provisional Airport Authority had awarded the contract for the new airport terminal to a British company, which had submitted the most expensive proposal. The media questioned whether Lu's remarks would become a "daily event" until his return to Beijing.

Lu employed the "divide and rule" method among the democrats to distinguish between possible supporters and opponents, and took advantage of a public forum to consolidate the position of the Chinese Communists against the British. This tactic was called "megaphone diplomacy" by the local media, and resembled the strategy of the Communists in the 1930s and 1940s when they announced their policies toward the Nationalists and Japanese, aiming at securing the widest possible united front against their enemies. The Communists identified enemies, broadcast their views, and sought to win allies. In the previous few years, Lu had used the same tactic, and his complaints were similar. When he was in Guangzhou in December 1990, shortly before the airport talks, he delivered severe criticisms of the Hong Kong government. He expressed his disapproval in the same manner in January 1991 when he met the Hong Kong governor in Beijing.[39] Although the topic was different, Lu used the same megaphone strategy to put the British on the defensive regarding critical matters and talks concerning Hong Kong.[40] The upcoming issues included the future of Radio Television of Hongkong (RTHK) after 1997—corporatization or a government news agency—and the Hong Kong government budget before the handover.

Before the new governor, Chris Patten, took office in July 1992, both Beijing and the local Communists (HK Xinhua) warned him against creating a hostile political atmosphere in the territory. For some weeks, Beijing openly objected to the possibility of appointing members of the United Democrats to Exco. On the eve of Patten's arrival, the leftist media and HK Xinhua asked him not to launch major political reforms, to ensure Hong Kong's stability and prosperity and a smooth transition to Chinese rule in 1997.[41] On both the national (through Beijing's spokesman) and local (through leftist sources) levels, the Chinese Communists employed the megaphone tactic to announce their position, prepare for Patten's future actions, and provide justification for future attacks, if necessary, against Patten's administration.

The Chinese Communists advised on Hong Kong matters in response to Chris Patten's high-handed action in calling for faster democratization of the territory, in direct contrast to the policy of his predecessors. Beijing was concerned about the government structure. Meeting in July 1992 with delegates from the pro-Beijing party—the Democratic Alliance for the Betterment of Hong Kong (DAB), Lu Ping commented that foreign passport holders could stand for election in the 1995 Legco elections, and, if they won, could constitute at most 20 percent of the lawmaking body. Lu's comments were in line with earlier proposals of the DAB.[42] Through the DAB delegation, he also forwarded messages to Patten. In August, Patten assured China of the continuation of an executive-led administration.[43] The new governor also met with Zhou Nan, the director of HK Xinhua and the most senior official from mainland China he had seen so far. Although Zhou was not in competition with Lu to advise on Hong Kong matters, the local media still called the former "the shadow governor" of the transition period. Proclaiming their position on various issues, the Chinese Communists aroused suspicion that they were setting up "their own stove" in Hong Kong, namely, creating with their allies another authority against the local administration.

The megaphone diplomacy of the Chinese Communists was evident on both national and local levels, as they launched offensives against the governments in London and Hong Kong. Criticized by the British for interfering in Hong Kong matters, Beijing asserted that it had "the right and responsibility" to do so.[44] In mid-1992, the Chinese head of the Sino-British Joint Liaison Group (JLG), Guo Fengmin, stated that Beijing would not want to see the appointment of United Democrats to Exco. Subsequently, China's ambassador to London, Ma Yuzhen, dismissed British objections to Guo's comments, and stated that China was acting in accordance with the provisions of the Joint Declaration to ensure the successful transfer of the Hong Kong administration. Ma was reiterating the Chinese position on a statement from China's Foreign Ministry in response to the British opposition. Beijing and London became entangled in Hong Kong issues. Obviously, China's snub increased the tension between the two sides, which argued about Exco appointments and democratization in 1995.[45] China's media joined the debate as *Wenhuibao* (*Wen Wei Po*) staged attacks against the British Foreign Office, while Beijing considered the British criticism of Guo invalid.

Patten unveiled his reform package for Hong Kong for the remaining years before the handover in a speech at the opening session of the Legco on October 7, 1992. His proposals for constitutional change covered the District Boards, Legco, and Exco. Regarding the 1995 Legco elections, Patten said he would need to discuss them with Beijing. He pressed for the direct election of twenty out of sixty Legco seats in 1997. According to the Basic Law, the election committee would choose ten Legco seats, and functional constituencies the remaining thirty. Patten also proposed the establishment of nine new functional constituencies, and the direct election of all District Board members, who would constitute the election committee. He was making a head start in his reform proposals and had already arranged to visit Beijing later the same month.[46] The governor was well prepared for Chinese objections even before he announced his plan, but calculated that Beijing would not want to jeopardize stability by refusing to discuss the proposals.[47]

Only an hour after Patten had left Beijing following his first official visit there, Lu Ping held a press conference in the Chinese capital and asserted China's position on various issues. Lu revealed to the media that there had previously been an understanding between London and Beijing on the 1995 Legco elections. He also cautioned the Hong Kong government and London against not seeking China's approval on the new airport and making unilateral decisions. Commenting on Patten's visit, Lu said that the governor had refused to respect China's opinion on constitutional issues in Hong Kong, and that there had been no advancement in relations with the other side. He said that confrontation was expected, and that if that happened, China would not hesitate to take drastic actions including the establishment of its own administration to take over Hong Kong in 1997.[48] The Beijing leaders engaged in open debates with the new governor. The media observed that China "had the whip hand in influencing public opinion in the territory, sending chills through the economy at will" and generating controversy among local groups as to what might constitute the best interests of the territory.[49] They interpreted Lu's warnings at the beginning of the Patten administration as "opening shots in what could be a long war."[50]

5. Beijing's United Front Allies

While Beijing and the Patten administration were revealing their differences in opinion, Hong Kong society did not merely stand by and watch. Local groups took action. By late 1992, the Business and Professionals Federation (BPF), headed by Vincent Lo, was seen as a possible mediator between Beijing and Patten, to resolve the deadlock between the two sides. A *South China Morning Post* headline read: "Business Could Help End Political Impasse."[51] There were rumors that the BPF would take on the role of a political party. If that were the case, the paper suggested, then the BPF could be an alternative force to the democrats and liberals, as its members were business and community elite with much political influence, and many were Legco members and former Basic Law drafters. There was speculation whether the BPF could "unblock the logjam" between Patten and China over constitutional reform. Under the current circumstances, neither the liberals nor pro-Beijing forces such as DAB could offer a solution to the dispute. The business elite might succeed where others had failed—the Patten administration seriously needed productive discussions with groups in Hong Kong society to find effective ways to break the impasse.[52]

Nevertheless, business leaders soon emerged as conservative critics of the Patten administration. The BPF's attacks against Patten's political reform package dashed any hopes that the business elite would act as a mediator between Beijing and the local administration. Rather than acting as a go-between, Vincent Lo criticized Patten's two main proposals related to the 1995 elections, those concerning the election committee and functional constituencies.[53] The BPF refuted the longstanding rumor of its intention to form a political party, but claimed that business had the responsibility to express its concern over political reform in Hong Kong.[54] According to Lo, the BPF aimed at forestalling Patten's reform package, and had the support of Chinese-owned companies in Hong Kong. This move signified that local Chinese business members were important allies of Beijing's united front effort.[55]

As a close ally of China's united front, the BPF stepped forward and denounced Patten's policy address on October 7, 1992. Lo claimed that if Patten went ahead with his political reform and Legco supported the related bills early the next year, then Hong Kong society would suffer enormously in the four and a half years before the handover.[56] Because of its fear that Hong Kong's stability and prosperity were in danger, the BPF issued a public statement against the governor. Lo even acknowledged that the BPF decision was atypical of the conservative business elite—businessmen and professionals had traditionally avoided public confrontations.[57] Nevertheless, the BPF, owing to the possible consequences of Patten's reform package, had to voice its opinion. Commentators said that the BPF as a whole was courageous to make a public declaration and oppose Patten's faster democratization of Hong Kong.[58]

China's united front allies learned to use megaphone politics. Another group that brought matters into the open was the DAB. DAB's chairman, Tsang Yok-sing, disproved rumors that China would establish a shadow government in Hong Kong, asserting that Lu Ping had denied such an intention during the visit of DAB to Beijing in December 1992.[59] After meeting with Beijing leaders, the DAB warned Patten against continuing to use confrontational tactics, and emphasized that only cooperation with China would ensure the smooth transfer of Hong Kong to Chinese rule in 1997. Otherwise, Tsang claimed, amid the current political impasse Patten would soon lose support from the majority of the local population.[60] He said that Patten had not received the right advice and was wrong to believe that he could achieve more through confronting Beijing.[61]

The Co-operative Resources Centre (CRC) and its convener—Legco member Allen Lee—joined the opposition against Patten's constitutional reform. CRC members claimed that like most people of Hong Kong, they were very concerned about the potential crises resulting from Patten's reform package.[62] According to the CRC, the existing crisis in relations between Beijing and the Hong Kong government was having a negative impact on local confidence in the future. Echoing the BPF, Lee said that there was a great deal of anxiety in Hong Kong society, and observed that CRC members could no longer "afford to stay nonchalant" as they had in the old days.[63] He warned the public about the adverse effects of the dispute, such as the polarization of the local community, conflicts among District Board members, stock market fluctuations, fears, and anxieties. Interestingly, he commented on megaphone politics and the exchange of accusations between the Beijing and Hong Kong governments, saying that Hong Kong people were filled with emotion as a result of the megaphone politics of Beijing and dreadful accusations in local society.[64]

As a counterproposal, Lee suggested that the composition of the election committee follow that outlined in the Sino-British correspondence dated February 1990. He urged that the demarcation of the nine new functional constituencies be based on the same principles as those of the existing 21 functional constituencies, as expressed in the 1984 and 1988 White Papers on the development of representative government. He opposed the abolition of appointed seats for the District Boards.[65] With this in mind, the CRC looked forward to a visit to Beijing to explain the current situation to the Communist leaders and hopefully end the controversy. In February 1993, on the eve of the Beijing visit, Lee explained that the CRC had two objectives: to resolve the political impasse between the Chinese and British governments, and to explore the possibility of arranging talks between both sides. He said that Hong Kong's relationship with China was not only political, resting on the "one country, two systems" principle, but also characterized by concerns about the economic prosperity of the territory after 1997.[66] Lee stressed that Hong Kong could not afford continued resistance to China.[67]

In early 1993, China announced the appointment of forty-nine additional Hong Kong Affairs Advisers, and the selection showed that Beijing was widening its united front to target different sectors of society, with the inclusion of political (17) and business (14) representatives, academics (11), professionals (4), and, what was most surprising, former government officials (3). Two persons of non-Chinese ethnicity were among these advisers.[68]

Belonging to the "minority" group, Sir David Akers-Jones was a British citizen and former Hong Kong government official. He now became one of the Chinese Communists' united front allies. Aged sixty-five at the time of his appointment, Sir David was the outgoing head of the Housing Authority, and had been Chief Secretary and briefly, acting Governor. He was then a member of the BPF's advisory council, and thus was projected to have a conservative outlook.[69] Sir David said his intention was to promote cooperation and communication between mainland China and Hong Kong. Responding to criticism of his decision to side with Beijing, the former senior official said that he saw the role of advisers as "important at a time when other channels of communication are failing to open up fresh channels ... the appointment of a wider range of advisers can help by substantially increasing the scope for communication."[70] He believed that as an expatriate, he could contribute new perspectives and suggestions in handling issues. Sir David said that all of his Chinese friends welcomed the appointment, and that he trusted that his example would provide assurance to foreigners in Hong Kong that they could engage in conversations with the Beijing government. With his previous experience in the District Boards, Municipal Councils, and functional constituencies, he was well acquainted with Hong Kong's social matters and needs. Having been a government official for thirty years (1957–1987), Sir David was also concerned about the morale of the civil service during the transition, especially given the bitter squabbles between the Beijing and British leaders. As an adviser to the BPF, he supported the business group's rejection of Patten's proposed reform package. He said that as a longtime resident of Hong Kong, he felt very sorry and regretted that relations between Beijing and the Hong Kong government had deteriorated to such an extent.[71] He reiterated that China had made known that negotiations were possible between the two sovereign powers.

The other non-Chinese to join the second group of advisers was the leader of the local Indian community (24,000 members), Hari Harilela. He was the honorary president of the Indian Chamber of Commerce, and in charge of the Holiday Inn hotels. Like Sir David, the Indian leader's concern was communication with Beijing, to safeguard the stability of Hong Kong. He named his two priorities: first, there was the need to let Beijing know of the concerns of Hong Kong people and how its leaders should respond to such matters; second, the Indian community must be informed of what would happen after 1997 and its responsibilities.[72] He said that some of his fellow Indians were worried about the future and felt insecure, as many of them would become stateless after the handover. Harilela was also a prominent member of the BPF. While he advised Beijing to support local infrastructure projects, such as the construction of the airport and container terminals, he also urged it to take note of the opinion of the civil service. He emphasized that expatriates had a role to play, and told the Communist leaders that the Customs and Excise and Inland Revenue departments and the Independent Commission Against Corruption (ICAC) could benefit from having non-Chinese as heads.

By the end of 1993, local leaders in Hong Kong had begun to make their move. The *South China Morning Post* reported, "A group of 200 prominent Chinese community leaders in Hong Kong have banded together to launch what could be the largest united front body in the territory."[73] The group called itself the Association of Overseas Chinese and Chinese in Hong Kong, and aimed at fostering the "spirit of brotherhood" and working for the transition to Chinese rule in 1997. Members included Wang Gung-wu (vice chancellor of the University of Hong Kong), Hilton Cheong-Leen (former chairman of the Urban Council), Ng Hong-mun (NPC representative), Maria Tam (lawyer), and Xu Simin (editor of the leftist magazine *Mirror* and a CPPCC Standing Committee member). They emphasized the necessity to unite, communicate, and cooperate. As the group's chief organizers were members of China's NPC and CPPCC (a united front organization), its being heard by Beijing leaders was beyond doubt. Members claimed that their association would be "a liaison mechanism for local Chinese and Chinese from other parts of the world."[74] The controversy surrounding Patten's political reform and resulting disputes had prompted various parties to publicize their stand and assert their position.

In late 1993, Beijing used the megaphone strategy and charged the British with behaving yet again like "old colonists." The Communist leaders claimed that they had already given in on certain aspects of political reform: the lowering of the voting age, the British "single-seat single-vote" proposal, and the replacement of appointments to the District Boards in 1994 with direct elections.[75] Employing the old united front tactic of rebuking the enemy, HK Xinhua said that China had always been sincere and willing to talk, whereas the British had treated the Chinese as weak and easy to frighten. To amass supporters in Hong Kong, Beijing set up the PWC, the forerunner of the SAR Preparatory Committee. The PWC was under the leadership of the Chinese Foreign Minister and advised the Beijing government on matters related to the handover. Following the united front principle of collaborating with local leaders, PWC representatives included NPC deputies and Hong Kong professionals and politicians. There were in total fifty-seven PWC members, thirty of whom were local dignitaries, namely, business and community leaders. The PWC had two avowed concerns: a smooth transition and transfer of sovereignty, and consideration of the interests of the people of Hong Kong.[76] The PWC strove to prepare for "fresh elections in 1997" and was prepared for disagreement between the Chinese and British on political reform for Hong Kong.[77] The PWC had political, economic, legal, cultural, education, and law and order subgroups. China's foreign minister, Qian Qichen, emphasized the contribution of the PWC and "the need to make a united effort to make the 1997 changeover a success."[78]

Observers considered the PWC to be China's way of gaining leverage in its handling of British demands, a tool in Sino-British diplomacy. However, with Sino-British relations going nowhere, the PWC could assume greater significance, as the Beijing leaders were asking for ways to consolidate and expedite the work to facilitate the handover in 1997. Commentators said that Beijing had set up a "second stove" in Hong Kong to interfere in matters related to the transition to Chinese rule. This observation seemed to hold true when a mainland co-convenor of a PWC subgroup called upon the Hong Kong government to speed up the airport construction to ensure that the project would be cost effective.[79] Not long before, the HKMAO had announced that Beijing would not accept the "through train" arrangement; in other words, Legco, District Board, and Municipal Council members elected before 1997 would not hold their seats after the handover.[80] Subsequently, Beijing announced that elections for positions on the District Boards and Municipal Councils would be unnecessary in 1997 should the functions of these governing bodies remain unchanged; however, the Communist leaders believed that elections for Legco positions would be essential. This decision was supported by the Hong Kong members of the PWC political subgroup.[81] The development of the PWC became such a sensitive issue that the Hong Kong government refused to allow its officials to attend PWC meetings. According to Patten, as communication channels already existed between the local administration and Beijing, one must take PWC invitations to meetings with "a pinch of salt."[82] Such was the case in January 1994 when Hong Kong's Secretary for Economic Services, Gordon Siu, canceled a trip to Beijing to attend a meeting of the PWC economic subgroup. The PWC had taken the initiative to invite Siu. However, the Hong Kong government denied having any policy to discourage contact between local officials and the PWC. The point here is that Patten would not recognize either the status or role of the PWC, nor meet with PWC representatives to discuss economic, political, and other matters related to Hong Kong's domestic development.

6. The Development of the United Front

The united front comprised staunch supporters of the Chinese Communists, new allies, and even neutral observers. Its basic tactics were to disclose differences with its enemies and make charges against them to justify the policies and actions of the Communists. During the Patten administration, China's rejection of the governor's reform package resulted in attacks from the other side. The pattern that emerged was frequent charges by both sides against each other. In January 1994, Patten lashed out at the Beijing leaders for rejecting his reform package and the resulting political impasse. He accused China of "being irrational and illogical in deadlocked talks" concerning Hong Kong's future.[83] Speaking to the media, Patten said that he considered China's response to be "largely rhetorical" and "devoid of argument."[84] It was obvious that diplomatic talks were impossible between Beijing and the Hong Kong government; Patten put it this way—Beijing officials regarded consultation as vetoing every item of his reform package.[85] He added that this was unbearable. Verbal attacks came from both sides, resulting in a political deadlock that worried various sectors of society and provided the rationale and material for some business and community leaders to side with Beijing.

Beijing's relations with the Hong Kong administration were arousing considerable concern. The deadlock strategy seemed to be working, however, as even some Hong Kong hands from the British side disapproved of Patten's actions. One of them was Sir Percy Cradock, who was a former British ambassador to Beijing and foreign policy adviser to both Margaret Thatcher and John Major. Sir Percy took part in the Sino-British negotiations leading to the 1984 Sino-British Joint Declaration, and warned Patten against launching his reforms unilaterally, as this would be "indefensibly reckless" and might provoke "a vicious backlash" from China, which would be disastrous to Hong Kong's future stability and prosperity.[86] Locally, Sir David Akers-Jones launched a war of words with Patten, who had earlier spoken against the ex-official. Patten had quoted Sir David as saying "The Chinese style is not to rig elections. But they do like to know the result before they're held."[87] Sir David claimed that the governor had taken his words out of context to discredit him and the Beijing government. He said that he was not referring to elections for the District Boards or Legco, and that Patten was repeating his words like a "cheap joke."[88] Borrowing a Chinese adage, Sir David accused Patten of having "a small-minded man's mentality to gauge a gentleman's intentions."[89]

The icy relations between Beijing and Patten over Hong Kong matters were mirrored in Sino-Anglo relations over other events. According to the *South China Morning Post*, the Foreign Affairs Committee of China's NPC sent "an angry letter," which delivered harsh charges against the British, announcing that the latter had severely interfered in its domestic matters and ignored the normal practice of international politics. China pointed to the British attack regarding the issue of human rights in Tibet.[90] Typical of the Chinese response to foreign charges, Beijing claimed that the British Parliament had upset the Chinese people, ignored their national feelings, and damaged the bilateral relations between the two countries. Reflective of the foreign mentality, British Foreign Secretary Douglas Hurd said that China's human rights record had implications for how Beijing would handle Hong Kong in the future.

To consolidate its position in Hong Kong before the handover, Beijing created another group of allies—the District Affairs Advisers. In early

February 1994, the local media learned that HK Xinhua, which had district offices in Hong Kong Island, Kowloon, and Shatin, would make the announcement of the appointment of these advisers. The director of HK Xinhua, Zhou Nan, was ready for the move.[91] Unlike the Hong Kong Affairs Advisers, who came under the direction of both HK Xinhua and HKMAO, this new group of advisers would answer only to HK Xinhua. The first batch of District Affairs Advisers included those who belonged to the lower tier of the colonial administration of Hong Kong, namely, members of the District Boards, Area Committees, and Mutual Aid Committees. At the same time, this group accepted personnel from the Kaifong (Cantonese romanization, meaning "neighborhood") Associations and other district bodies. The District Affairs Advisers would give their opinions in their personal capacity.

The first group of District Affairs Advisers included 128 members of the District Boards and Municipal Councils (one out of four of the total number) and 146 local leaders.[92] Of these 274 advisers, sixty-two had CCP affiliations. Forty-three members of DAB, often labeled as pro-China, were among the first group of appointees, as were members of some of the so-called liberal parties, with seven from the Liberal Party, six from the Liberal Democratic Federation, four from the Association for Democracy and People's Livelihood, and two from the Meeting Point. As usual, to avoid controversy and opposing views, HK Xinhua refused to name any United Democrat as an adviser.

Beijing had constructed a hierarchy with three levels of united front allies. The District Affairs Advisers formed the lowest level of supporters, the local Hong Kong Affairs Advisers belonged to the second level (China soon announced a third batch), and local PWC members were the top consultants.[93] On the one hand, China wanted to ensure the smooth transfer of the administration of Hong Kong in 1997 through establishing strong relationships with local allies. On the other hand, it had promised the territory autonomy after 1997, and had indicated its confidence in the principle of "Hong Kong people governing Hong Kong." It had repeatedly said that it had not and would not meddle in local Hong Kong politics. In March 1994, HKMAO director Lu Ping said that no people could interfere with Hong Kong's business and affairs, and that China had already taken measures to forestall such activity.[94] The appointment of the three tiers of advisers was a way to cultivate friendships with the leaders of the future SAR. Beijing announced the third and fourth batches of Hong Kong Affairs Advisers in 1994 and 1995 respectively.[95]

At the same time, Beijing's Foreign Ministry said it would consider asking Hong Kong civil servants to indicate whether they would stay in the government after the handover. It was a move to please them, as the spokesman of the Foreign Ministry said they should "put their hearts at ease," and have faith that China would uphold the Sino-British Joint Declaration and the Basic Law.[96] As for the top leadership of the government, Beijing asserted that the British did not have a say in the matter as such would infringe upon Chinese sovereignty over Hong Kong. According to the Foreign Ministry, only the Beijing government and Hong Kong SAR chief executive had the right to nominate and appoint the principal officials of the SAR government.[97] Beijing assured the civil servants of their importance in the Hong Kong government both before and after the handover. Subsequently, there were reports that HK Xinhua had been inviting senior officials (deputy secretaries and principal assistants) to dinner "to get to know each other."[98] Whether Beijing was successful in wooing the senior civil servants is questionable: some of them became irritated when they were described as having served the British administration for a long time, and advised to be prepared to indicate where their loyalty lay. One was annoyed as he did not think it was necessary to have such meetings to prove the ability of civil servants. Only a few days later, Beijing withdrew its request and said that only civil servants planning to resign after the handover should inform the future SAR government.[99]

7. Concluding Remarks: Toward the Handover in 1997

The PWC had fulfilled its objectives by the middle of 1995 when it held its last plenary meeting. It had made recommendations to Beijing concerning the Preparatory Committee for the Hong Kong SAR. These were that the Preparatory Committee, which was responsible for preparing for the establishment of the SAR, should comprise mainland Chinese and local members, with offices in Beijing and Hong Kong, and should begin to function in January 1996.[100] The Preparatory Committee would form the Selection Committee, which would elect the first chief executive of the Hong Kong SAR, and its members were to come from four sectors—industrial, commercial, and financial groups; professionals; labor, grassroots, and religious groups; and political groups. The Selection Committee turned out to be "overwhelmingly big business," with members including Li Ka-shing, Stanley Ho, and Gordon Wu.[101] The Legco elected in 1995 could only function until the last day of British rule—June 30, 1997.

7

The Selection of the Chief Executive, May–December 1996

1. Introduction

Tung Chee-hwa was elected the chief executive of the Hong Kong SAR in December 1996. There had already been much speculation about Hong Kong's future. Its return to China was unprecedented, as this did not bring about independence for the territory but rather resulted in its subordination under an ideologically different system. Beijing had boasted that the "one country, two systems" concept was a great innovation that would be beneficial to Hong Kong's "prosperity and stability," and if successfully implemented, would have implications for reunification with Taiwan. The world watched the handover, but Hong Kong people had lived with anxiety about this event for more than a decade, and were ready to work with China. This chapter attempts to see how the three different parties—Beijing, the election candidates, and the local people—took advantage of the situation in 1996 to prepare for Chinese rule of the SAR, and exerted influence on the course of events leading to the election of the chief executive in December.

In the second half of 1996, the election race for the position of chief executive dominated Hong Kong headlines. As then Director of the HKMAO Lu Ping emphasized, the candidate must be a patriot who loved China.[1] This was the first time in the territory's history that the highest policymaker would come from its own population, and that the local people could, in a limited way, participate in the process, as a four hundred-member Selection Committee was responsible for choosing Hong Kong's first chief executive. The media frequently used the word "selection" rather than "election" in describing the process, as the electoral college was pro-China and Beijing was considered to have already handpicked Tung. Nevertheless, a local

Chinese could not have risen to the highest position in Hong Kong if it had remained a British colony. An opinion poll, released on election day, December 11, showed that Tung had a 70.1 percent approval rating.[2] Typical of any election winner, his popularity immediately rose after his victory.

This chapter argues that the three parties involved (Beijing, the election candidates, and the Hong Kong public) had to work within the limits of their power while making their views known and having their role in the process acknowledged. By election day, they believed that they had satisfied each other's demands and established among themselves a working relationship. Beijing had promoted as chief executive a local ally, the candidates had campaigned for their causes and persuaded the Selection Committee members to vote for them, and the Hong Kong people had made sure that the chief executive was accepted by them and able to communicate their views to leaders in Beijing.

In addition, this chapter stresses the similarities between what Beijing hoped to see and what the local population desired. In the chief executive selection process, pragmatism was the guiding principle. The different sides were willing to accommodate one another to ensure the stability and prosperity of the territory. With Hong Kong officially returning to China on July 1, 1997, the local people paid close attention to the newly elected chief executive-designate, and felt in December 1996 that they were prepared for the coming SAR administration. The election in 1996 had implications for Beijing's post-handover leadership, and for the wishes and expectations of the people of Hong Kong.

2. Three Aspects of the Selection Process: (1) Decisive Role of Beijing; (2) Management of Public Opinion; and (3) Concerns of the Local Population

Three aspects of the selection process are addressed: (1) Beijing's decisive role; (2) its response to public opinion; and (3) the concerns of the local population. First, Beijing played a decisive role in the selection process. In January 1996 in the Great Hall of the People, China's President Jiang Zemin met with members of the NPC's Preparatory Committee for the establishment of the SAR. When he was about to leave the room, he suddenly approached Tung Chee-hwa, who was in the front row, and shook hands with him. The next day, a newspaper headline read: "Jiang Encounter Marks Magnate as Candidate."[3] The Hong Kong media speculated that Beijing had chosen Tung to be chief executive. From then on, the 59-year-old shipping tycoon received growing attention. That he won the election seemed to confirm the speculation resulting from this famous handshaking incident.

Beijing's significant role in the process benefited business interests, which symbolized the united front effort of the Chinese Communists for many years. The close tie between business and politics was an abiding feature of Hong Kong history. The decade before the handover witnessed business people changing from a pro-British to a pro-China position, and openly supporting Beijing. Since the drafting of the Basic Law in the 1980s, there had been charges of "the business monopoly of politics." In 1996, Tung's business background had different implications. Although his business outlook brought criticism against him, his impressive victory in the November Selection Committee nominations made people rethink his fitness for the position of chief executive. His conservatism and main-land China connections seemed crucial for the smooth transition of the territory to Chinese rule. As the head of a shipping enterprise, Tung had multiple connections, and as a Shanghainese, he was well acquainted with Jiang Zemin and spoke with the latter in their local dialect. Tung also took advantage of his father's linkages in Taiwan. He was active in high circles overseas, and among his friends were former American President George Bush and then Assistant Secretary of State Winston Lord. He also advised the Council on Foreign Relations and the Hoover Institution.[4]

Second, Beijing had become more skillful in responding to public opinion, which was important for the establishment of both its legitimacy and that of the SAR government in the rule of Hong Kong. Regarding its legitimacy, Beijing had the right to re-exercise sovereignty over the territory. Nevertheless, the SAR government needed to secure the trust of the people in its administration and promote public confidence. Only by demonstrating that it worked for local interests and agreeing to "a high degree of autonomy" for the local population could Beijing assert its authority in the territory.

Although Beijing played a major role in the event, it repeated that the election would satisfy the wishes of the people of Hong Kong. Although the four hundred-member Selection Committee was responsible for choosing the chief executive, the local population would have *some* influence on the process. Beijing said that the chief executive must be accepted by the Hong Kong people. In fact, those who failed to obtain a public following did not have a chance to run for the position. Some who had already made known their intention to enter the election race withdrew from the process after realizing that they had little support and thus could not expect the Selection Committee to nominate them as official candidates in the election. In the November nominations, a former judge failed to secure enough votes owing to his lack of public support. The chief executive would be *a person accepted by both Beijing and the Hong Kong people.*

Throughout the process, the contenders campaigned for their causes, met with people from all walks of life, and showed their eagerness to gain public support. They made known their expectations of the job of chief executive, elaborated on the role of the future office holder, and announced their policy platforms. Beijing and the Hong Kong government also talked about the responsibilities of the chief executive. This served to educate people and to give the impression that the chief executive was in a position to determine Hong Kong's future. In addition, the campaigns enabled Hong Kong society to identify its own needs, and to articulate its demands regarding the SAR administration. They also contributed to Beijing's united front work with the local population to secure more public support. In the last few months of 1996, public confidence began to rise. By the end of the election race, the chief executive-designate had emerged as a popular figure.

Third, the increase in public confidence reflected the mentality of the people. Before the November nominations, Tung was losing ground against his major opponent, Chief Justice Sir Yang Ti-liang, in terms of public support. However, in December, after Tung had won a decisive victory in the nomination process, public opinion polls showed he had an approval rating of 70.1 percent.[5] This showed that people did not have a fixed opinion regarding the future chief executive and thus were ready to accept the obvious outcome. Earlier criticism of Tung had concerned his business background rather than his political platform, himself, or his campaign style. The priority of the public was the maintenance of the status quo, and people were ready to accept someone who could safeguard the territory's stability and prosperity, which were *the* major concerns of Hong Kong society.

3. The Making of Public Opinion and the Appearance of the "Dream Team"

In May 1996, Lo Tak-shing became the first to announce his intention to run for chief executive. The 61-year-old lawyer was then a Preparatory Committee member. He had served in the past on Exco and Legco of the Hong Kong government, and was well-known for having changed sides—previously pro-British, he became pro-China. He had also admitted that he found the post very attractive after the proclamation of the Basic Law in 1990.[6] He emphasized that, having been a BLCC member, he had a longstanding working relationship with Beijing.

Other Preparatory Committee members, however, were thinking of alternative candidates. A "pro-Tung Chee-hwa group" within the committee planned ahead. Uncertain whether Tung would stand for election, the group made use of the Preparatory Committee's general meeting in Zhuhai, Guangdong Province, to prepare for future moves,[7] and consider other possible candidates. One of its choices was Sir Chung Sze-yuen, a former Exco member. At that time, Tung refused to talk about the election, and a rumor arose that he might not run for chief executive. His supporter, Li Ka-shing, another prominent tycoon, also declined to comment on the election.[8]

In the midst of the ongoing speculation, Beijing clarified the election procedures. The director of HK Xinhua, Zhou Nan, emphasized that the Selection Committee would choose the chief executive. Since this committee had not yet been formed, Zhou claimed that current reports were merely "the boiling of water," a colloquial Hong Kong expression meaning "empty talks."[9] Selection Committee members would be nominated by their own groups, and chosen at the Preparatory Committee's general meeting.[10] The Preparatory Committee would report on the election timetable and the responsibilities of the chief executive-designate before the handover.

Jiang Zemin emphasized that the chief executive had to be accepted by the general public, and fully represent its interests. In his meeting with British Deputy Prime Minister Michael Heseltine, Jiang said that Beijing would not unilaterally decide on the chief executive, as the Selection Committee would solicit the views of various classes of society.[11] His statement was well received in the territory, and seemed to offer the promise that the chief executive election would be "substantive" rather than "a mere formality."[12] Jiang made a calculated move in underscoring the importance of popular opinion in the selection process—a united front strategy of "making friends" with the local population—to enhance the legitimacy of the election and chief executive.

A breakthrough came in early June when Tung resigned from Exco, the governor's cabinet. He explained that he did so to avoid a conflict of interest between his positions in Exco and the Preparatory Committee, but observers believed that he was preparing to run for chief executive.[13] His supporters, who regarded his move to be a response to Lo Tak-shing's declaration of his intention to run, were excited.[14] Although Tung had always disagreed with Governor Chris Patten, he received much praise from the latter for his work in Exco and devotion to local interests. Patten described Tung as a person of integrity and knowledge, and well-known in international circles.[15]

Tung's resignation suggested his intention to enter the election, and the *South China Morning Post* immediately sought public opinion of possible candidates for chief executive. In a poll conducted from May 27 to 31, 1996, 56.5 percent of the respondents supported Chief Secretary Anson Chan, the head of the civil service, as chief executive.[16] The poll also showed that

49 percent were skeptical of "business people's support for individual rights" in view of a recent conflict between business and the governor.[17] The business elite was seen to be conservative and pro-establishment. Despite his positions in Exco and the Preparatory Committee, Tung had been an obscure figure in politics, and even the media knew very little about him. The impression was that he was a "low-key" person. After his resignation from Exco, Tung needed to cultivate a favorable public image to run for chief executive.

Rumors spread that China had decided on a "dream team" for the future SAR, which would comprise Tung and Chief Secretary Chan.[18] Beijing stressed that the chief executive should have the support of the civil service.[19] When interviewed earlier by CNN, Chan had refused to say whether she would run for election, but indicated her willingness to work for the SAR government no matter who became its head.[20] Toward the end of July, another poll showed that Tung and Chan topped the ratings as the most popular choices for chief executive.[21] In early August, Preparatory Committee and former BLDC member Louis Cha referred to Tung as the best candidate for the post.[22] He believed that Tung could coordinate the different interests and maintain good working relations with the various parties (characteristic of the united front strategy of the Chinese Communists). He also hoped that Chan would continue to lead the civil service after the handover, as she was knowledgeable about the government situation. He seemed to be promoting the dream team. He was not optimistic about the possibility that Lo, Chan, or Sir Sze-yuen would become chief executive. According to Cha, Lo had poor personal relations and a poor public image. While Cha urged Chan to stay on as head of the civil service, he thought that Chan and Sir Sze-yuen knew too little about Beijing's mentality to become chief executive. Later, when asked whether he was speaking on behalf of Beijing, Cha denied doing so.[23] In a poll conducted from August 19 to 22, 1996, Chan came in first place with an approval rating of 60.1 percent, and Tung ranked second with a rating of 10.4 percent.[24] In addition, 41.7 percent of the respondents said that they would accept Tung if he became chief executive.

4. Business Competitors and Judicial Counterparts

Tung's resignation from Exco appeared to signify his intention to join the election race. Although he had not yet made a public declaration, Tung was cautiously following a plan in the step-by-step manner that he later described as his working style. In September, he revealed the business undertakings between his company and those of his Taiwanese brother-in-law.

It was speculated that Tung made the public announcement to avoid the possibility that the relationship would be brought to light in the course of the election campaign and used against him.[25]

While the dream team garnered most of the attention, another name appeared. Sir Yang Ti-liang, a 67-year-old Supreme Court Chief Justice, announced his intention to run for chief executive when he was on vacation in London. He received the support of Xu Simin, who was the editor of the leftist mouthpiece *Mirror* and a Preparatory Committee member. Yang's supporters emphasized his judicial background, and said that he would provide an honest and just administration for the SAR. The media immediately speculated that the criticism of Tung's business background had prompted Beijing to look for other interested parties. Hence, Xu openly sided with Yang. The concern for public opinion suggested that the Chinese Communist leaders wanted the process to appear not only competitive but also legitimate. They certainly welcomed Yang's entry into the race.[26] The united front strategy had always been to "win as many friends" as possible.

On September 19, 1996, following Lo and Yang, Tung announced his intention to join the election race. There were rumors that China had helped Tung's company in the mid-1980s when it faced a serious financial crisis. Aware of this, Tung argued that a candidate's background was not as important as his character, and that the chief executive should be a person of ability, strength, and integrity.[27] While there were now three people in the race, the real competition was between Tung and Yang.[28] Although Tung faced criticism because of his business background, he had the support of the civil servants.[29] At that time, the situation seemed to be "either Tung or Yang."

A former High Court judge became the fourth person to join the race. Also a Preparatory Committee member, 71-year-old Arthur Garcia was popular in some judiciary circles, and the media described him as an opponent of Yang.[30] His supporters wanted him to run against Yang to reduce the chance that the latter would win the election.

The fifth interested party was Peter Woo, the 50-year-old son-in-law of the late shipping tycoon Sir Pao Yue-kong, and the honorary chairman of Wharf Holdings. Whereas Garcia was an opponent of Yang, Woo seemed to be a threat to Tung as both had substantial support from business.[31] Although Woo was the last to enter the race, he took the lead in announcing a detailed policy platform.[32] The others immediately followed suit. In addition, Woo began his media campaign by holding press receptions and talking about his private life.[33] Known to be close to Beijing circles, former Basic Law drafter Louis Cha acknowledged that Woo had asked for his opinion. Cha held that the race would be among Tung, Yang, and Woo[34] because, as noted, he thought that Lo had a poor public image. At that time, Garcia remained an obscure figure.

Poll results supported Cha's prediction regarding the main leadership contenders. Public opinion had changed rapidly. Although Chief Secretary Chan obtained the highest rating (40 percent) in an October poll, her popularity had dropped since August.[35] In contrast, Tung and especially Yang enjoyed an increase in popularity, with respective approval ratings of 14.7 percent and 21.5 percent. In a previous poll in August, Chan had received 60.1 percent of the votes, and Tung slightly more than 10 percent.[36] Also at that time, 21.6 percent of the respondents opted for Tung and 9.8 percent for Yang if Chan did not run in the race.

In October, however, Yang was able to beat Tung. When Chan was removed from consideration, Yang received 45.7 percent of the votes, Tung 24.4 percent, Woo 9.5 percent, and Lo and Garcia only 0.8 percent and 0.2 percent, respectively. Although Chan was the most popular choice, her apparent reluctance to enter the election race meant that people had to think about other available candidates. The poll results indicated that the public preferred Yang, a Chief Justice, to Tung, a business tycoon with mainland China connections.[37] Analysts observed: "People are becoming more realistic but they still are hesitant about having a businessman ruling Hong Kong."[38]

The media described the process as "the selection of the chief executive" rather than "his election," as the Selection Committee was responsible for casting the votes.[39] The difference in ratings between Tung and Yang might not affect the election outcome, but the lack of public support accounted for the failure of Lo and Garcia. Although the Selection Committee was not a mirror of public opinion, it had to be sensitive to popular sentiment. At least, according to Jiang, the chief executive should be acceptable to the Hong Kong people. Possibly because they had not received public support, Garcia and Lo withdrew from the race on October 11 and 17, respectively. They did not expect the Selection Committee to nominate them as official candidates. Entering the race now was 74-year-old Li Fook-sean, a Preparatory Committee member and a former appeals court judge. It had earlier been speculated that Li would consider entering the election, not to win, but, like Garcia, to reduce the number of votes for Yang.[40] The contest was now between two businessmen and two people with a judicial background. In a poll on October 19, Yang took the lead, receiving 33 percent of the votes, followed by Tung (25 percent), Woo (8 percent), and Li (5 percent).[41] In a poll one week earlier, however, Tung had ranked first, Yang second, and Woo a distant third.[42] The actual competition was still between Tung and Yang.

5. Expectations of the Future Chief Executive

While it is natural to talk about the expectations held of any public office holder, the position of chief executive was entirely new in Hong Kong. Having expectations of the chief executive implied having confidence in someone who could make independent decisions and convey the wishes of the local people to the Beijing leaders. These expectations placed the chief executive in a better light, gave the post a clearer profile, and increased the respect for the chief executive among the general populace. At the same time, the selection process educated the public on the responsibilities of the chief executive, and more importantly, the would-be office holder.

In October, Tung announced his policy platform, entitled "Building a 21st Century Hong Kong Together," and talked about the role of the chief executive. He asked people to prepare for future risks while they enjoyed the present prosperity, and to unite and work together toward the twenty-first century.[43] As usual, Tung emphasized the notions of "one country, two systems," "Hong Kong people governing Hong Kong," and "a high degree of autonomy of the future SAR." He said that Hong Kong should be proud of returning to China and taking part in the Chinese modernization effort.

Tung also talked about the role of the SAR government. He stressed the importance of negotiation, consensus rather than confrontation, and the establishment of working relations with China "based on mutual understanding and trust."[44] He repeatedly asked people to think more about their duties than their rights. Tung appeared to be the core member of Beijing's united front in Hong Kong.

Less than a week after Tung revealed his platform, Chief Secretary Chan announced that she would not enter the election. She did, however, outline "the criteria the Hong Kong people and the civil service considered essential for the chief executive."[45] The top concern was the person's character and ability, as he needed to be a person of integrity, courage, and principle. The second and third criteria were the upholding of the Sino-British Joint Declaration and the Basic Law, respectively. Chan asked that the chief executive follow the two documents, implement the "one country, two systems" policy, and preserve local rights and freedoms. The fourth criterion was to effectively communicate with Beijing to promote mutual understanding and respect. Lastly, the chief executive was to pay attention to local needs and anxieties. Chan made her declaration in her capacity as Chief Secretary, head of the civil service. Thus, she set forth the conditions on which civil servants would accept the chief executive. Although she seemed to speak on behalf of government employees, she was only repeating often-stated principles and concerns. Rather than making new demands, Chan actually related Hong Kong's stability and prosperity to successful leadership by the chief executive. In doing so, she acknowledged the importance of the post and the selection process, and established the authority of the chief executive.[46]

The selection process was gathering momentum, and people continued to focus on Tung and Yang. A poll conducted from October 23 to 24 showed that Tung received 30.2 percent of the votes, Yang 27.5 percent, Woo 8.7 percent, and Li 3.3 percent.[47] Another poll at this time indicated that Tung was leading the race, with 46.5 percent of the votes, whereas Yang had only 37.7 percent Although Tung was able to beat Yang, their positions reversed shortly afterwards. A poll released on November 7 showed that Yang had 33.5 percent support, Tung 32.4 percent, Woo 4 percent, and Li 2 percent.[48] The difference in ratings between Tung and Yang decreased while support for Woo and Li steadily dwindled.

6. Final Outcomes

While Tung, Yang, Woo, and Li received the most attention, they were among thirty-one applicants who wanted to run for chief executive. Interestingly, other applicants included political "nobodies," including a bus terminal manager. On November 2, the Preparatory Committee endorsed eight applications, including those of Tung, Yang, Woo, and Li. It declared the rest invalid owing to reasons such as an incomplete application or the double nationality of the applicant.[49] On the same occasion, the Preparatory Committee elected the Selection Committee. Three hundred and forty people were chosen, and together with the 26 local deputies of the NPC and the thirty-four representatives of the CPPCC, formed the Selection Committee.

The composition of the Selection Committee indicated the direction of the chief executive election. The twenty-nine Legco members appointed to the committee were mainly from pro-China political parties, such as the Democratic Alliance for the Betterment of Hong Kong (DAB) and the business-oriented Liberal Party. The leftist Federation of Trade Unions (FTU) was also represented. Of the Selection Committee members, very few were independent, with most having the support of parties and affiliated groups. These included, in addition to those already mentioned, the Association for Democracy and People's Livelihood, Liberal Democratic Federation, Heung Yee Kuk, New Territories Association of Societies, Former Senior Civil Servants' Association, Business and Professionals Federation (BPF), Chinese General Chamber of Commerce, Hong Kong Progressive Alliance, and Civic Force. The Liberal Party and BPF openly declared their support for Tung, while the Former Senior Civil Servants' Association, Civil Force, and Liberal Democratic Federation showed favoritism toward the shipping tycoon.[50] The above were either staunch supporters of the united front or parties with whom the united front aimed to form alliances.

The eight successful applicants needed to secure 50 nominations from the Selection Committee before they could become official candidates in the election. In a poll conducted before the first meeting of the Selection Committee, 45 percent of the respondents said that they would like to see Tung, Yang, Woo, and Li nominated as official candidates.[51] When asked about their preference, 66 percent voted for Yang, 63 percent for Tung, 50.3 percent for Woo, and 44.8 percent for Li.

The Selection Committee met for the first time on November 15. Tung received 206 votes, Yang 82, and Woo 54. Surprisingly, Li failed in his nomination bid, receiving just 43 votes.[52] As Tung already had more than one half of the votes and Yang and Li were far behind him, the likelihood of his being elected in December was high. Analysts argued that since more than 80 percent of the Selection Committee members came from business sectors—the chief components of the united front—"Tung's impressive win demonstrated the strength of these circles."[53] Before the nominations, there were reports that Tung was the most popular of the candidates among business groups.[54]

Although the nomination outcomes did not correspond with the relative positions of Tung and Yang in the polls, public opinion explained the defeat of Li. A journalist wrote: "If opinion polls have any relevance to the chief executive race, the defeat of Simon Li Fook-sean in the qualifying vote was illuminating."[55] The journalist continued, "Mr Li, who joined the contest following the withdrawal of Lo Tak-shing, was the victim of a popularity disaster. A candidate whose popularity rating is barely above one per cent was always a non-starter."[56] Public opinion influenced the selection process, as a person of low popularity did not even have a place in the competition.

Tung had so far given "an impression of quiet strength and confidence."[57] He aimed to preserve the status quo and promote cordial relations with Beijing. Although his business outlook and Beijing relations brought criticism and attacks, in the polls he was always ranked first or second, and after his nomination, he began to receive the most support. This showed that people were ready to accept the obvious outcome, namely, Tung's leadership after 1997. It seemed that Tung would "almost certainly be Hong Kong's first post-1997 leader."[58] As the situation became clear, Tung's business background appeared to be favorable given the concern for the economic well-being and stability of the territory.

In one commentary, it was suggested that Tung's success could be attributed in part to his election campaign: "the extent of his backing still suggests that he has built on that by his performance in the campaigning of recent weeks."[59] Although the four hundred-member Selection Committee was responsible for choosing the chief executive, election campaigns gave people the impression that they were part of the process. That the candidates made open appeals to the public made the competition appear legitimate and upright. Such activities demonstrated that Beijing was willing to listen *to some extent* to the voices of Hong Kong people. The united front was more tolerant of different opinions at this time. This was better than Beijing's mere denial of rumors that China had already decided on the chief executive.

A significant phenomenon was Tung's rise in popularity after his nomination. His approval rating beforehand was 32.9 percent, whereas in a poll conducted from November 18 to 19, it had increased to 40.1 percent. In contrast, Yang's rating dropped from 42.6 percent to 40.7 percent. Woo's rating remained at 4.0 percent.[60] One week later, with a rating of 42.3 percent, Tung beat Yang, who had only 36.8 percent, and Woo, with 3.4 percent.[61] After Tung had secured an overall majority of votes in the Selection Committee nominations, the public began to focus on him and his platform. Although his China connections and business outlook were criticized, Tung appeared to be able to establish channels of communication between Beijing and Hong Kong. He had shown confidence, determination, and affability. Although he openly asserted his pro-China position, his conservatism seemed to guarantee the maintenance of the status quo, and was the main reason that people were willing to accept the united front. The changes in the poll results demonstrated that people had begun to accept the obvious outcome, namely, the selection of Tung as chief executive.

Toward the end of November, the confidence of Hong Kong people was on the rise.[62] The selection process contributed to this sense of optimism, as the candidates remained in the limelight campaigning for their causes. Although Tung was sure to win the election, he continued to appeal for public support. The candidates and their lobbying teams tried to influence the Selection Committee members but also approached the public, making their claims and asserting their position.[63]

Tung was very confident about winning the election, for he complained about the bad *fengshui* of Government House, and said that he did not feel like moving in if he became the chief executive.[64] Even Xu Simin, who had supported Yang, bluntly stated that the judge was not likely to win.[65] In early December, a poll showed that Tung's popularity had soared, with his approval rating reaching 46.7 percent. Yang's was much lower, at only 28.8 percent.[66] Another poll at this time showed that Tung received 48.5 percent of the votes as the favorite choice for chief executive, whereas Yang had only 41.3 percent and Woo 9.5 percent.[67]

As expected, Tung won the election on December 11 after receiving an overwhelming majority of votes—320. Yang and Woo received just 42 and

36 votes, respectively. Speaking to the media after his landslide victory, Tung asked people to unite and work together. He said that Hong Kong had been heavily burdened by political issues in the past, and that his administration would concentrate on economic matters and social problems.[68]

Tung had worked with both Beijing and the British Hong Kong government. He was widely respected in international circles, and seen to be "a conciliator, a master of the quiet compromise."[69] Observers regarded him as "a quietly effective power broker" who could convey local interests to Beijing.[70] Tung repeatedly said that he preferred compromise to confrontation, and his desire for consensus seemed crucial to the territory's smooth transition to Chinese rule. This atmosphere of assurance led to an approval rating for Tung of 70.1 percent in a poll released on election day.[71]

For the first time in history, the Hong Kong people had participated, at least in a limited way, in the selection of their head of government. Although they could not directly vote for the chief executive, their opinions influenced Beijing, the selection process, and the candidates themselves, and found expression in polls, public debates, the media, and the candidate question and answer forums. The lack of public support of Lo, Garcia, and Li led to their dropping out of the leadership race, and confirmed what Foreign Minister Qian Qichen had said in his opening speech for the chief executive election, namely, that Beijing would "respect the wishes of the Hong Kong people."[72] Popular opinion had a bearing on not only the process but also the united front strategy.

7. Conclusion

As the time of the handover drew near, the world was paying increasing attention to developments in Hong Kong. Beijing knew that anything disastrous happening in Hong Kong would mean a major crisis for China. If Beijing had the will to live up to its promise, to maintain the territory's "stability and prosperity," then did it also have the ability to do so? In an unprecedented event in 1996, when Hong Kong people for the first time chose their chief executive through the Selection Committee, Beijing was able to respond to popular sentiment, with the priority being the maintenance of the status quo. At the end of the process, public confidence was on the rise. Changes in the polls showed that the local population did not have a specific candidate in mind. Rather, they were eager to know what the election outcome would be and to prepare for it. Hence, the increase in support for Tung after the November nominations meant that he was a suitable choice for the people, in the sense that he could work with the Beijing leaders. Both Hong Kong people and Beijing knew that the chief executive had to be acceptable to both sides. After the December election, both sides felt that their needs and opinions had been respected. The challenge now was how the future Hong Kong SAR would be governed.

The united front in Hong Kong comprised mainly business sectors. Their concern was the preservation of the status quo, which was the main reason people were willing to accept Tung as the chief executive of the SAR. Maintenance of the status quo meant the continuation of freedom in political, economic, and social activities. To the people of Hong Kong, the domination of the business elite in the united front meant at least that the economic prosperity of Hong Kong would be preserved after the handover. If the united front was not able to form alliances with the more liberal-minded, then at least it was able to dispel worries, suspicions, and unwanted speculation about the future prosperity of the territory. This was true before Hong Kong became part of China on July 1, 1997. The united front symbolized conservatism, a factor that had positive implications for the handover. At least, it suggested that Hong Kong would not change much in the foreseeable future.

Tung Chee-hwa and the Last Days of Colonial Hong Kong, December 1996–June 1997

1. Introduction

Hong Kong attracted enormous attention worldwide when the British colony, a model of capitalism and a laissez-faire economy, was returned to China, a Socialist regime. It was estimated that about eight thousand foreign reporters and journalists were in Hong Kong at the time of the handover on July 1, 1997. For months before this historic event, the media overseas reported extensively on Hong Kong: every move of the newly elected chief executive, his cabinet of advisers, the Provisional Legislature, and the squabbles among the different parties in the territory. Even before Hong Kong reverted to Chinese sovereignty, the Western press had proclaimed its death.[1] A *New York Times* headline asserted, "Farewell to Hong Kong's Freedom," and the related article stated that the situation in the territory after the handover would become very similar to that of China.

A negative slant in the reporting of Hong Kong's reversion to China was evident in international magazines.[2] The handover ceremony seemed to be considered the funeral for the territory. Early in 1995, *Fortune*'s cover story, titled "The Death of Hong Kong," declared that "the old colony's days as a global business center are numbered." In a later issue in May 1997, the magazine's cover showed a pair of red chopsticks picking up a pearl, clearly signifying the forthcoming control of Hong Kong by the Communists. In addition, as a local newspaper pointed out, the same story was covered in various ways to cater for different audiences.[3] For example, the international issue of *Newsweek* sold locally in Hong Kong had a gold cover with the title "Hong Kong: The City of Survivors," whereas the American edition with the same content about the territory showed a Chinese girl blindfolded by China's five-star flag, and asked, "Can Hong Kong Survive?" Before the handover, the Western and Asian viewpoints were respectively pessimistic and confident. The Western media expressed concern about the future of Hong Kong's capitalist system. In contrast, according to the Hong Kong-based *Far Eastern Economic Review*, Asian countries regarded the handover as signifying the end of colonialism and the creation of more opportunities for establishing economic relations with China.[4]

As Hong Kong's return to Chinese rule directly affected the local people, this chapter examines the course of events in the territory from the election of the chief executive in December 1996 to the handover on July 1, 1997. In doing so, it attempts to understand the views of the people of Hong Kong on their future and the newly elected chief executive, and to analyze the implementation of the united front policy of the Chinese Communists. It discusses the new administration that Tung Chee-hwa proposed for the SAR after he won the election. What was the composition of his cabinet and the Provisional Legislature? Were there any changes made to the bureaucracy? This chapter outlines Tung's political and administrative position, his expectations for the SAR government, the priorities of his administration, and his promises. Most importantly, the chapter describes how all of the above reflected Tung's relations with Beijing and his role in the united front work of the Chinese Communists with Hong Kong capitalists. It also addresses the problems that Tung and the new SAR administration faced in ruling Hong Kong as of July 1, 1997.

This chapter concludes with the observation that local confidence depended very much on Tung's ability to implement the "one country, two systems" policy. After his election in December 1996, the chief executive-designate enjoyed a short "honeymoon" period of popularity as a result of his conservative image and ability to communicate with Beijing leaders, both of which seemed crucial for the maintenance of the status quo and the stability of the territory. Tung symbolized the united front between Beijing and the local capitalists. Later, in February 1997, controversies over the Provisional Legislature and civil liberties legislation undermined his image of trustworthiness. However, in the same month, Tung announced his list of key government officials, and his approval rating bounced back as the confidence of the local population was restored. Tung's choices seemed to allow for the smooth transition of the civil service and preservation of the status quo.

The concern about the maintenance of the status quo was an indicator of the anxiety over whether Tung could preserve Hong Kong's system within the one country framework. This chapter argues that whereas the people of Hong Kong were confident about their future before the handover, their trust in Tung wavered in response to different events. Tung needed to pay greater attention to the differences between the "two systems" to maintain the status quo of Hong Kong, while assuaging public concern about the dominance of "one country." Although the Hong Kong SAR administration would not take control of the territory until July 1, 1997, the chief executive-designate had already become Hong Kong's shadow head in the months before the handover.

2. Tung's Assertion of Authority and the United Front Strategy

On December 11, 1996, Tung won an overwhelming majority of votes and became the SAR chief executive-designate. The local media called the process a "selection" as a four hundred-member Selection Committee, formed by the Preparatory Committee, was responsible for choosing the chief executive. Although Beijing said that Hong Kong had entered into a new era of democracy, some local critics refused to acknowledge the legitimacy of the Selection Committee, as its members had a pro-China background and were staunch supporters of the united front with the Chinese Communists.[5] In the selection, Tung received 320 votes, whereas his main competitors Chief Justice Sir Yang Ti-liang and tycoon Peter Woo received small numbers of votes.[6] Local academic Lau Siu-kai commented: "Though Tung was not popularly elected, but instead was 'elected' by a 400-strong Selection Committee dominated by Hong Kong's social and economic elites, Hongkongers still heaved a sigh of relief at the electoral outcome."[7] As Lau explained, "Tung projected the image of a decent, benevolent and honest gentleman" who had "a sense of commitment to the place and a duty to the country."[8]

Tung, a shipping magnate, was already well acquainted with members of China's leadership. His long friendship with President Jiang Zemin dated back to the time when the latter was still the Shanghai party secretary. The famous incident in the Great Hall of People when Jiang unexpectedly shook hands with Tung in front of a large crowd of Hong Kong delegates and reporters was often cited by the media. Local commentators suspected that Jiang had hand-picked Tung to be the chief executive. It was alleged that Beijing had provided financial support for the tycoon in the 1980s, when his company faced a serious crisis. Before Tung declared his interest in running for the post of chief executive, he had held an important position in the British Hong Kong government as a member of Exco, the governor's cabinet. He subsequently resigned from Exco to run for election. Tung was also an insider in China's governmental framework. He was a member of the NPC's Preparatory Committee for the establishment of the Hong Kong SAR and the National Committee of the Eighth CPPCC, and an adviser to HK Xinhua and the HKMAO.[9] Tung could work with both the British and Chinese sides, which was attributed to his preference for mediation over confrontation.

Like most election winners, Tung enjoyed an upsurge in popularity for some time after his election. On the eve of the election, when it was certain that he would win as he had already secured a majority of votes in the Selection Committee nomination, an opinion poll showed that about 70 percent of respondents were willing to support him as the chief executive. Tung's election campaign contributed to his popularity (which declined substantially during his subsequent rule of Hong Kong). A foreign journalist in Hong Kong wrote: "Over the past few months, the amiable Tung has painted himself as a fatherly patriot with traditional Chinese values who prefers private consensus-building to public outspokenness."[10] The public called him "Uncle Tung." His crew cut hairstyle, loyalty to his family and business, and regular lifestyle gave him a conservative and traditional image.

From the beginning of his campaign in September 1996, Tung consistently employed three "isms" to explain his vision for Hong Kong: Confucianism, elitism, and nationalism. He asked for adherence to Confucian values, and called for the service of "the best and the brightest" in the government. To minimize internal conflicts, he urged people to think of the good of Hong Kong and China[11]—to consider not just their rights but also their obligations. Drawing upon Confucian teachings, he emphasized that his fundamental objectives were to eliminate differences in society and bring about overall unity. Tung said that in the SAR government (an executive-led administration), he and his advisers would direct the course of Hong Kong's institutional development and its political outlook. Thus, he wanted a reliable Exco to serve as his cabinet. He stated that Exco members should be (1) the elite of society, (2) have strong political awareness and be able to advise the government, and (3) be ready to promote the policies and decisions of the administration. In speeches throughout his campaign, Tung stressed his loyalty to the nation. He asserted he would not allow any future references to the independence of Taiwan and Tibet. He reiterated that the people of Hong Kong should love their motherland, China.

Tung had only six months following the election to establish the SAR government and his own authority. His first move was to meet with those who could challenge his authority: Governor Chris Patten, Chief Secretary Anson Chan, and the most outspoken critic of both him and Beijing, the Democratic Party. This was similar to the united front strategy of winning over other sectors or opinions of society. Tung's every move was aimed to create an image of affability and of public relations value.

Tung was a shadow chief, challenging the outgoing governor. Less than two weeks after he had won the election, Tung made a well-publicized attempt to convince Patten to accept the Provisional Legislature and provide government assistance to its work. The sixty-member Provisional Legislature was elected by the Selection Committee in December 1996, and would replace the existing Legco at midnight on June 30, 1997. Of the existing Legco members, thirty-four took part in the election, and thirty-three were elected. The Democratic Party was not a part of the united front, and its members were naturally critical of any events and matters concerning the Provisional Council. Hence, the nineteen Democrats who were in Legco were not involved in the Provisional Legislature election.[12]

The Provisional Legislature was created to counteract Patten's efforts to expedite the democratization process and his introduction of more elected seats in Legco in 1995. To Beijing, Patten had violated the 1990 deals between the Chinese and British governments. Had the agreements been implemented, they would have allowed for a "through-train" for legislators elected before 1997.

On December 23, Tung met Patten privately at Government House but failed to persuade the governor to stop his open opposition to the Provisional Legislature. The occasion ended with Tung and Patten appearing together before the press, cordially shaking hands and smiling for the camera.[13] The picture made it look as though they had come to an agreement when just the opposite was true. Nevertheless, both promised to meet regularly in the future. Tung announced that his next meetings would be with the Chief Secretary and Financial Secretary.

Five days later, Tung had a two-hour breakfast meeting with Chief Secretary Anson Chan at his private villa. Chan had been the public's first choice for the chief executive post although she declined to join the race. Her leadership would have ensured a smooth transition of the civil service and served as a guarantee of the stability of the SAR. At the meeting, Chan accepted Tung's invitation to continue in her position in the post-handover government. The meeting, however, was merely a formality. Although Chan had earlier made known her intention to stay on, both took advantage of the situation to attempt to establish "a very co-operative working relationship" for the future.[14] The long talked-about "dream-team" of a Tung-Chan partnership materialized. It was a managed occasion to allow for the presence of the press, to emphasize the concern for the stability and prosperity of Hong Kong and promote the confidence of the civil service and territory. A local newspaper wrote: "Just as Mr Tung has come to epitomise a set of prudent, businesslike values and a non-confrontational style for the future, so Mrs Chan stands for the continuity of good and effective administration, . . ."[15] Tung's alliance with Chan accounted in part for his early honeymoon period.

Tung also had to deal with the Democrats. The Democratic Party was the largest winner in the 1995 Legco election. Its leader, Martin Lee, was one of the popular choices for chief executive in opinion polls. Tung had accused the Democrats of being "uncritically anti-China," but said that he would like to meet them.[16] At their meeting, Tung asked the Democrats "to stop challenging the legality of the provisional legislature, saying they risked damaging Hong Kong's image."[17] He urged them to be a "constructive party," and to avoid creating a bad impression of Hong Kong among overseas spectators who might know very little about the local situation.[18] In response, Lee said he would continue to inform international circles of Hong Kong's situation. However, the Democrats called Tung "a political conservative who was sincere and dedicated" to the territory.[19]

Tung became the shadow head of the territory. Claiming that his official title should be "the chief executive" rather than "the chief executive-designate" prior to July 1, 1997, Tung aroused debate regarding his role before the handover. He also appointed a shadow cabinet. Because the Hong Kong SAR government was to be an executive-led administration, Tung's first major institutional task was to consolidate the executive branch and name his advisers. Toward the end of January 1997, Tung announced the composition of his cabinet. It had fifteen members, including Tung himself, with an Administrative Secretary, a Financial Secretary, and Secretary of Justice as permanent members. It included a senior politician with long experience working with the British, two industrialists, two accountants, a solicitor, a banker, a businessman, a former chief justice, a current Exco member, and a leftist unionist. Only three had a party affiliation. Tung's selection of his cabinet members was typical of China's united front strategy to form alliances with conservative, business, and industrial elites and local leaders. Eight of the members were in their forties, two were in their sixties, and one was in his late seventies.

3. Tung and China's Leadership

Tung's early popularity could be attributed to not only his alliance with Anson Chan but also his close relations with the Beijing leadership. The speculation that he had been "handpicked" by Jiang Zemin worked both for and against him at different times. During his campaign, this cost Tung some votes in the polls and attracted criticism from the press and his opponents. Nevertheless, his ascendance also gave assurance that the chief executive would be able to effectively communicate with Beijing, and that the views of Hong Kong people would be passed on to China's leadership. In other words, the early worry that Tung would play a subservient role was superseded by an upsurge in public confidence that the voice of the chief executive would be heard in Beijing. He belonged to Beijing's united front with the local elites and leaders.

After Tung won the election, his meetings with Beijing leaders were broadly publicized, a common united front strategy, and conducted in a cordial manner. He attended a ceremony at Diaoyutai state guest house, at which Order 207 of the State Council officially made Tung the Hong Kong SAR chief executive. In his first visit to Beijing after the election, Tung also met with Jiang and talked about Hong Kong. The latter emphasized that Hong Kong would be administered separately, with the rule of law strictly implemented.[20] He also said that Beijing would keep its promise to safeguard a high degree of autonomy for Hong Kong and fully support the new chief executive. China's firms would not have special privileges in the territory, which would continue to operate as a capitalist market economy. On the same occasion, Tung urged China's NPC to issue a statement on the legality of the Provisional Legislature, as its 1994 decision ended the colonial Legco but did not mention the Provisional Legislature. He later told reporters that he could contact the State Council at any time, but it would normally be unnecessary for him to do so. He wished to avoid the impression that he acted on Beijing's directives.

During Tung's honeymoon period, rather than criticizing his business background and Beijing connections, the public saw the merits of his conservatism and his ability to work with the Communist leaders. Tung's outlook seemed to be a guarantee of Hong Kong's future stability and prosperity. His high-profile meetings in Beijing and exceptional acquaintance with Jiang seemed to be a source of confidence among the local population. These meetings represented the successful implementation of the longstanding united front strategy of the Chinese Communists of "making friends" with Hong Kong leaders. In Tung's meeting with Jiang, the latter reiterated that Beijing would not interfere in matters of the Hong Kong SAR and provide assistance only at its request.[21] Afterward, Tung had infrequent meetings with Beijing officials in Hong Kong, which included a visit from the Chinese members of the Sino-British Joint Liaison Group in early January.

4. The Challenges

Tung was soon challenged on three issues: the existence of the Provisional Legislature, the revision of civil liberties laws, and his relations with key government officials. These issues had implications for his actual powers, ability to counteract the decisions of Beijing, and role in the united front strategy. In other words, the concept of "Hong Kong people governing Hong Kong" was apparently being put to the test even before the handover.

4.1. The Provisional Legislature Controversy

The focus of the debate on the Provisional Legislature was the legality of the body. According to the decision adopted by the NPC on April 4, 1990, which was included in the Basic Law, *the first legislature of the Hong Kong SAR* would have sixty members, twenty chosen by geographical constituencies through direct election, ten by an election committee, and thirty from functional constituencies. Unlike the later legislatures, which would have four-year terms, the first SAR legislature was to last for only two years.[22] The Basic Law, which was the mini-constitution of the Hong Kong SAR, did not mention the establishment of a provisional legislature *before the election of the first SAR legislature.* Thus, the formation of the Provisional Legislature called into question its legal basis and rationale. From Beijing's perspective, Patten's political reform violated the earlier deals between the Chinese and British governments, which would have allowed for a "through-train" of Legco members elected in 1995 to continue after 1997. Thus, it was necessary to assemble a provisional legislature to succeed the outgoing Legco on July 1, 1997, to avoid a legal vacuum. In late December 1996, the Selection Committee that was responsible for electing the chief executive also chose the 60 members of the Provisional Legislature, which would last until 1998.

There were arguments against the establishment of the Provisional Legislature. One of them was that the Basic Law indicated the temporary nature of the first SAR legislature by limiting it to a two-year term. The mini-constitution, however, did not mention a provisional legislature. According to this argument, there was no legal rationale for the establishment of the Provisional Legislature before the election of the first SAR legislature, which would also be a temporary body.[23] From the perspective of the Hong Kong Bar Association (the professional organization of local barristers), the "absence of a through-train for the last Legislature Council could only mean that the last Legislative Council will terminate on 30 June 1997. It cannot justify the composition and formation of the First Legislation [sic] Council in a manner different from that prescribed in ... the 1990 NPC Decision."[24]

Because the 1990 NPC decision did not talk about a provisional legislature, the Selection Committee was not authorized to establish any other legislative body the nature and appearance of which were different from the first SAR legislature already outlined. Even a later 1994 NPC decision failed to mention a provisional legislature, although it empowered the NPC's Preparatory Committee for the establishment of the SAR to prescribe the method for forming the first SAR legislature. As the 1990 NPC decision already described in detail the formation of the first SAR legislature, the Bar Association believed that the Provisional Legislature "would be a flagrant distortion of the meaning of the Basic Law and an affront to the Rule of Law."[25]

The chief executive-designate once again headed to Beijing, this time "for meetings seeking ways to strengthen the legality of the provisional legislature."[26] On this second trip to Beijing after his election, Tung met with Foreign Minister Qian Qichen and Director of the HKMAO Lu Ping. During the visit, Tung reiterated his call for an NPC resolution on the legality of the Provisional Legislature.[27] As the British Hong Kong government refused to support the Provisional Legislature, questioning its legal basis, Beijing promised to provide funding until June 30 and to later retrieve the money from the SAR. To avoid complicating the legality issue and facing the embarrassment of protests, the Provisional Legislature met in Shenzhen, Guangdong Province, instead of Hong Kong. Consistent with his reputation for preferring compromise over confrontation, Tung repeatedly urged the opponents of the Provisional Legislature to seek consensus and provide support for the body. He seemed to have the same idea as the later elected Provisional Legislature member Rita Fan, namely, that the SAR legislature should refrain from being too "politicized." Tung also repeated his election pledge that the administration would work toward the resolution of local socioeconomic problems rather than concentrating on political debates, as the Patten government had done.[28]

Indeed, the Provisional Legislature acquired the status of a shadow body. Some of the staff of the Legco Secretariat resigned from their positions and moved over to the Provisional Legislature.[29] At the same time, there was confusion and controversy as to whether this body had the right to enact laws before the handover. Whereas a member of Tung's cabinet insisted that it should be able to do so, legal experts said otherwise. In addition to legal concerns, there were fundamental technical difficulties. The colonial Legco publicized its bills in government gazettes for public consultation before the first, second, and third readings. This was done in accordance with its Standing Orders and followed strict procedures. As a law professor pointed out, the colonial government did not support the Provisional Legislature and thus the latter could not have its bills printed in the gazette.[30] However, because the Provisional Legislature met in Shenzhen, the British Hong Kong government could not challenge it, even if it did not follow the rules. The professor commented, "It's like a private club; they can form their own rules. The public has no status and cannot challenge any non-observance of the rules."[31] Nevertheless, the legality of any law passed would be questioned. In April, there were queries as to whether the Provisional Legislature could conduct readings on the right of abode legislation.[32] The British Hong Kong government suggested that the Provisional Legislature issue a white paper for public consultation and consider the bill only after July 1.

To address the issue of the legality of the laws passed by the Provisional Legislature, the Tung office decided to imitate Singapore's method. When Singapore declared its independence, it passed independence legislation, which confirmed the transfer of sovereignty, administrative, and judiciary powers and the continuation of the existing administrative and judiciary bodies. On July 1, the Provisional Legislature members would swear an oath and pass a "Reunification Bill" to confirm all of their earlier decisions. Sir Yang Ti-liang, the former Supreme Court judge who lost in the chief executive election, explained that this bill would not only confirm the Provisional Legislature decisions but also eliminate the possibility of legal controversy in the future.[33] The Provisional Legislature was a part of Beijing's united front with its loyal supporters in Hong Kong.

4.2. Revision of Civil Liberties Legislation

Tung's popularity faced another serious challenge when Beijing sought to repeal and modify certain Hong Kong laws that were described as inconsistent with the Basic Law. In January 1997, the legal subgroup of the NPC's Preparatory Committee reviewed 624 laws and recommended that 16 be repealed and nine modified. The subgroup asked that articles 2(3), 3, and 4 of the Bill of Rights Ordinance be abolished. Of particular concern was the proposal to reinstate the original pre-1995 Public Order Ordinance and pre-1992 Societies Ordinance, which had later been amended.[34] The subgroup's proposal provoked strong reaction from the governor, who regarded it as legal nonsense and accused China of ignoring the impact that it would have on the territory's image abroad. Patten added that the British would raise the issue through various diplomatic channels.[35]

According to the Public Order Ordinance then in force, those who organized demonstrations of more than 30 people needed only to *notify* the police beforehand. The pre-1995 version, however, required the application for *permission* from the police for demonstrations of more than 20 people. As for the existing Societies Ordinance, new societies needed only to *notify* the Societies Officer within one month after establishment. The pre-1992 version required the *registration* of new societies within fourteen days of establishment. The existing Societies Ordinance asked the government to submit reasonable evidence and obtain court approval before it could break into a society's gatherings. Before 1992, however, the government did not have to submit any reasonable evidence to explain its actions. The earlier law also forbade societies from establishing connections with foreign political forces.[36]

On February 1, 1997, the NPC's Preparatory Committee discussed how to handle the Public Order Ordinance and the Societies Ordinance. Only about one week earlier, Tung had insisted that the two ordinances would be reinstated from July 1 onward, and stated that the first SAR legislature, after extensive consultation in 1998, would pass replacement laws. At the February 1 Preparatory Committee meeting, however, Tung changed his mind, and said that the public would need to decide whether to amend the two ordinances before the handover. He presented two choices: the public could either amend the ordinances before July 1 and adopt the amended versions after the handover, or not amend them before July 1 but rather temporarily reinstate their original versions after the handover.[37]

Subsequently, British Foreign Secretary Malcolm Rifkind joined Patten in criticizing events in Hong Kong. Meeting with his Chinese counterpart, Qian Qichen, he asked Beijing to recognize and carefully consider the international concern over the "retrograde step" on human rights in the territory.[38] The British side was merely reiterating its democratic position, as Rifkind frankly admitted that it was impossible for London to change China's decision. The local Democratic Party leader, Martin Lee, warned that Hong Kong's civil liberties would be eroded after China's takeover. In this incident, Tung acted much like a shadow head and accused Lee of "badmouthing" the territory.[39] The issue of the revision of the civil liberties legislation aroused debate worldwide. While foreign governments expressed their concern over the matter, local forces were anxious to make a good impression abroad. Speaking at a Los Angeles university, Mr. Justice Benjamin Liu, a Hong Kong appeal court judge, argued that Beijing's decisions would not have a negative impact on the interests of the territory.[40]

The month of February ended the honeymoon period of the newly elected chief executive. According to an opinion poll conducted by the University of Hong Kong, public support for Tung dropped from 64.9 percent in early December to 58.5 percent by early February. As reported, more "alarming" was that Tung's popularity had fallen below Patten's. With an approval rating of only 58.7 percent in early December, Patten enjoyed a small rise in support to 59.1 percent in early February.[41] The debate regarding the revision of the civil liberties legislation, coupled with the ongoing controversy about the legality of the Provisional Legislature, produced a temporary decline in public confidence. It seemed that current issues easily affected the public mood, as the announcement of Tung's choices for key government officials just two weeks later, at the end of February, resulted in a rise in Tung's popularity (refer to section 4.3, "The Tung Leadership").

In early April, when the future Hong Kong SAR Secretary of Justice, Elsie Leung, moved into her new office, the Provisional Legislature announced that it would consider the proposed changes to the civil liberties laws in the form of "blue bills." It would conduct three readings of the blue bills to avoid what it called "a legal vacuum" after the handover.[42] Although Tung kept his earlier promise that the public would be consulted on what to do regarding the two ordinances, he set a deadline by which the changes had to be made. In April, the chief executive-designate's office revealed its proposed changes to the ordinances in the form of a 36-page document and invited public opinion until the end of the month. Under the proposed amendments to the Public Order Ordinance, organizers of demonstrations of more than thirty people had to apply for "a notice of no objection" from the police seven days beforehand, or if this were impossible, no later than 48 hours prior to the event. The period of notification remained the same, but the police would have more powers as it could refuse the application on the grounds of "the interests of national security or public safety, public order, the protection of public health or morals or the protection of the rights and freedoms of others."[43]

With regard to the Societies Ordinance, the proposed amendments required that societies apply to register with the police within one month of establishment. Based on reasons similar to those outlined in the proposed amendments to the Public Order Ordinance, the police could refuse the application for registration. The most controversial item was that the proposal forbade local political societies from receiving financial contributions from either "foreign organizations" or "aliens," and from establishing "direct or indirect affiliation with" foreign political bodies.[44] Immediately, the concern was that it would sometimes be difficult for societies to check whether or not donations came from aliens. For example, a Hong Kong resident who gave money to party fundraisers on the street might have a foreign passport. In addition, the nature of a local body might be hard to define if it engaged in nonpolitical activities but one or more of its members took part in elections.

At the end of the consultation period, several criticisms had emerged. The British Hong Kong government argued that existing laws already guaranteed public security and order, and that the concept of "aliens" was inconsistent with the Basic Law. It also said that the requirement to obtain "a notice of no objection" was equivalent to asking for permission from the authorities. The Hong Kong Bar Association called for the clarification of such terms as "foreign political organizations" and "affiliation" and the relaxation of the restriction with regard to aliens. In its opinion, the concept of "national security" was vague. It said that if the authority did not issue a notice of objection, then that would automatically mean that there were no objections to the application. As the proposed changes also prohibited local political bodies from accepting Taiwanese donations, the BAR Association joined others in asking that mainland Chinese contributions also be forbidden. The Democrats added that the restrictions on demonstrations violated the International Covenant on Civil and Political Rights. Even the Liberal Party, the leaders of which belonged to the Provisional Legislature, contended that the application for "a notice of no objection" was unnecessary.[45]

In response to these criticisms, the chief executive-designate's office made eleven amendments to its proposal for changes to the Societies and Public Order ordinances. With regard to the much debated concept of "national security," the office pointed to the protection of territorial integrity and the independence of the PRC. It added that the notion of "national security" must take into consideration the standards of "a democratic society." The office did not specify, however, what a democratic society was. The amended proposal also deleted the phase "public health or morals."[46]

As for the restriction on financial contributions from aliens and foreign groups, the office narrowed it to only foreign political organizations. In addition, foreign political bodies no longer included international political organizations. With regard to local "political societies," this term would mean political parties, or those whose main functions were to promote and support candidates for elections.[47] The earlier proposal had applied the restriction on foreign organizations to those of Taiwan as well. To eliminate this ambiguity and the embarrassment of treating Taiwan as a foreign place, the office created a separate item to prohibit donations from Taiwanese political organizations. There would also be a special staff responsible for answering enquiries regarding societal affairs.[48]

In addition, the office eliminated the requirement that demonstrations give at least 48 hours' prior notice. Instead, the police would consider special cases that were reported less than seven days prior to the event. If organizers informed the police seven days beforehand and did not receive an objection 48 hours prior to the event (or three days beforehand with no objection received 24 hours prior to the event), then the demonstration could be held. The office added that demonstrations that corresponded with public interests would be allowed.[49]

With regard to the relaxation of restraints on protests and funding, Hong Kong society responded in two different ways. While the Democrats argued that "the amendments were cosmetic, saying the right to voice dissent remained at threat," political parties within the Provisional Legislature were satisfied with the updated proposal. A local newspaper commented that the forces in the territory were polarized.[50] Critics worried that the emphasis on "national security" would force local groups into self-censorship. They were afraid that after July 1, 1997, no one would dare to talk about independence for Tibet and that "national security could be used as a pretext to disband groups disliked by the Government."[51]

4.3. The Tung Leadership

After Tung won the election, his open alliance with Anson Chan allayed some anxieties about the transition of the civil service. There was a popular wish that 20 or more of its key officials could ride a "through-train," namely, continue in their positions after the handover.[52] On February 20, 1997, immediately after his return from Beijing and with the approval of the Chinese leadership, Tung announced the list of key SAR officials. Except for Elsie Leung, the future Secretary for Justice, all were current civil servants. One of them, Lily Yam, received a promotion and would head the Independent Commission Against Corruption (ICAC). Tung was careful to add that he would respect the impartiality of the civil service, especially with regard to his present conflict with Patten.[53]

After Tung's announcement, the *South China Morning Post* commissioned Asian Commercial Research Limited (ACR) to conduct a survey of public opinion. ACR interviewed 586 people from February 22 to 26. The results were encouraging for the chief executive, as 48.1 percent of the interviewees believed that "Tung's popularity was on the rise," 24.4 percent said it was in decline, 19.5 percent thought it was "relatively stable," and 7 percent did not have any opinion.[54] Regarding the reliability of the chief executive, 35 percent said "they trusted Mr Tung more now than they did in December [1996]," 30 percent had the opposite opinion, and 26.1 percent "were adopting a wait-and-see attitude and declined to comment."[55] These highly favorable figures resulted from the general endorsement of Tung's civil service appointments. Of the interviewees, 90 percent supported his choices, and only 1.9 percent thought differently. The poll showed an overall approval for Tung's decisions, which indicated a preference for the status quo and fear of any minor disturbances.

More interestingly, the same poll asked about public feelings on the handover. Its "Happiness Index" showed an increase in public confidence since it had first been measured in October 1994.[56] It also showed that 26 percent "expected to be happy" on June 30, 37 percent "to be sad," and 37 percent to be unsure. In May 1996, those who expected to be sad still outweighed those who expected to be happy by 11 percent. However, the picture had changed by July 1996, "with an excess of 10 percentage points for happy over sad."[57] In October, three months later, the number of people expecting to be happy was 18 percent higher than the number of those expecting to be sad.

In February 1997, 66 percent of interviewees thought that they would be happy whereas only 11 percent felt that they would be sad. Thus, the heading of this news report even read: "Polls Point to a New-Found Confidence." The report stated: "The major reasons why Mr Tung is thought more popular include the simple fact that he will hold the Chief Executive's job. Other factors mentioned are that he is fluent and appealing in the media; that people believe in him and like the way he is acting; and that he has good relations with China."[58] However, the "major reasons why he is thought less popular are that he follows China's wishes; that he will abolish human rights legislation; and that he is not perceived as being democratic."[59]

Nevertheless, the results of another poll commissioned by the *South China Morning Post* in early April showed that Tung's popularity had drastically fallen. Only 30.8 percent of the interviewees said that they trusted him more, while 45.3 percent said that they placed "less trust" in him.[60] These results corresponded with the existing controversy about the Public Order Ordinance and the Societies Ordinance. One month later, in early May, the public seemed to have accepted the revision of the civil liberties legislation and evaluated more highly Tung's ability and trustworthiness.[61] The poll gave him 5.0 points for his ability (compared to 4.7 in April) and 4.9 points for trustworthiness (compared to 4.4 in April).

Even in April, when the Happiness Index dropped to 57 percent (indicating the percentage of the 586 interviewees who would expect to be happy on June 30), the figure was higher than those of previous years.[62] Although the public seemed to be bothered occasionally by current events, their level of confidence in the future had increased in recent years.

In June, relations between Chan and Tung were reported to be strained as a result of Chan's interview with *Newsweek*. The controversial point was the implication that she would resign if she could no longer be guided by her conscience. She said: "The way the civil service works and the way we've been brought up, you're not just there to implement decisions. You're there to give your frank and honest views without bias. Where a consensus is not possible, then I accept that the governor presently and the chief executive in the future has the prerogative to make the final decision."[63] Chan continued: "But of course there might be issues that are points of principle, and as a matter of conscience, you feel you can't accept those decisions. And when that happens often enough, you start asking yourself, do I stay or do I go? And I think most people would know what my answer would be."[64]

The easily shaken public reacted. One local newspaper immediately wrote: "Chan's words 'indicate looming crisis.'"[65] Although the media continued to report conflicts between Tung and Chan, the fact that Chan's role and power would be reduced in the SAR administration had long been common knowledge. In June Paul Yip, the chief executive-designate's special adviser, said that Chan would need to adjust to Tung's different style. Since his appointment as governor in 1992, Patten had been involved mainly in diplomatic matters. Fully occupied with squabbles with Beijing, he gave power and many decision-making opportunities on livelihood matters to the Chief Secretary. Thus, Chan's authority and responsibilities were on the increase after Patten's arrival. However, Yip warned that Tung's working style was very different from that of the governor. Yip described the chief executive-designate as a conscientious person with his own views, who would be eager to get involved in major matters. Thus, there would be a different "division of labor" between the chief of the civil service and Tung after the handover. In the top echelons of the civil service, there was already talk that "the good days" of Chan would soon pass and that her power and freedom of action would decline.[66] Tung repeatedly called for the development of "consensus politics," and emphasized that civil servants should concentrate on their work rather than taking sides in political matters, as had been the case in the Patten administration.[67]

5. Conclusion

Although the Western media tended to see Hong Kong's return to China as the death of the territory, the level of confidence of the local people in the months before the handover was higher than it had been for years. The people of Hong Kong would be closely watching Tung's administration. The ability of the chief executive to preserve the status quo of the territory would indicate the viability of the "one country, two systems" concept, at least in the eyes of the local population. Thus, the fundamental challenge for Tung was how to implement the necessary changes while ensuring that the status quo was not threatened.

Tung represented the united front, which Beijing had been working on for years—since the 1997 question had surfaced. From the perspective of the public, Tung had direct communication channels with the Communist leaders, and this alone sufficed to illustrate the collaboration between Beijing and Hong Kong on "one country." On the one hand, the united front symbolized cooperation, mutual trust among the parties involved, and promises for the future. On the other hand, its existence suggested that opposing opinions and personalities would be on the fringe of the major decision-making process. Although the united front promised the maintenance of the status quo, critics felt that it was not too soon to warn people of the implications of implementing the "one country, two systems" policy for human rights and freedom of speech. The success of the policy depended on the success of the united front—whether Beijing could cultivate a camp of followers—and the ability to win over neutrals, bystanders, and observers.

The results of public opinion polls changed in accordance with the confidence placed in Tung, the chief executive-designate. Tung was a traditional Chinese, who strongly emphasized harmonious relations with Beijing and had already demonstrated his ability to achieve this objective. Tung himself belonged to the core of the united front of the Chinese Communists in Hong Kong. The united front was not demonstrated to be a threat to the public in general, as its existence promised a working relationship between Tung and Beijing even before the handover.

The "pro-Beijing" camp had proven its capacity and willingness to work with the Communist leaders. In Hong Kong, people knew who the staunch supporters of the united front were. Their identity was no secret. The only concern was whether the united front, which aimed at maintaining Beijing's perception of the status quo, would actually turn the clock back to the old colonial days when human rights and individual freedoms were not so much an issue to society as a whole. Nevertheless, local public confidence was much higher than that depicted by the Western media on the eve of the handover. The difference between the local point of view and Western descriptions of it might be attributed to the difference in the perception of the Communist united front in Hong Kong. The term "united front" seemed to have aroused suspicion and criticism in Western circles, but the practices of the united front did not seem to scare many people away from Hong Kong.

The main focus of Beijing was the upper-class capitalists in Hong Kong. This correlated with the objective of amassing maximum support for China's modernization effort. Chinese Communists and Hong Kong capitalists shared some common outlook. Both of them were (1) politically conservative, being concerned about the status quo, (2) critical and even hostile to the Democrats, and (3) supportive of economic reform rather than political change. The Hong Kong media charged the business elite and professionals with being "pro-China" and loyal friends of the Beijing government. The Chinese Communists' united front policy in Hong Kong differed from their traditional practice on the mainland. Their intention was not warlike or revolutionary, unlike the Guomindang-CCP united front against the Japanese in the 1940s and subsequent mass campaigns. There were no external threats of aggression against China and no internal rivals to the CCP. Instead, the prestige of the PRC depended very much on its ability to continue to achieve modernization. Hong Kong had provided the financial, banking, and commercial resources, as well as expertise for the mainland. Of particular importance were the local capitalists, who controlled the most economic power of the territory.

Acknowledgment: This chapter is an expanded and updated version of the author's article: "Tung Chee-hwa and His Challenges: A Look at Hong Kong's Last Colonial Days, December 1996–June 1997," *Asian Perspective* 22, no. 2 (1998): 169–91. The author would like to thank *Asian Perspective* for permission to publish this chapter.

Notes

Chapter 1

1. Ian Scott, *Political Change and the Crisis of Legitimacy in Hong Kong* (Honolulu: University of Hawaii Press, 1989), p. 18; Mark Roberti, *The Fall of Hong Kong: China's Triumph and Britain's Betrayal* (New York: John Wiley & Sons, 1994), pp. 22–24.
2. Kevin P. Lane, *Sovereignty and the Status Quo: The Historical Roots of China's Hong Kong Policy* (Boulder, CO: Westview Press, 1990), pp. 3–4.
3. *Vienna Convention on the Law of Treaties 1969* (Done at Vienna on May 23, 1969. Entered into force on January 27, 1980. United Nations, *Treaty Series*, vol. 1155, p. 331) (United Nations, 2005).
4. Editorial, "Lun Zhong Ying guanxi yu Xianggang de qiantu" [Discuss Sino-British relations and the future of Hong Kong], *Wen Wei Po* [Wenhuibao], May 6, 1949, p. 2.
5. James Tuck-Hong Tang, *Britain's Encounter with Revolutionary China, 1949–54* (New York: St. Martin's Press, 1992), p. 186.
6. Y. C. Jao, "Hong Kong's Role in Financing China's Modernization," in *China and Hong Kong: The Economic Nexus*, ed. A. J. Youngson (Hong Kong: Oxford University Press, 1983), p. 17.
7. Derek Davies, "China Earns from Hongkong," *Far Eastern Economic Review*, June 20, 1963, pp. 689 & 691.
8. Ibid., p. 692.
9. James T. H. Tang and Frank Ching, "The MacLehose-Youde Years: Balancing the 'Three-Legged Stool,' 1971–86," in *Precarious Balance: Hong Kong Between China and Britain, 1842–1992*, ed. Ming K. Chan (Armonk, NY: M. E. Sharpe, 1994), pp. 153–54.
10. Alvin Y. So, *Hong Kong's Embattled Democracy: A Societal Analysis* (Baltimore & London: John Hopkins University Press, 1999), p. 261.
11. Wai-kwok Wong, "Can Co-optation Win Over the Hong Kong People? China's United Front Work in Hong Kong Since 1984," *Issues & Studies* 33, no. 5 (May 1997): 102–37.
12. Christine Loh, *Underground Front: The Chinese Communist Party in Hong Kong* (Hong Kong: Hong Kong University Press, 2010).
13. Suzanne Pepper, *Keeping Democracy at Bay: Hong Kong and the Challenge of Chinese Political Reform* (Lanham, MD: Rowman & Littlefield, 2008), p. 254.

14. Chan Lau Kit-ching, *From Nothing to Nothing: The Chinese Communist Movement and Hong Kong, 1921–1936* (Hong Kong: Hong Kong University Press, 1999).
15. Ibid., p. 1.
16. Ibid., p. 5.
17. Scott, *Political Change and the Crisis of Legitimacy in Hong Kong*, p. 18; Roberti, *The Fall of Hong Kong*, pp. 22–24.
18. Robert Cottrell, *The End of Hong Kong: The Secret Diplomacy of Imperial Retreat* (Hong Kong: John Murray, 1993).
19. Ibid., p. 177.
20. Ibid., pp. 182–83.
21. Books on Hong Kong's story to 1997 include: Caroline Courtauld and May Holdsworth, *The Hong Kong Story* (Hong Kong: Oxford University Press, 1997); Roger Buckley, *Hong Kong: The Road to 1997* (Cambridge: Cambridge University Press, 1997).
22. Roberti, *The Fall of Hong Kong*, pp. 305–9.
23. David Wen-wei Chang and Richard Y. Chuang, *The Politics of Hong Kong's Reversion to China* (New York: St. Martin's Press, 1998), p. 17.
24. Albert H. Yee, *A People Misruled: Hong Kong and the Chinese Stepping Stone Syndrome* (Hong Kong: API Press, 1989).
25. Ibid., pp. 228–29.
26. Frank Welsh, *A History of Hong Kong* (London: HarperCollins, 1994), p. 511.
27. Ibid., p. 540.
28. John Flowerdew, *The Final Years of British Hong Kong: The Discourse of Colonial Withdrawal* (Houndmills: Macmillan, 1998), p. 219.
29. Ibid., p. 215.
30. Ibid., p. 220.
31. Gerald Segal, *The Fate of Hong Kong: The Coming of 1997 and What Lies Beyond* (New York: St. Martin's Press, 1993), pp. 207–11.
32. Steve Tsang, *Hong Kong: An Appointment with China* (London: I. B. Tauris, 1997), p. 111.
33. Ibid., pp. 111–12, 133–35.
34. Ibid., pp. 111–12.
35. Steve Tsang, "Realignment of Power: The Politics of Transition and Reform in Hong Kong" in *Political Order and Power Transition in Hong Kong*, ed. Li Pang-kwong (Hong Kong: Chinese University Press, 1997), pp. 31–51.
36. Jamie Allen, *Seeing Red: China's Uncompromising Takeover of Hong Kong* (Singapore: Butterworth-Heinemann Asia, 1997), pp. xvi–xviii.
37. Ibid., pp. xiv–xviii.
38. Richard Evans, *Deng Xiaoping and the Making of Modern China* (London: Penguin Books, 1995), p. 311.
39. Lane, *Sovereignty and the Status Quo*, p. 9.
40. Michael Yahuda, *Hong Kong: China's Challenge* (London: Routledge, 1996).
41. Yik-yi Chu, "Overt and Covert Functions of the Hong Kong Branch of the Xinhua News Agency, 1947–1984," *Historian* 62, no. 1 (Fall 1999): 32–33.

42. Ibid., pp. 31–32.
43. Cindy Yik-yi Chu, "The Origins of the Chinese Communists' Alliance with the Business Elite in Hong Kong: The 1997 Question and the Basic Law Committees, 1979–1985," *Modern Chinese History Society of Hong Kong Bulletin* 9–10 (October 1999): 51–67; Yik-yi Chu, "The Failure of the United Front Policy: The Involvement of Business in the Drafting of Hong Kong's Basic Law, 1985–1990," *Asian Perspective* 24, no. 2 (2000): 173–98.
44. David Shambaugh, ed., *Greater China: The Next Superpower?* (Oxford: Oxford University Press, 1995).
45. Sonny Shiu-Hing Lo, *The Dynamics of Beijing-Hong Kong Relations: A Model for Taiwan?* (Hong Kong: Hong Kong University Press, 2008), pp. 169–75.
46. Ibid., p. 181.
47. Deng Xiaoping, "Jiefang sixiang, shishi qiushi, tuanjie yizhi xiangqiankan" [Liberate thinking, learn from the facts, unite together to look forward] (dated December 13, 1978), in *Deng Xiaoping wenxuan 1975–1982* [Selected works of Deng Xiaoping 1975–1982] (Hong Kong: renmin chubanshe, 1983), pp. 130–43.
48. *Zhongguo tongyi zhanxian quanshu* [The complete book on China's united front] (Beijing: Guoji wenhua, 1993), p. 681.
49. Deng Xiaoping, "Xinshiqi de tongyi zhanxian he renmin zhengxie de renwu" [The new era's united front and the tasks of the people's political conference] (dated June 15, 1979), in *Deng Xiaoping wenxuan*, p. 171.
50. Ibid., p. 173.
51. *Zhongguo tongyi zhanxian quanshu*, p. 682.
52. Zhonggong Zhongyang Tongzhanbu Yanjiushi, ed., *Tongyi zhanxian zhishi wenda* [Questions and answers for the knowledge of united front] (Beijing: Zhongguo wenshi chubanshe, 1988), p. 56.
53. *Zhongguo tongyi zhanxian quanshu*, p. 687.
54. Deng Xiaoping, "Aiguo tongyi zhanxian qiancheng yuanda dayou kewei" [The prospects of the "patriotic united front" are great and rewarding] (dated November 24, 1982), in *Deng Xiaoping lun tongyi zhanxian* [Deng Xiaoping discusses the united front], ed. Zhonggong Zhongyang Tongyi Zhanxian Gongzuobu and Zhonggong Zhongyang Wenxian Yanjiushi (Beijing: Zhongyang wenxian chubanshe, 1991), p. 250.
55. Zhao Chunyi, Sun Youkui, and Bai Yuming, eds. *Xinshiqi tongyi zhanxian lilun yu shijian* [The theory and practice of the new era's united front] (Changchun: Jilin daxue chubanshe, 1986), pp. 11–15.
56. United Front Department of the Beijing City Committee, Beijing, April 18, 1995.
57. Yuan Lizhou, ed., *Tongzhan zhishi yu zhengce* [Facts and policies of the united front] (Harbin: Harbin gongye daxue chubanshe, 1985), pp. 44–45.
58. Ibid.; Kwok-sing Li, comp., *A Glossary of Political Terms of the People's Republic of China*, trans. Mary Lok (Hong Kong: Chinese University Press, 1995), pp. 452–53.
59. Zhao Chunyi, Sun Youkui, and Bai Yuming, ed. *Xinshiqi tongyi zhanxian lilun yu shijian*, p. 17.

60. Beijing Shehui Zhuyi Xueyuan, ed., *Zhongguo Gongchandang tongyi zhanxian shi* [A history of the united front of the Chinese Communist Party] (Beijing: Zhongguo wenshi chubanshe, 1993), p. 329.

61. Yuan Lizhou, ed., *Tongzhan zhishi yu zhengce*, p. 45.

62. Kwok-sing Li, comp., *A Glossary of Political Terms of the People's Republic of China*, p. 451.

63. J. D. Armstrong, *Revolutionary Diplomacy: Chinese Foreign Policy and the United Front Doctrine* (Berkeley: University of California Press, 1977), p. 33.

64. Lyman P. Van Slyke, *Enemies and Friends: The United Front in Chinese Communist History* (Stanford: Stanford University Press, 1967), p. 2.

65. Ibid., p. 3.

66. Ibid.

67. Van Slyke, *Enemies and Friends*, p. 9.

68. Ibid.

69. Van Slyke, *Enemies and Friends*, p. 93.

70. Mao Tse-tung, "The Situation and Tasks in the Anti-Japanese War After the Fall of Shanghai and Taiyuan" (dated November 12, 1937), in Mao Tse-tung, *Selected Works of Mao Tse-tung*, vol. 2 (Peking [Beijing]: Foreign Language Press, 1965), pp. 69–70.

71. Shum Kui-Kwong, *The Chinese Communists' Road to Power: The Anti-Japanese National United Front, 1935–1945* (Hong Kong: Oxford University Press, 1988).

72. Suzanne Pepper, *Civil War in China: The Political Struggle, 1945–1949* (Berkeley: University of California Press, 1978).

73. Peter Van Ness, *Revolution and Chinese Foreign Policy: Peking's Support for Wars of National Liberation* (Berkeley: University of California Press, 1970).

74. Ibid., p. 28.

75. Ibid.

76. Lin Piao, "Long Live the Victory of People's War! In Commemoration of the 20th Anniversary of Victory in the Chinese People's War of Resistance against Japan," *Peking Review* 8, no. 36 (September 3, 1965): 24.

77. Ibid.

78. Yuan Lizhou, ed., *Tongzhan zhishi yu zhengce*, pp. 51–52.

79. Ibid.

80. United Front Department of the Beijing City Committee, Beijing, April 18, 1995.

81. Beijing Shehui Zhuyi Xueyuan Bangongshi, ed., *Gandan xiangzhao rongru yugong: shehui zhuyi chuji jieduan tongyi zhanxian yu duodang hezuo* [Mutual understanding, mutual support: the united front and multiparty collaboration in the early stage of Socialism] (Beijing: Shishi chubanshe, 1989), pp. 121–25; Qin Yefeng, Bai Yuwu, and Feng Lianju, *Guogong hezuo de guoqu yu weilai* [The past and future of the Guomindang-CCP collaboration] (Harbin: Heilongjiang jiaoyu chubanshe, 1991), pp. 396–97.

82. Zhonggong Zhongyang Tongzhanbu Yanjiushi, ed., *Tongyi zhanxian zhishi wenda*, p. 97.

83. Beijing Shehui Zhuyi Xueyuan Bangongshi, ed., *Gandan xiangzhao rongru yugong*, pp. 121–25; Qin Yefeng, Bai Yuwu, and Feng Lianju, *Guogong hezuo de guoqu yu weilai*, pp. 396–97.

84. Ibid.

85. Deng Xiaoping, "Zhongguo dalu he Taiwan heping tongyi de shexiang" [Thoughts about the peaceful unification between mainland China and Taiwan] (dated June 26, 1983), in *Deng Xiaoping lun tongyi zhanxian*, ed. Zhonggong Zhongyang Tongyi Zhanxian Gongzuobu and Zhonggong Zhongyang Wenxian Yanjiushi, pp. 251–53.

86. Beijing Shehui Zhuyi Xueyuan Bangongshi, ed., *Gandan xiangzhao rongru yugong*, p. 123; Qin Yefeng, Bai Yuwu, and Feng Lianju, *Guogong hezuo de guoqu yu weilai*, p. 397.

87. Van Slyke, *Enemies and Friends*, p. 8.

88. Ibid.

89. Van Slyke, *Enemies and Friends*, pp. 8–9.

90. Mao Tse-tung, "On the People's Democratic Dictatorship" (dated June 30, 1949), in Mao Tse-tung, *Selected Works of Mao Tse-tung*, vol. 4 (Peking [Beijing]: Foreign Language Press, 1975), p. 417.

91. Jin Yaoru, "Chongwen Zhou Enlai zongli Xianggang zhengce: kan jinri Gang-Ao gongzuo zhi 'zuo'—wo de huiyilu zhi er" [To look at the "leftism" of today's Hong Kong and Macao work: remembering Premier Zhou Enlai's Hong Kong policy, the second part of my memoirs], *Dangdai yuekan* [*Contemporary monthly*], June 15, 1992, pp. 33–34.

92. "Zhonggong kan Xianggang jieji jiegou" [The Chinese Communist Party looks at the Hong Kong class structure], *Dangdai yuekan* [*Contemporary* monthly], October 15, 1991, p.17.

Chapter 2

1. The phrase "a borrowed place in a borrowed time" comes from the title of Richard Hughes' famous book, *Borrowed Place, Borrowed Time: Hong Kong and Its Many Faces*, 2nd rev. ed. (London: André Deutsch, 1976). The first edition, with a slightly different title—*Hong Kong: Borrowed Place—Borrowed Time*—was published by the same publisher in 1968.

2. Emily Lau, "The Rising Red Tide: Under the Surface China Is Establishing Its Own Structure," *Far Eastern Economic Review*, August 1, 1985, p. 23.

3. *Zhongguo tongyi zhanxian quanshu* [The complete book on China's united front] (Beijing: Guoji wenhua, 1993), p. 15.

4. Chan Lau Kit-ching, *From Nothing to Nothing: The Chinese Communist Movement and Hong Kong, 1921–1936* (Hong Kong: Hong Kong University Press, 1999), p. 1.

5. Ibid.

6. Lyman P. Van Slyke, *Enemies and Friends: The United Front in Chinese Communist History* (Stanford: Stanford University Press, 1967), p. 93.

7. Ibid.
8. Ibid.
9. Mao Tse-tung, "The Situation and Tasks in the Anti-Japanese War After the Fall of Shanghai and Taiyuan" (dated November 12, 1937), in Mao Tse-tung, *Selected Works of Mao Tse-tung*, vol. 2 (Peking [Beijing]: Foreign Language Press, 1965), pp. 69–70.
10. Ibid., p. 69.
11. Ibid.
12. Ibid.
13. Mao Tse-tung, "The Situation and Tasks in the Anti-Japanese War After the Fall of Shanghai and Taiyuan," p. 70.
14. Ibid.
15. Ibid.
16. Van Slyke, *Enemies and Friends*, pp. 111–12.
17. Ibid., pp. 143–44.
18. Mao Tse-tung, "On the Question of Political Power in the Anti-Japanese Base Areas" (dated March 6, 1940), in *Selected Works of Mao Tse-tung*, vol. 2, p. 418.
19. Chen Xin and Guo Zhikun, eds., *Xianggang quanjilu* [Illustrated chronicle of Hong Kong], vol. 1 (Hong Kong: Zhonghua shuju, 1997–1998), p. 212.
20. Ibid., pp. 211 & 214.
21. Li Guoqiang and Zhang Peixin, *Xianggang zai kang Ri qijian* [Hong Kong's anti-Japanese period] (Hong Kong: Xianggang wenshi chubanshe, 2005), pp. 32–36.
22. Liang Shangyuan, *Zhonggong zai Xianggang* [The Chinese Communists in Hong Kong] (Hong Kong: Wide Angle Press, 1989), pp. 1–3. This is a memoir of a former member of the Office of the Eighth Route Army in Hong Kong; pages 1–87 deal with the history of the Office in Hong Kong. See also Chan Lau Kit-ching, *From Nothing to Nothing*, p. 7.
23. Liang Shangyuan, *Zhonggong zai Xianggang*, p. 2; Chen Xin and Guo Zhikun, eds., *Xianggang quanjilu*, vol. 1, p. 216.
24. Liang Shangyuan, *Zhonggong zai Xianggang*, pp. 11–13; Chen Xin and Guo Zhikun, eds., *Xianggang quanjilu*, vol. 1, p. 216.
25. "Balujun zhu Xianggang banshichu" [The Office of the Eighth Route Army in Hong Kong], in *Zhonggong dangshi ziliao zhuanti yanjiuji: kan Ri zhanzheng shiqi (2)* [Historical materials on the history of the Chinese Communist Party: anti-Japanese war period (2)] (Beijing: Zhonggong dangshi ziliao chubanshe, 1989), pp. 157–58.
26. Ibid., pp. 158–59, 173.
27. Ibid., p. 174.
28. Liang Shangyuan, *Zhonggong zai Xianggang*, pp. 2–3.
29. Ibid., p. 4.
30. Yuan Xiaolun, *Yue Gang kangzhan wenhuashi lungao* [A history of anti-Japanese war effort among cultural circles in Guangdong and Hong Kong] (Guangzhou: Guangdong renmin chubanshe, 2005), pp. 34–36.

31. Ibid., p. 35.
32. Liang Shangyuan, *Zhonggong zai Xianggang*, pp. 4–6.
33. Ng Lun Ngai-ha and Yee Yim Kwong, *Zhongguo mingren zai Xianggang: 30, 40 niandai zai Gang huodong jishi* [China's celebrities in Hong Kong: A record of their activities in Hong Kong in the 1930s and 1940s] (Hong Kong: Hong Kong Educational Publishing, 1997), p. 22.
34. Liang Shangyuan, *Zhonggong zai Xianggang*, pp. 4–9, 27–28.
35. Kurt W. Radtke, *China's Relations with Japan 1945–83: The Role of Liao Chengzhi* (Manchester: Manchester University Press, 1990), p. 64.
36. Ibid., pp. 65–66.
37. Ibid., p. 67.
38. Chan Lau Kit-ching, *From Nothing to Nothing*, p. 8.
39. Liang Shangyuan, *Zhonggong zai Xianggang*, pp. 17–20.
40. Liao Chengzhi, "Jiaqiang huaqiao xuanchuan gongzuo" [To strengthen the propaganda work with overseas Chinese; dated September 27, 1940], in *Liao Chengzhi wenji* [Collected works of Liao Chengzhi], vol. 1 (Hong Kong: Joint Publishing (HK), 1990), pp. 78–79.
41. Chan Lau Kit-ching, *China, Britain and Hong Kong 1895–1945* (Hong Kong: Chinese University Press, 1990), p. 266.
42. Liang Shangyuan, *Zhonggong zai Xianggang*, pp. 31–40; Zhong Zheng, "Qianxi Song Qingling de kang Ri guoji tongyi zhanxian sixiang" [An analysis of Song Qingling's thought on the anti-Japanese international united front], *Luoyang shifan xueyuan xuebao* [Newsletter of Luoyang Normal School] 4 (2003): 99.
43. *Dagongbao*, February 25, 1939, p. 6; July 26, 1939, p. 6.
44. Zheng Canhui, Ji Hongsheng, and Wu Jingping, *Song Qingling yu kang Ri jiuwang yundong* [Song Qingling and the anti-Japanese movement for national survival] (Fuzhou: Fuzhou renmin chubanshe, 1986), pp. 190, 193–95.
45. "Balujun zhu Xianggang banshichu," p. 170.
46. Tsai Jung-fang, *Xianggangren zhi Xianggangshi 1841–1945* [The Hong Kong people's history of Hong Kong] (Hong Kong: Oxford University Press, 2001), p. 191.
47. *Dagongbao*, October 19, 1939, p. 6.
48. Tsai Jung-fang, *Xianggangren zhi Xianggangshi 1841–1945*, p. 193; Lu Weiluan, *Xianggang wenzong—Neidi zuojia nanlai ji qi wenhua huodong* [Hong Kong's literary circles: the arrival of mainland writers and their cultural activities] (Hong Kong: Wah Hon, 1987), pp. 53–54; Chan Lau Kit-ching, *From Nothing to Nothing*, p. 8.
49. Xuanyuan Lu, "Xinhuashe Xianggang fenshe de zaoqi lishi" [The early history of the Hong Kong Branch of Xinhua News Agency], *Guangjiaojing yuekan* [*Wide Angle* monthly], June 16, 1986, p. 20.
50. Tsai Jung-fang, *Xianggangren zhi Xianggangshi 1841–1945*, p. 194.
51. Ibid., pp. 194, 217–18.
52. Du Junhua, "Liao Chengzhi yu Xianggang kangzhan baozhi" [Liao Chengzhi and antiwar newspapers in Hong Kong], *Wenshi zazhi* [Journal of literature

and history], no. 1 (2002): 61; Ng Lun Ngai-ha and Yee Yim Kwong, *Zhongguo mingren zai Xianggang*, pp. 21–23.

53. *Liao Chengzhi wenji*, vol. 1, pp. 96–97.
54. "Balujun zhu Xianggang banshichu," p. 165.
55. Ibid., pp. 167–68.
56. Mao Dun, *Wo zouguo de daolu* [My path], vol. 3 (Hong Kong: Chung Hwa, 1981), pp. 228–29.
57. Liang Shangyuan, *Zhonggong zai Xianggang*, pp. 63–64.
58. Ibid.
59. Wu Zhongcai and Zhang Yuxia, "Dui 1939 nian Nanfangju zuochu chexiao 'Guangxisheng Gongwei' dengxiang jueding de tantao" [An investigation into the decision of the Southern Bureau to terminate the "Guangxi Work Committee" in 1939 and others], in *Nanfangju dangshi yanjiu lunwenji* [A collection of essays on the history of the Southern Bureau], ed. Zhonggong Sichuan Shengwei Dangshi Yanjiushi and others (Chongqing: Chongqing chubanshe, 1993), pp. 75–82.
60. Ibid., pp. 80–82.
61. Ibid., pp. 82–83.
62. Zhang Diming and Liu Xingquan, "Jixu he fayang Nanfangju miqie lianxi qunzhong de lishi jingyan" [Continue and develop the historical experience of the Southern Bureau in its intimate relations with the masses], in *Nanfangju dangshi yanjiu lunwenji*, ed. Zhonggong Sichuan Shengwei Dangshi Yanjiushi and others, pp. 138–39.
63. Tsai Jung-fang, *Xianggangren zhi Xianggangshi 1841–1945*, p. 215.
64. Zhang Diming and Liu Xingquan, "Jixu he fayang Nanfangju miqie lianxi qunzhong de lishi jingyan," pp. 146–48.
65. Ibid., p. 147.
66. Peng Chengfu and Li Rong, "Nanfangju dui kangzhan shiqi Guotongqu minzhu yundong de yingxiang he lingdao" [The Southern Bureau's impact on and leadership over democratic movements in Guomindang-controlled areas during the anti-Japanese war], in *Nanfangju dangshi yanjiu lunwenji*, ed. Zhonggong Sichuan Shengwei Dangshi Yanjiushi and others, p. 165.
67. Ibid., pp. 165–66.
68. *Guangdongqu dang, tuan yanjiu shiliao, 1937–1945* [Research materials on the party and the league in Guangdong region, 1937–1945], vol. 1 (Guangzhou: Guangdong renmin chubanshe, 1988), pp. 362–65 (dated September 1936–November 1939).
69. Ibid., pp. 365–66.
70. Li Jiayuan, *Xianggang baoye zatan* [Essays on the newspaper industry in Hong Kong] (Hong Kong: Joint Publishing, 1989), p. 155.
71. Ibid., pp. 155–57.
72. Philip Snow, *The Fall of Hong Kong: Britain, China and the Japanese Occupation* (New Haven & London: Yale University Press, 2003), pp. 49–50; Radtke, *China's Relations with Japan 1945–83*, p. 71.
73. "Yu Yuandong Yingjun tanpan hezuo kang Ri, gei Zhonggong zhongyang de dianbao" [Negotiating with the Far Eastern British military for cooperation

against the Japanese: telegrams to the Communist Central Committee; dated October 25–December 7, 1941], in *Liao Chengzhi wenji*, vol. 1, pp. 105–9.

74. Ibid., p. 110, n. 1.

75. Ibid., p. 110, n. 2.

76. Liang Shangyuan, *Zhonggong zai Xianggang*, p. 86; Zhou Shuzhen, *1949 piaoyao Gangdao* [Hong Kong and 1949] (Beijing: Shishi chubanshe, 1996), pp. 28–29; Radtke, *China's Relations with Japan 1945–83*, p. 71; "Balujun zhu Xianggang banshichu," pp. 181–84.

77. *Guangdongqu dang, tuan yanjiu shiliao, 1937–1945*, vol. 2, p. 447 (dated February 16, 1942).

78. Xu Yueqing, ed., *Yuan Dongjiang zongdui Gang Jiu duli dadui* [The original independent force of Hong Kong and Kowloon of the East River Column] (Hong Kong: Gang Jiu dadui (jianshi) bianjizu, 1999), p. 13; Chan Lau Kit-ching, *From Nothing to Nothing*, p. 9.

79. Liu Zhipeng and Zhou Jiajian, *Tunsheng renyu: Rizhi shiqi Xianggangren de jiti huiyi* [Fell silent: the collective memory of Hong Kong people during the Japanese occupation] (Hong Kong: Chung Hwa Book, 2009), pp. 279–81; Zhang Huizhen and Kong Qiangsheng, *Cong shiyiwan dao sanqian: lunxian shiqi Xianggang jiaoyu koushu lishi* [From 110,000 to 3,000: an oral history on Hong Kong's education under the Japanese occupation] (Hong Kong: Oxford University Press, 2005), pp. 11–19, 25–36.

80. *Dongjiang zongdui zhi* [Anecdotes of the East River Column] (Beijing: Jiefangjun chubanshe, 2003), p. 342.

81. Gordon Y. M. Chan, "Hong Kong and Communist Guerilla Resistance in South China, 1937–1945," *Twentieth-Century China* 29, no. 1 (November 2003): 53; Edwin Ride, *BAAG: Hong Kong Resistance, 1942–1945* (Hong Kong: Oxford University Press, 1981), pp. 52–53; Xie Yongguang, *Sannian ling bageyue de kunan* [Misery of three years and eight months] (Hong Kong : Mingbao chubanshe, 1994), pp. 366–67.

82. James T. H. Tang, "World War to Cold War: Hong Kong's Future and Anglo-Chinese Interactions, 1941–55," in *Precarious Balance: Hong Kong Between China and Britain, 1842–1992*, ed. Ming K. Chan (Armonk, NY: M. E. Sharpe, 1994), pp. 115–16; Zhou Shuzhen, *1949 piaoyao Gangdao*, pp. 30–32.

83. Zhang Han, "Lishi shang de Zhonggong Xianggang fenju" [The Hong Kong Central Branch Bureau in history], *Wenshi zazhi* [Journal of literature and history], no. 3 (1997):14–15.

84. Xuanyuan Lu, "Xinhuashe Xianggang fenshe de zaoqi lishi," pp. 19–20.

85. In the 1970s, Qiao Guanhua became involved in important diplomatic matters. As deputy foreign minister in 1971, he headed the Chinese delegation to the United Nations, a historical event initiated by Mao Zedong. In February 1972, Qiao was responsible for drafting the Shanghai Communiqué with Henry Kissinger. Liang Kuifeng, "Renjian ziyou zhenqing zai—Qiao Guanhua yu Li Hao" [There was true friendship in the world—Qiao Guanhua and Li Hao], in *Wo yu Qiao Guanhua* [Qiao Guanhua and I], by Zhang Hanzhi and others (Beijing: Zhongguo qingnian chubanshe, 1994), pp. 244–45, 254.

86. Xie Yongguang, *Xianggang kang Ri fengyunlu* [A record of Hong Kong's anti-Japanese activities] (Hong Kong: Cosmos Books, 1995), p. 13.
87. Feng Yidai, "Yi Qiao Guanhua" [Remember Qiao Guanhua], in *Wo yu Qiao Guanhua*, by Zhang Hanzhi and others, pp. 174–75.
88. Xu Chi, "Di'erci shijie dazhan yu caihua hengyi de Qiao Guanhua" [The Second World War and the brilliant Qiao Guanhua], in *Wo yu Qiao Guanhua*, by Zhang Hanzhi and others, pp. 180–82.
89. Ibid., p. 192.
90. Feng Yidai, "Yi Qiao Guanhua," pp. 174–75.
91. Xuanyuan Lu, "Xinhuashe Xianggang fenshe de zaoqi lishi," p. 20.
92. Steve Tsang, "Maximum Flexibility, Rigid Framework: China's Policy Towards Hong Kong and Its Implications," *Journal of International Affairs* 49, no. 2 (Winter 1996): 419.
93. Zhou Shuzhen, *1949 piaoyao Gangdao*, pp. 40–42.
94. Jin Yaoru, "Chongwen Zhou Enlai zongli Xianggang zhengce: kan jinri Gang-Ao gongzuo zhi 'zuo'—wo de huiyilu zhi er" [To look at the "leftism" of today's Hong Kong and Macao work: remembering Premier Zhou Enlai's Hong Kong policy, the second part of my memoirs], *Dangdai yuekan* [*Contemporary monthly*], June 15, 1992, p. 32.
95. Lau, "The Rising Red Tide," p. 23.

Chapter 3

1. John P. Burns, "The Structure of Communist Party Control in Hong Kong," *Asian Survey* 30, no. 8 (August 1990): 749–52, 755, 763–64.
2. Kevin P. Lane, *Sovereignty and the Status Quo: The Historical Roots of China's Hong Kong Policy* (Boulder, CO: Westview Press, 1990), pp. 91–93; Ian Scott, *Political Change and the Crisis of Legitimacy in Hong Kong* (Honolulu: University of Hawaii Press, 1989), pp. 176–77.
3. Qiao Songdu, *Qiao Guanhua and Gongpeng: wo de fuqing muqing* [My parents Qiao Guanhua and Gongpeng] (Beijing: Zhonghua shuju, 2008), pp. 92–93; Wen Zhuofei, "Xianggang Xinhuashe ruhe touguo zuobao zuo xuanchuan gongzuo" [How the Hong Kong Xinhua News Agency conducted promotional work through leftist newspapers], in *Jiuqi xiaoying: Xianggang, Zhongguo yu Taipingyang* [The 1997 effect: Hong Kong, China and the Pacific], ed. Wu Guoguang (Hong Kong: Taipingyang shiji yanjiusuo, 1997), p. 29.
4. See Liang Kuifeng, "Renjian ziyou zhenqing zai—Qiao Guanhua yu Li Hao" [There was true friendship in the world—Qiao Guanhua and Li Hao], in *Wo yu Qiao Guanhua* [Qiao Guanhua and I], by Zhang Hanzhi and others (Beijing: Zhongguo qingnian chubanshe, 1994), pp. 244–45; James T. H. Tang, "World War to Cold War: Hong Kong's Future and Anglo-Chinese Interactions, 1941–55," in *Precarious Balance: Hong Kong Between China and Britain, 1842–1992*, ed. Ming K. Chan (Armonk, NY: M. E. Sharpe, 1994), pp. 115–16; Zhou Shuzhen, *1949 piaoyao Gangdao* [Hong Kong and 1949] (Beijing: Shishi chubanshe, 1996),

pp. 30–32, 34–37; Xuanyuan Lu, "Xinhuashe Xianggang fenshe de zaoqi lishi" [The early history of the Hong Kong Branch of Xinhua News Agency], *Guangjiaojing yuekan* [*Wide Angle* monthly], June 16, 1986, pp. 19–20.

5. Steve Tsang, "Maximum Flexibility, Rigid Framework: China's Policy Towards Hong Kong and Its Implications," *Journal of International Affairs* 49, no. 2 (Winter 1996): 419–20.

6. Zhou Shuzhen, *1949 piaoyao Gangdao*, p. 37.

7. Ibid., pp. 38–39.

8. Ibid., pp. 42–46.

9. Ibid., pp. 39–40.

10. Ibid., pp. 40–42.

11. Xuanyuan Lu, *Xinhuashe toushi* [An insight into the Xinhua News Agency] (Hong Kong: Wide Angle Press, 1987), pp. 13–16.

12. Qiao Songdu, *Qiao Guanhua and Gongpeng*, p. 93.

13. Jin Yaoru, "Chongwen Zhou Enlai zongli Xianggang zhengce: kan jinri Gang-Ao gongzuo zhi 'zuo'—wo de huiyilu zhi er" [To look at the "leftism" of today's Hong Kong and Macao work: remembering Premier Zhou Enlai's Hong Kong policy, the second part of my memoirs], *Dangdai yuekan* [*Contemporary* monthly], June 15, 1992, p. 32.

14. Ibid.

15. Jin Yaoru, "Chongwen Zhou Enlai zongli Xianggang zhengce," p. 33.

16. Yu Jiwen, "Zhonggong zai Gang de gongzuo xitong" [The Chinese Communist work system in Hong Kong], *Nineties* [Jiushi niandai yuekan], October 1985, pp. 56–57; Xuanyuan Lu, *Xinhuashe toushi*, pp. 25–26.

17. Liang Shangyuan, *Zhonggong zai Xianggang* [The Chinese Communists in Hong Kong] (Hong Kong: Wide Angle Press, 1989), pp. 132–33.

18. Zhong Shimei, "Zhonggong ruhe guanli Xianggang?" [How did the Chinese Communists administer their work in Hong Kong?], *Dangdai shishi zhoukan* [*Contemporary* weekly], November 25, 1989, p. 20; Burns, "The Structure of Communist Party Control in Hong Kong," p. 750.

19. Zhong Shimei, "Zhonggong ruhe guanli Xianggang?" p. 20.

20. *Hong Kong: Economic Prospects to 1987*, Special Report no. 156 (London: Economist Intelligence Unit, 1983), p. 49; Jin Yaoru, "Chongwen Zhou Enlai zongli Xianggang zhengce," pp. 33–34.

21. Jin Yaoru, "Chongwen Zhou Enlai zongli Xianggang zhengce," pp. 33–34; Kan Tang, *Hongkong and Macao: History in Search of a Future* (Taipei [Taibei]: World Anti-Communist League, China Chapter: Asian Peoples' Anti-Communist League, Republic of China, 1989), pp. 17–18.

22. Jin Yaoru, "Chongwen Zhou Enlai zongli Xianggang zhengce," p. 34.

23. Felix Patrikeeff, *Mouldering Pearl: Hong Kong at the Crossroads* (London: George Philip, 1989), p. 38.

24. Xuanyuan Lu, *Xinhuashe toushi*, p. 29.

25. Ibid., pp. 36–39, 44; Zhong Shimei, "Gongwei qian Gang tongyi lingdao—Zhonggong ruhe guanli Xianggang?" [The work committee moved to Hong Kong and consolidated the leadership—how did the Chinese Communists

administer their work in Hong Kong?], *Dangdai shishi zhoukan* [*Contemporary weekly*], December 2, 1989, p. 20.

26. Xuanyuan Lu, *Xinhuashe toushi*, pp. 41–42.
27. Situ Huifen, "Meiguo, Xianggang jingyan he Zhongguo de gaige" [The United States, Hong Kong experience and China's reform], *Guangjiaojing yuekan* [*Wide Angle* monthly], September 1988, p. 62; *Hong Kong: Economic Prospects to 1987*, p. 49.
28. Situ Huifen, "Meiguo, Xianggang jingyan he Zhongguo de gaige," p. 62; Xuanyuan Lu, *Xinhuashe toushi*, pp. 39–41; *Hong Kong: Economic Prospects to 1987*, pp. 45 & 49; William F. Beazer, *The Commercial Future of Hong Kong* (New York: Praeger, 1978), p. 129.
29. Zhong Shimei, "Gongwei qian Gang tongyi lingdao," p. 20.
30. Liang Shangyuan, *Zhonggong zai Xianggang*, pp. 138–41; Xuanyuan Lu, *Xinhuashe toushi*, pp. 44–47.
31. Liang Shangyuan, *Zhonggong zai Xianggang*, p. 140; Xuanyuan Lu, *Xinhuashe toushi*, pp. 45–47; Zhong Shimei, "Gongwei qian Gang tongyi lingdao," pp. 20–21.
32. "Kwangtung Set Up Committee in Support of HK Compatriots," *Ta Kung Pao* (*Dagongbao*), English Edition, June 7, 1967, p. 3.
33. "Struggle Committee Warns HK Authorities," *Ta Kung Pao* (*Dagongbao*), English Edition, June 10, 1967, p. 1.
34. "PLA Garrison Demonstrates on the Border," *Ta Kung Pao* (*Dagongbao*), English Edition, June 10, 1967, p. 3.
35. Richard Evans, *Deng Xiaoping and the Making of Modern China* (London: Penguin Books, 1995), p. 263.
36. Ibid.; Jürgen Domes, "The Impact of the Hong Kong Problem and Agreement on PRC Domestic Politics," in *Hong Kong: A Chinese and International Concern*, ed. Jürgen Domes and Yu-ming Shaw (Boulder, CO: Westview Press, 1988), p. 85.
37. Evans, *Deng Xiaoping and the Making of Modern China*, p. 263.
38. Domes, "The Impact of the Hong Kong Problem and Agreement on PRC Domestic Politics," p. 85.
39. Immediate Hong Kong to Commonwealth Office, Telno. 1276, August 21, 1967, FCO 40/113 "Hong Kong: Legal Affairs—Action against Communist Press," Special Collection Microfilm, University of Hong Kong Library.
40. Hong Kong to Commonwealth Office, August 20, 1967, FCO40/113.
41. Ibid., Telnos. 1384 and 1387, September 14, 1967, FCO 40/113.
42. Ibid., Telno. 1358, September 8, 1967, FCO 40/113.
43. Confidential: Draft Submission: "Measures against the Communist Press," August 3, 1967, FCO 40/113; Commonwealth Office to Hong Kong, Telno. 1840, September 6, 1967, FCO 40/113.
44. Immediate Hong Kong to Commonwealth Office, Telno. 1316, August 29, 1967, FCO 40/113.
45. John D. Young, "The Building Years: Maintaining a China-Hong Kong-Britain Equilibrium, 1950–71," in *Precarious Balance*, ed. Ming K. Chan, pp. 142–44; *Hong Kong: Economic Prospects to 1987*, pp. 49–50.

46. Liang Shangyuan, *Zhonggong zai Xianggang*, p. 173; Xuanyuan Lu, *Xinhuashe toushi*, pp. 53–55.

47. *Zhongguo tongyi zhanxian quanshu* [The complete book on China's united front] (Beijing: Guoji wenhua, 1993), p. 331.

48. Ibid.

49. Zhong Shimei, "Dui Gang fangzhen, zheng chu duo men—Gang Ao Ban yu Gongwei de maodun" [Different policies toward Hong Kong: conflicts between the Hong Kong and Macao Affairs Office and the Hong Kong and Macao Work Committee], *Dangdai shishi zhoukan* [*Contemporary* weekly], December 9, 1989, pp. 20–21.

50. Emily Lau, "The Rising Red Tide: Under the Surface China Is Establishing Its Own Structure," *Far Eastern Economic Review*, August 1, 1985, pp. 22–23; Xu Jiatun, *Xu Jiatun Xianggang huiyilu* [Xu Jiatun's Hong Kong memoirs], vol. 1 (Hong Kong: Xianggang lianhebao, 1994), pp. 48–49; Zhong Shimei, "Dui Gang fangzhen, zheng chu duo men," p. 21.

51. Xu Jiatun, *Xu Jiatun Xianggang huiyilu*, vol. 1, pp. 4–12; Xuanyuan Lu, *Xinhuashe toushi*, pp. 78–79.

52. Xu Jiatun, *Xu Jiatun Xianggang huiyilu*, vol. 1, pp. 1–2.

53. Xuanyuan Lu, *Xinhuashe toushi*, pp. 74–75.

54. Xu Jiatun, *Xu Jiatun Xianggang huiyilu*, vol. 1, pp. 2–3.

55. Yu Jiwen, "Zhonggong zai Gang de gongzuo xitong," p. 57; Xuanyuan Lu, *Xinhuashe toushi*, pp. 104 & 106.

56. Xuanyuan Lu, *Xinhuashe toushi*, pp. 77, 101–7.

57. Lau, "The Rising Red Tide," p. 23; Yu Jiwen, "Zhonggong zai Gang de gongzuo xitong," pp. 58–59.

58. Lau, "The Rising Red Tide," p. 23; Xuanyuan Lu, *Xinhuashe toushi*, pp. 106–7.

59. Xu Jiatun, *Xu Jiatun Xianggang huiyilu*, vol. 1, p. 5.

60. Xuanyuan Lu, *Xinhuashe toushi*, pp. 77–78.

61. Xu Jiatun, *Xu Jiatun Xianggang huiyilu*, vol. 1, pp. 32–35.

62. Xuanyuan Lu, *Xinhuashe toushi*, pp. 83–99.

63. Lau, "The Rising Red Tide," p. 22.

64. Zhang Jiefeng and others, *Bubian, wushi nian?: Zhong Ying Gang jiaoli Jibenfa* [No change for fifty years?: China, Britain and Hong Kong wrestled with the Basic Law] (Hong Kong: Langchao chubanshe, 1991), p. 38.

65. Xu Jiatun, *Xu Jiatun Xianggang huiyilu*, vol. 1, p. 131.

66. Ibid., p. 132.

67. Ibid., pp. 127–32; Scott, *Political Change and the Crisis of Legitimacy*, pp. 204–5.

68. Philip Bowring, "Heaven's Command: Index Arise," *Far Eastern Economic Review*, February 23, 1984, p. 77; Teresa Ma, "Capitalism, China-style: 'Big Boss' Wang Outdoes Hongkong Entrepreneurs with a Series of Deals Which Shake Up the Territory," *Far Eastern Economic Review*, March 1, 1984, p. 68; *Hong Kong: Economic Prospects to 1987*, p. 45. The first largest banking group in Hong Kong was the Hong Kong Bank group.

69. Xu Jiatun, *Xu Jiatun Xianggang huiyilu*, vol. 1, pp. 173–76.

70. Zhang Jiefeng and others, *Bubian, wushi nian*, pp. 36–39.
71. Joseph Cheng, "Democrats Have Lost Their Way," *South China Morning Post*, March 4, 1989, Review, p. 6.
72. Xu Jiatun, *Xu Jiatun Xianggang huiyilu*, vol. 2, pp. 368–69.
73. Ibid., pp. 437–56.
74. Chris Yeung, "Tycoons' Plan for Self-Rule 'Treasonous': HK$10b Post-1997 Lease Sought for City," *South China Morning Post*, July 4, 2007, p. 1.
75. Zong Daoyi and others, eds., *Zhou Nan koushu: shen zai jifeng zhouyu zhong* [Zhou Nan recounted: in strong winds and rain] (Hong Kong: Joint Publishing [HK]., 2007), p. 355.

Chapter 4

1. Yin Qian, *Dynamics vs. Tradition in Chinese Foreign Policy Motivation: Beijing's Fifth Column Policy in Hong Kong as a Test Case* (Commack, NY: Nova Science, 1999), p. 171.
2. As local scholars suggest, petitions to the Hong Kong Branch of the Xinhua News Agency represented "China's increasing influence over Hong Kong's internal affairs." See Anthony Bing-leung Cheung and Kin-sheun Louie, *Social Conflicts in Hong Kong, 1975–1986: Trends and Implications,* Occasional Paper no. 3 (Hong Kong: Hong Kong Institute of Asia-Pacific Studies, Chinese University of Hong Kong, April 1991), pp. 23–24.
3. Jamie Allen, *Seeing Red: China's Uncompromising Takeover of Hong Kong* (Singapore: Butterworth-Heinemann Asia, 1997), p. 75.
4. Ibid., p. 77.
5. Ibid., p. 79.
6. Kevin P. Lane, *Sovereignty and the Status Quo: The Historical Roots of China's Hong Kong Policy* (Boulder, CO: Westview Press, 1990), p. 8; Li Changdao and Gong Xiaohang, *Jibenfa toushi* [A look into the Basic Law] (Hong Kong: Chung Hwa 1990), p. 22.
7. Li Changdao and Gong Xiaohang, *Jibenfa toushi*, pp. 21–22.
8. Xu Jiatun, *Xu Jiatun Xianggang huiyilu* [Xu Jiatun's Hong Kong memoirs], vol. 1 (Hong Kong: Xianggang lianhebao, 1994), pp. 82–83.
9. Brian Hook, "Political Change in Hong Kong," in *Greater China: The Next Superpower?* ed. David Shambaugh (Oxford: Oxford University Press, 1995), p. 188, n. 1.
10. Sze-yuen Chung, *Hong Kong's Journey to Reunification: Memoirs of Sze-yuen Chung* (Hong Kong: Chinese University Press, 2001), pp. 30–31.
11. Ibid., p. 31.
12. Ian Scott, *Political Change and the Crisis of Legitimacy in Hong Kong* (Honolulu: University of Hawaii Press, 1989), p. 176; Lane, *Sovereignty and the Status Quo*, pp. 91–92.
13. Margaret Thatcher, *The Downing Street Years 1979–1990* (London: HarperCollins, 1993; New York: HarperPerennial, 1995), p. 259.

14. Ibid., p. 261.
15. Ibid., p. 259.
16. Scott, *Political Change and the Crisis of Legitimacy in Hong Kong*, p. 181.
17. Zhang Jiefeng and others, *Bubian, wushi nian?: Zhong Ying Gang jiaoli Jibenfa* [No change for fifty years?: China, Britain and Hong Kong wrestled with the Basic Law] (Hong Kong: Langchao chubanshe, 1991), p. 32; "Taiwan Not Same Issue as Hongkong," *Beijing Review*, August 27, 1984, p. 8.
18. Scott, *Political Change and the Crisis of Legitimacy in Hong Kong*, Appendix A: "Chronology of the Sino-British Negotiations," pp. 338–40.
19. Thatcher, *The Downing Street Years*, p. 489 (italics hers).
20. Ibid., p. 490.
21. Ibid.
22. Scott, *Political Change and the Crisis of Legitimacy in Hong Kong*, p. 340 (Appendix A).
23. Michael Specter, "Colonial Constituency: An Election Proposal May Mean a New Phase in Sino-British Talks," *Far Eastern Economic Review*, January 19, 1984, pp. 12–14.
24. Teresa Ma and Philip Bowring, "Amber, but Not Green: An Upsurge of Optimism over the Future May Be Premature," *Far Eastern Economic Review*, February 9, 1984, pp. 10–11.
25. Teresa Ma, "Debatable Proposition: The Territory's Usually Docile Councillors Want at Least a Say in What the Future Is to Be," *Far Eastern Economic Review*, March 8, 1984, p. 26.
26. Philip Bowring, "Heaven's Command: Index Arise," *Far Eastern Economic Review*, February 23, 1984, p. 77.
27. Teresa Ma, "Capitalism, China-style," *Far Eastern Economic Review*, March 1, 1984, p. 68.
28. Ibid.; Philip Bowring, "Elec and Eltek—El-cheapo," *Far Eastern Economic Review*, March 8, 1984, p. 101.
29. Lu Jingli, "Zhongzi jigou zai Gang fazhan de xin zhuanbian" [New changes of mainland companies in Hong Kong], *Economic Digest* [*Jingji yizhou*], February 13, 1984, pp. 4–6.
30. Ibid., p. 6.
31. Emily Lau, "The Rising Red Tide: Under the Surface China Is Establishing Its Own Structure," *Far Eastern Economic Review*, August 1, 1985, p. 22.
32. Derek Davies, "A Leap into the Dark: Britain Concedes Sovereignty but Wants All Agreements Guaranteed," *Far Eastern Economic Review*, May 3, 1984, pp. 14–15.
33. Philip Bowring and Teresa Ma, "Promises, Promises: Britain and China Talk on about an Agreement, but without Guarantees It Is Not Likely to Mean Much," *Far Eastern Economic Review*, May 17, 1984, pp. 18–19.
34. Philip Bowring, "Peking's Little List," *Far Eastern Economic Review*, May 17, 1984, pp. 18–19.
35. Scott, *Political Change and the Crisis of Legitimacy in Hong Kong*, p. 204.
36. "Deng Xiaoping on Hongkong Issue," *Beijing Review*, July 23, 1984, p. 16.

37. Ibid., p. 17.
38. Ibid., pp. 16–17.
39. Scott, *Political Change and the Crisis of Legitimacy in Hong Kong*, p. 204.
40. "Deng on Problems about Hong Kong," *Beijing Review*, June 4, 1984, p. 6.
41. Emily Lau, "Left, Right and Centre," *Far Eastern Economic Review*, September 13, 1984, pp. 29–30.
42. "Leaders: HK Policy Will Not Be Altered," *Beijing Review*, October 15, 1984, p. 6.
43. "Accord Brings Stability to Hongkong," *Beijing Review*, December 24, 1984, p. 8.
44. "HK Agreement Hailed Worldwide," *Beijing Review*, October 8, 1984, pp. 10–11.
45. Louise do Rosario, "The Door Opens Wide: Entrepreneurial Entrepôt Hongkong Profits from the Opening of China's Trade with the World," *Far Eastern Economic Review*, February 28, 1985,. pp. 96–97.
46. Elizabeth Cheng, "Lending Credibility: The Bank of China Moves Further into the International Capital Markets by Arranging a Hongkong Property Loan," *Far Eastern Economic Review*, May 9, 1985, pp. 84–85.
47. Emily Lau, "Scramble for Power: The Territory's Non-Civil Servant Leaders Begin the Race to the Top," *Far Eastern Economic Review*, April 18, 1985, pp. 43–44.
48. Ibid., p. 43.
49. Ibid., pp. 43–44.
50. Xu Jiatun, *Xu Jiatun Xianggang huiyilu*, vol. 1, chap. 4.
51. Ibid., pp. 120–21.
52. Ibid., p. 121.
53. Ibid., p. 122.
54. Ibid.
55. Ibid.
56. Xu Jiatun, *Xu Jiatun Xianggang huiyilu*, vol. 1, pp. 122–24.
57. Ibid., pp. 127–29.
58. Ibid., pp. 129–31.
59. "Zhonggong kan Xianggang jieji jiegou" [The Chinese Communist Party looks at the Hong Kong class structure], *Dangdai yuekan* [*Contemporary* monthly], October 15, 1991, pp. 16–18.
60. Ibid., p. 17 (italics mine).
61. Ibid., p. 18.
62. Zhang Jiefeng and others, *Bubian, wushi nian*, pp. 32–33.
63. Robert Cottrell, *The End of Hong Kong: The Secret Diplomacy of Imperial Retreat* (London: John Murray, 1993), p. 99.
64. Lu Fanzhi, *Lu Fanzhi lun Xianggang qiantu (2): Ping Zhong Ying shuangfang yu jibenfa wenti* [A discussion on Sino-British Relations and the Basic Law question] (Hong Kong: Beichen xueshe, Jixianshe, 1985), p. 147.
65. Terry Cheng, "Basic Law Group Becomes Official: Now for First Draft Session," *South China Morning Post*, June 19, 1985, pp. 1 & 14.
66. Zhang Jiefeng and others, *Bubian, wushi nian*, pp. 36–39.
67. William McGurn, ed., *Basic Law, Basic Questions: The Debate Continues* (Hong Kong: Review Publishing, 1988), Appendix D: "Full List of Basic Law Drafting Committee (BLDC) Members," pp. 165–68.

68. "Jibenfa qicao weihui mingdan zhengshi gongbu" [The announcement of the membership list of the Basic Law Drafting Committee], *Wah Kiu Yat Po*, June 19, 1985, p. 1; "Huoren jibenfa qicao weihui chengyuan" [The appointed Basic Law Drafting Committee members], *Ta Kung Pao (Dagongbao)*, June 19, 1985, p. 4.

69. Zhang Jiefeng, *Bubian, wushi nian*, p. 37.

70. "Huoren jibenfa qicao weihui chengyuan," *Ta Kung Pao (Dagongbao)*, June 19, 1985, p. 4.

71. Emily Lau, "Basic-Law Makers: Peking Announces the Make-Up of a Drafting Committee Geared to Develop a Mini-Constitution for the British Territory," *Far Eastern Economic Review*, July 4, 1985, pp. 16.

72. "Gangren pinglun jibenfa qicao weihui renxuan" [Hong Kong people commented on the selection of the Basic Law Drafting Committee], *Wah Kiu Yat Po*, June 19, 1985, p. 1.

73. Cheng, "Basic Law Group Becomes Official: Now for First Draft Session," pp. 1 & 14.

74. Zhang Jiefeng, *Bubian, wushi nian*, p. 38.

75. Lau, "Basic-Law Makers," p. 16.

76. Shi Jianwen, "Tan jibenfa qicao weihui mingdan" [On the Basic Law Consultative Committee membership list], *Ta Kung Pao (Dagongbao)*, June 22, 1985, p. 6.

77. Ambrose Y. C. King, "The Hong Kong Talks and Hong Kong Politics," *Issues & Studies* 22, no. 6 (June 1986): 69–71.

78. Ibid., p. 70.

79. Ibid.

80. Ibid.

81. Ibid.

82. "Ji Pengfei huiyishang jiang jincheng" [Ji Pengfei talked about the schedule in the meeting], *Wah Kiu Yat Po*, July 2, 1985, p. 1.

83. Zhang Jiefeng, *Bubian, wushi nian*, pp. 46–51.

84. Emily Lau, "The Early History of the Drafting Process," in *The Basic Law and Hong Kong's Future*, ed. Peter Wesley-Smith and Albert H. Y. Chen (Hong Kong: Butterworths, 1988), p. 93.

85. Scott, *Political Change and the Crisis of Legitimacy in Hong Kong*, pp. 281–82.

86. Emily Lau, "Capitalist Delegates to People's Congress," *Far Eastern Economic Review*, August 1, 1985, pp. 24 & 26.

87. Emily Lau, "Shadow in the Wings: Peking's Xinhua Sets Up Power Centre in the Territory," *Far Eastern Economic Review*, January 9, 1986, p. 32.

Chapter 5

1. Ming K. Chan, "Democracy Derailed: Realpolitik in the Making of the Hong Kong Basic Law, 1985–90," in *The Hong Kong Basic Law: Blueprint for "Stability and Prosperity" under Chinese Sovereignty?*, ed. Ming K. Chan and David J. Clark (Armonk, NY: M. E. Sharpe, 1991), p. 13.

2. Lau Siu-kai, "From Elite Unity to Disunity: Political Elite in Post-1997 Hong Kong," in *Hong Kong in China: The Challenges of Transition*, ed. Wang Gungwu and John Wong (Singapore: Times Academic Press, 1999), p. 52.

3. Ian Scott, *Political Change and the Crisis of Legitimacy in Hong Kong* (Honolulu: University of Hawaii Press, 1989), p. 206.

4. Zhang Jiefeng and others, *Bubian, wushi nian?: Zhong Ying Gang jiaoli Jibenfa* [No change for fifty years?: China, Britain and Hong Kong wrestled with the Basic Law] (Hong Kong: Langchao chubanshe, 1991), p. 38.

5. Xu Jiatun, *Xu Jiatun Xianggang huiyilu* [Xu Jiatun's Hong Kong memoirs], vol. 1 (Hong Kong: Xianggang lianhebao, 1994), p. 131. The HKMWC was actually the CCP in Hong Kong. For a secondary account of Xu Jiatun's united front policy toward the business elite, read Wai-kwok Wong, "Can Co-optation Win Over the Hong Kong People? China's United Front Work in Hong Kong Since 1984," *Issues & Studies* 33, no. 5 (May 1997): 116–19.

6. Xu Jiatun, *Xu Jiatun Xianggang huiyilu*, vol. 1, p. 132.

7. Ibid.

8. Richard Hughes, *Borrowed Place, Borrowed Time: Hong Kong and Its Many Faces*, 2nd rev. ed. (London: André Deutsch, 1976), p. 23.

9. Ambrose Y. C. King, "The Hong Kong Talks and Hong Kong Politics," *Issues & Studies* 22, no. 6 (June 1986): 69–71.

10. Cindy Yik-yi Chu, "The Origins of the Chinese Communists' Alliance with the Business Elite in Hong Kong: The 1997 Question and the Basic Law Committees, 1979–1985," *Modern Chinese History Society of Hong Kong Bulletin*, nos. 9–10 (October 1999): 60–63; John Flowerdew, *The Final Years of British Hong Kong: The Discourse of Colonial Withdrawal* (Houndmills: Macmillan, 1998), p. 59.

11. *Jibenfa de dansheng* [The birth of the Basic Law] (Xianggang [Hong Kong]: Wenhui chubanshe, 1990), pp. 212–28.

12. "Editorial Welcomes Basic Law Consultative Committee" (HK270707 Hong Kong, *South China Morning Post*, November 27, 1985, p. 2), in Foreign Broadcast Information Service, *China Report: Political, Sociological, and Military Affairs* (JPRS-CPS-86-010), January 21, 1986, p. 85.

13. "Hong Kong Paper Views Affiliations of Law Committee Members" (HK070758 Hong Kong, *Hong Kong Standard*, December 7, 1985, p. 5), *China Report*, January 21, 1986, p. 105.

14. "Composition of Basic Law Standing Committee Criticized" (HK070640 Hong Kong, *Hong Kong Standard*, December 7, 1985, pp. 1 & 20), *China Report*, January 21, 1986, p. 108.

15. "Hong Kong Paper Views Affiliations of Law Committee Members," *China Report*, January 21, 1986, p. 106.

16. "Composition of Basic Law Standing Committee Criticized," *China Report*, January 21, 1986, p. 107.

17. "Hong Kong Paper Views Affiliations of Law Committee Members," *China Report*, January 21, 1986, p. 106.

18. Zeng Zhongrong and Chen Shaojuan, "Yao fanrong buyao minzhu: Shangjia zhuanzheng shi qilu? shi tantu?" [Prosperity but not democracy: Is the

business monopoly of politics a rough road? A smooth journey?], *Pai Shing Semi-monthly*, November 16, 1986, pp. 9–11.

19. Business and Professional Group, Consultative Committee for the Basic Law of the Hong Kong Special Administrative Region, "How to Elect the Chief Executive of the Future Hong Kong SAR Government: A Proposal by the Business and Professional Group of the BLCC" (Gift from Shui On Group Ltd.; Hong Kong Collection, Main Library, University of Hong Kong, 1986), pp. 1–6.

20. Ibid.

21. "How to Elect the Chief Executive of the Future Hong Kong SAR Government," p. 1.

22. Ibid.

23. Ibid.

24. "How to Elect the Chief Executive of the Future Hong Kong SAR Government," p. 4.

25. Ibid., p. 2.

26. Ibid., p. 3.

27. Ibid., pp. 3–4.

28. Ibid., p. 5.

29. "Examples of Constituents for the Grand Electoral College Proposed by the Business & Professional Group (BPG) of Members of BLCC for the Election of the Chief Executive and 25% of the Legislature" (Gift from the BPG; Hong Kong Collection, Main Library, University of Hong Kong, received in 1988), p. 4.

30. Ibid., Part IV. Lists of Examples, no page numbers.

31. Ibid., Part IV. Lists of Examples (Sector: Professionals), no page numbers.

32. "Hong Kong Legislative Council Split over Direct Elections," (HK280518 Hong Kong, *South China Morning Post*, November 28, 1985, p. 1), *China Report*, January 21, 1986, p. 87.

33. Ibid., p. 88.

34. Zeng Zhongrong, "Kan! shangjiamen zai xiang shenme?" [Look! What are the businessmen thinking?], *Pai Shing Semi-monthly*, November 16, 1986, pp. 14–15.

35. Tan Li, "Gongshang zhuanyejie ziwei chunqiang shejian hui jizhe" [The BLCC members of the industrial, business, and professional sectors met with the reporters and skillfully answered the questions], *Pai Shing Semi-monthly*, November 16, 1986, pp. 13–14.

36. He Yumian, "Zhengzhi yingxiangli shei yu shangjia bi" [Who could compete with the political influence of the business elite?], *Pai Shing Semi-monthly*, November 16, 1986, p. 16.

37. James T. H. Tang and Frank Ching, "The MacLehose-Youde Years: Balancing the 'Three-Legged Stool,' 1971–86," in *Precarious Balance: Hong Kong Between China and Britain, 1842–1992*, ed. Ming K. Chan (Armonk, NY: M. E. Sharpe, 1994), p. 150.

38. He Yumian, "'Gongshang jie,' 'minzhu pai': zhengzhi lunzhan maixiang gaochao" [The "industrial and business sectors," the "pro-democracy party": The

debates over the political system reaches the high wave], *Pai Shing Semi-monthly*, November 16, 1986, p. 12.

39. Chen Xiaoman, "Shijia caituan jiebanren, nianqing wushi qiyejia: zhengtan xinxing yaobuyao minzhu?" [The successors of big families and big corporations, the young and practical entrepreneurs: Do the new political stars want democracy?], *Pai Shing Semi-monthly*, November 16, 1986, p. 20.

40. Chen Jianping, "Zhengdang zhengzhi dui wending buli: Lu Ping zuo dui Gang ji tan geren yijian" [Party politics was harmful to stability: Lu Ping expressed his views to Hong Kong reporters], *Wen Wei Po*, July 3, 1986, p. 4.

41. Yik-yi Chu, "Overt and Covert Functions of the Hong Kong Branch of the Xinhua News Agency, 1947–1984," *Historian* 62, no. 1 (Fall 1999): 39.

42. "Joint Declaration of the Government of the United Kingdom of Great Britain and Northern Ireland and the Government of the People's Republic of China on the Question of Hong Kong," in *A Draft Agreement between the Government of the United Kingdom of Great Britain and Northern Ireland and the Government of the People's Republic of China on the Future of Hong Kong* (Hong Kong: Government Printer, September 26, 1984), p. 18.

43. "Jibenfa xuyan caogao gongbu" [The release of the Draft Preamble of the Basic Law], *Wen Wei Po*, February 19, 1987, p. 4.

44. Emily Lau and Michael Malik, "Modern Politics Come Late to Colonial Legco," *Far Eastern Economic Review,* April 16, 1987, pp. 40–43; *Jibenfa de dansheng*, pp. 212–28, 232–43.

45. Zhang Jiefeng and others, *Bubian, wushi nian*, pp. 115–16.

46. Wong Siu-lun, "Business and Politics in Hong Kong During the Transition," in *Hong Kong in Transition 1992* (Hong Kong: One Country Two Systems Economic Research Institute, 1993), pp. 489–91.

47. Ibid., p. 500.

48. Ibid., p. 503.

49. Ibid., pp. 510–11.

50. Zhang Jiefeng and others, *Bubian, wushi nian*, pp. 153–57.

51. Ibid., p. 163.

52. Ibid., pp. 160–62.

53. Ibid.

54. Zhang Jiefeng and others, *Bubian, wushi nian*, pp. 157 & 161.

55. Ibid., p. 163.

56. Ibid., pp. 157, 161–62.

57. Joseph Cheng, "Democrats Have Lost Their Way," *South China Morning Post*, March 4, 1989, Review, p. 6.

58. Ibid.

59. Ibid.

60. "Zhengzhi tuanti tian shenglijun, 'Xin Xianggang lianmeng' chengli: mubiao pingheng ge jieceng liyi" [A new force to political groups, the "New Hong Kong Alliance" established: Its task is to balance the benefits of every class], *Sing Tao Daily*, March 6, 1989, p. 19.

61. Zhang Jiefeng and others, *Bubian, wushi nian*, pp. 168–69.

62. Ibid., pp. 168–70.

63. Ibid., pp. 170–73; "Beijing dachu 'liangyuanzhi' xinpai?" [Has Beijing showed its new card of a "bicameral system"?], *Yazhou zhoukan* [*Asia Weekly*], September 10, 1989, p. 16.

64. "Beijing dachu 'liangyuanzhi' xinpai?" p. 16.

65. Yang Sen, "Cong gongshang zhuanye renshi jiaodu ping 'yihui liangju' fang'an" [Comment on the "bicameral legislature" model from the point of view of the industrialists, businessmen and professionals], *Mirror* [Jingbao yuekan], October 1989, pp. 12–13.

66. "Beijing dachu 'liangyuanzhi' xinpai?" *Yazhou zhoukan,* September 10, 1989, p. 16.

67. Zhang Jiefeng and others, *Bubian, wushi nian*, pp. 167–68, 172, 174–75.

68. Ibid., pp. 175–77.

69. "Zhongfang zhendui san zhenying xietiao, yunniang tuichu wu-san-er fang'an" [In order to tackle the compromise of the three forces, the China side prepared to introduce a "five: three: two" model], *Ming Pao*, October 16, 1989, p. 5.

70. Ming K. Chan, "Democracy Derailed: Realpolitik in the Making of the Hong Kong Basic Law, 1985–1990," in *The Hong Kong Reader: Passage to Chinese Sovereignty*, ed. Ming K. Chan and Gerard A. Postiglione (Armonk, NY: M. E. Sharpe, 1996), p. 31.

71. Yuan Qiushi, ed., *Xianggang guodu shiqi zhongyao wenjian huibian* [A collection of the important documents of Hong Kong in the transitional period] (Hong Kong: Joint Publishing [HK], 1997), pp. 193–206.

72. Ibid., pp. 205–6.

73. *The Basic Law of the Hong Kong Special Administrative Region of the People's Republic of China* (Hong Kong: One Country Two Systems Economic Research Institute, 1992), p. 19.

74. Ibid.

75. *The Basic Law of the Hong Kong Special Administrative Region of the People's Republic of China*, p. 68.

76. Ibid.

77. *The Basic Law of the Hong Kong Special Administrative Region of the People's Republic of China*, pp. 59–60.

Chapter 6

1. John Flowerdew, *The Final Years of British Hong Kong: The Discourse of Colonial Withdrawal* (Houndmills: Macmillan, 1998), pp. 66–67.

2. Sze-yuen Chung, *Hong Kong's Journey to Reunification: Memoirs of Sze-yuen Chung* (Hong Kong: Chinese University Press, 2001), p. 172.

3. Flowerdew, *The Final Years of British Hong Kong*, pp. 66–67.

4. Ibid.

5. Chung, *Hong Kong's Journey to Reunification*, pp. 173–76.

6. Ibid., pp. 173, 175–76.

7. Ibid., pp. 174–75.
8. Ibid., pp. 175–76.
9. Alvin Y. So and Reginald Y. Kwok, "Socioeconomic Center, Political Periphery: Hong Kong's Uncertain Transition Toward the Twenty-first Century," in *The Hong Kong Reader: Passage to Chinese Sovereignty*, ed. Ming K. Chan and Gerard A. Postiglione (Armonk, NY: M. E. Sharpe, 1996), p. 213.
10. Ibid.
11. Flowerdew, *The Final Years of British Hong Kong*, p. 71.
12. "Zhonggong kan Xianggang jieji jiegou" [The Chinese Communist Party looks at the Hong Kong class structure], *Dangdai yuekan* [*Contemporary* monthly], October 15, 1991, pp. 16–18.
13. Ibid., pp. 16–17.
14. Ibid., p. 17.
15. Ibid., pp. 17–18.
16. Flowerdew, *The Final Years of British Hong Kong*, p. 71.
17. Chung, *Hong Kong's Journey to Reunification*, pp. 178–80.
18. Lau Siu-kai, "From Elite Unity to Disunity: Political Elite in Post-1997 Hong Kong," in *Hong Kong in China: The Challenges of Transition*, ed. Wang Gungwu and John Wong (Singapore: Times Academic Press, 1999), pp. 56–57.
19. John P. Burns, Victor C. Falkenheim, and David M. Lampton, *Hong Kong and China in Transition*, Canada and Hong Kong Papers, no. 3 (Toronto: University of Toronto-York University Joint Centre for Asia Pacific Studies, 1994), p. 26.
20. Ibid., p. 42.
21. Chung, *Hong Kong's Journey to Reunification*, pp. 180–81.
22. "Zhongfang pin guwen, Gangfu bu fandui" [China side appointed advisers, and the Hong Kong Government did not oppose], *Ming Pao*, January 24, 1992, p. 2.
23. Chris Yeung, Kent Chen, and Fanny Wong, "Alarm over China Plan on Advisers," *South China Morning Post*, January 16, 1992, p. 1.
24. Ibid.
25. "Zhongfang pin guwen, Gangfu bu fandui," p. 2.
26. Huang Kangxian, "Cong lianhe zhenxian dao huaqing jiexian: Zhonggong dui Xianggang zhengdang tongzhan de jibenfa" [From united front to drawing the line: the basic principles of the Chinese Communists' united front work among political parties in Hong Kong], *Hong Kong Economic Journal Monthly* [Xinbao caijing yuekan], April 1993, p. 49.
27. Geoffrey Crothall, "China's Leaders Greet 'Friends,'" *South China Morning Post*, March 12, 1992, p. 5.
28. Ibid.
29. Ibid.
30. Kent Chen and Geoffrey Crothall, "Reforms Emphasised in Speech to Advisers," *South China Morning Post*, March 13, 1992, p. 6.
31. Ibid.
32. Frank Ching, "The Beijing Bosses Look for the Right Kind of 'Advice,'" *South China Morning Post*, January 31, 1992, p. 17.

33. Ibid.
34. Willy Wo-lap Lam, "China's Men in HK Still Follow Mao," *South China Morning Post*, April 29, 1992, p. 21.
35. Ching, "The Beijing Bosses Look for the Right Kind of 'Advice,'" p. 17.
36. "Beijing's Recruiter: Appointment of 'Advisers' Panel Affirms Mainland Intentions toward the Territory," *South China Morning Post*, February 2, 1992, p. 11.
37. Lam, "China's Men in HK Still Follow Mao," p. 21; Chris Yeung and Kent Chen, "China to Appoint Liberals to Second Advisory Panel," *South China Morning Post*, March 9, 1992, p. 1.
38. "Lu Ping Brings Back Megaphone Diplomacy," *South China Morning Post*, March 7, 1992, p. 16.
39. Ibid.
40. Ibid.
41. David Wallen, "Patten in Hands-Off Warning to China," *South China Morning Post*, July 1, 1992, p. 1.
42. Doreen Cheung, "Foreign Passport Holders in Legco Fine: Lu Ping," *South China Morning Post*, July 23, 1992, p. 1.
43. "Assurance for Lu Ping: Executive-Led Government to Stay," *South China Morning Post*, August 8, 1992, p. 4.
44. John Kohut and Fanny Wong, "Beijing Insists It Has the Right to Express Views on Exco Line-up," *South China Morning Post*, June 25, 1992, p. 1.
45. Ibid.
46. Frank Ching and Stacy Mosher, "Shaken and Stirred: Governor Patten Unveils New Political Programme," *Far Eastern Economic Review*, October 15, 1992, p. 13.
47. Steve Tsang, *Hong Kong: An Appointment with China* (London & New York: I.B. Tauris, 1997), p. 188.
48. Fanny Wong and Geoffrey Crothall, "Beijing in Threat over Rule for '97," *South China Morning Post*, October 24, 1992, p. 1.
49. "China Turns up the Heat on Patten Plans," *South China Morning Post*, October 24, 1992, p. 14.
50. Ibid.
51. "Business Could Help End Political Impasse," *South China Morning Post*, November 7, 1992, p. 18.
52. Ibid.
53. Danny Gittings, "Discord in the Ranks as Business Raises Its Voice," *South China Morning Post*, November 8, 1992, p. 12.
54. Danny Gittings and Candy Wong, "Patten Gives Early Warning to Business," *South China Morning Post*, November 8, 1992, p. 2.
55. Flowerdew, *The Final Years of British Hong Kong*, pp. 124–25.
56. Vincent H. S. Lo, "The Danger of Patten's Reforms," *South China Morning Post*, November 22, 1992, p. 13.
57. Ibid.
58. "Opposition Mounts to Patten's Plans," *South China Morning Post*, November 10, 1992, p. 18.

59. Tsang Yok-sing, "Beijing Will Not Make Hongkong People Suffer," *South China Morning Post*, December 27, 1992, p. 11.
60. Ibid.
61. Ibid.
62. Allen Lee, "My Message to Leaders in London and Beijing," *South China Morning Post*, January 17, 1993, p. 13.
63. Ibid.
64. Ibid.
65. Ibid.
66. Allen Lee, "The Sooner Talks Begin the Better for Hongkong," *South China Morning Post*, February 28, 1993, p. 13.
67. Ibid.
68. "New Group for Beijing," *South China Morning Post*, March 30, 1993, p. 3.
69. Ibid.
70. Sir David Ackers-Jones, "How I Can Help Hongkong Communicate with China," *South China Morning Post*, March 28, 1993, p. 11.
71. Ibid.
72. Kevin Sinclair, "Forging Ties for a Future Uncertainty," *South China Morning Post*, September 28, 1993, p. 19.
73. "Chinese Community Leaders Unite to Launch New Group," *South China Morning Post*, December 1, 1993, p. 2.
74. Ibid.
75. So Lai-fun and Doreen Cheung, "New Political Row Brewing over Separating Elections," *South China Morning Post*, October 13, 1993, p. 2.
76. Doreen Cheung, "Beijing Lays Foundation to Shape HK Before 1997," *South China Morning Post*, December 10, 1993, p. 1.
77. Doreen Cheung, "Panel Set to Speed Up 1997 Polls," *South China Morning Post*, December 10, 1993, p. 6.
78. Chris Yeung, "Delegates Feel the Heat from the Second Stove," *South China Morning Post*, December 11, 1993, p. 23.
79. Linda Choy, "Construction Should be Speedy, Says PWC," *South China Morning Post*, January 7, 1994, p. 5.
80. Doreen Cheung, "Beijing Buries 'Through Train' Plan," *South China Morning Post*, December 28, 1993, p. 1.
81. Linda Choy, "Lower Tiers May Escape Fresh Elections after 1997," *South China Morning Post*, January 9, 1994, p. 2.
82. Linda Choy and Louis Ng, "Top Official Cancels Beijing Trip after PWC Invitation," *South China Morning Post*, January 8, 1994, p. 1.
83. "Patten Blasts Beijing over 'Vital' Reform," *South China Morning Post*, January 21, 1994, p. 5.
84. Ibid.
85. Ibid.
86. Ibid.
87. Louis Ng, "Sir David Hits Back at Patten over 'Cheap Jibe,'" *South China Morning Post*, January 22, 1994, p. 1.
88. Ibid.

89. Ibid.
90. David Healy, "Beijing Attacks UK Foreign Affairs Committee over Inquiry," *South China Morning Post*, January 30, 1994, p. 2.
91. Chris Yeung, "400 New Advisers Created," *South China Morning Post*, February 7, 1994, p. 1.
92. "Beijing Casts Net Wide for Advisers," *South China Morning Post*, March 5, 1994, p. 5.
93. Yeung, "400 New Advisers Created," p. 1.
94. So Lai-fun and Linda Choy, "China Promises Not to Meddle in HK Affairs," *South China Morning Post*, March 5, 1994, p. 1.
95. Lau, "From Elite Unity to Disunity: Political Elite in Post-1997 Hong Kong," p. 57.
96. Doreen Cheung, "Beijing Keeps Up Pressure on Civil Servants," *South China Morning Post*, April 1, 1994, p. 3.
97. Ibid.
98. S. Y. Yue, "Xinhua Woos Civil Servants for SAR," *South China Morning Post*, April 4, 1994, p. 1.
99. So Lai-fun, "Backdown on Civil Servants," *South China Morning Post*, April 7, 1994, p. 1.
100. Sir Sze-yuen Chung, "Mapping Out China's Shadow Rule," *South China Morning Post*, November 24, 1995, p. 8.
101. John M. Carroll, *A Concise History of Hong Kong* (Hong Kong: Hong Kong University Press, 2007), p. 202.

Chapter 7

1. Lu Ping, *Lu Ping koushu Xianggang huigui* [Lu recounted the return of Hong Kong] (Hong Kong: Joint Publishing [H.K.] 2009), p. 102.
2. Frank Ching, "A Milestone for Hong Kong," *Far Eastern Economic Review*, December 26, 1996 & January 2, 1997, p. 28.
3. Sandra Burton, "The Tycoon in a Taxi," *Time*, November 11, 1996, p. 25.
4. Tim Healy and Law Siu Lan, "'Highest Honor': A Landslide Vaults Tung Chee Hwa into the 1997 Leader's Hot Seat," *Asiaweek*, December 20, 1996, p. 26.
5. Ching, "A Milestone for Hong Kong," p. 28.
6. "Luo Decheng youyi wending xingzheng zhangguan" [Lo Tak-shing is interested in the chief executive post], *Ming Pao*, May 22, 1996, p. A1.
7. "Dongshi ruo fangqi, youshuo Zhong Shiyuan" [If Tung gives up, will persuade Chung Sze-yuen], *Ming Pao*, May 23, 1996, p. A2.
8. "Zhangguan houxuanren baodao shi 'baoshui'" [Reports on the candidates for chief executive are merely "boiling water"], *Ming Pao*, May 24, 1996, p. A4.
9. Ibid.
10. "Fandui linlihui nengfou ru tuiwei, chouwei you butong lijie" [The Preparatory Committee has a different understanding of whether to allow opponents of the Provisional Legislature enter the Selection Committee], *Ming Pao*, May 25, 1996, p. A6.

11. "Jiang Zemin: xingzheng zhangguan bifu Gangren yuanwang" [Jiang Zemin said that the chief executive must respect the wishes of the Hong Kong People], *Ming Pao*, May 25, 1996, p. A2.

12. Frank Ching, "Choosing Hong Kong's Leader: Chief Executive Must Understand 'One Country, Two Systems,'" *Far Eastern Economic Review*, July 18, 1996, p. 34.

13. "Dong Jianhua baituo jiaose chongtu, qingci xingzhengju" [Tung Chee-hwa avoids role conflict, and resigns from the Executive Council], *Ming Pao*, June 4, 1996, p. A1.

14. "Yi Xianggang de liyi wei yigui, Dong Jianhua yingde Pengdu zanshang" [Tung Chee-hwa received praise from Governor Patten for having taken care of the interests of Hong Kong], *Ming Pao*, June 4, 1996, p. A2.

15. "Pengdu zan Dong Jianhua zhengzhi jizhi" [Governor Patten praised Tung Chee-hwa for his integrity and wisdom], *Ming Pao*, June 5, 1996, p. A6. Frank Ching explains Tung's appointment to Exco in 1992: "After all, the British privately informed China of their plans to step up democratization in Hong Kong in 1992. To soften the blow, they told the Chinese that they would appoint a pro-China figure to serve as one of Governor Chris Patten's closest advisers in the Executive Council. It soon transpired that the pro-China person who had caught the British eye was Tung." For further details, read Frank Ching, "Tung: A Reluctant Candidate," *Far Eastern Economic Review*, July 25, 1996, p. 40.

16. Fung Wai-kong and Angela Li, "Tung 'Lacks Popular Support,'" *South China Morning Post*, June 5, 1996, p. 1.

17. "Opinion Split over Patten Business Row, Survey Shows," *South China Morning Post*, June 3, 1996, p. 1. This article reports on the same poll, which is mentioned in the citation in the previous note.

18. Willy Wo-lap Lam, "Executive Decisions," *South China Morning Post*, July 24, 1996, p. 19.

19. Song Ligong, "Cong teshou zhengba kan zhi Gang banzi de guanjian weizhi" [The chief executive competition and its implications for the ruling elite of Hong Kong], *Hong Kong Economic Journal Monthly* [Xinbao caijing yuekan], October 1996, p. 10.

20. "Chentai cheng leyi xuwei tequ zhengfu fuwu" [Mrs. Chan said that she is willing to serve the government of the Special Administrative Region], *Ming Pao*, June 5, 1996, p. A6.

21. "Dong Jianhua Chentai piaoshu lingxian" [Tung Chee-hwa and Mrs. Chan led the race], *Ming Pao*, July 26, 1996, p. A7.

22. "Zha Liangyong ping teshou renxuan, zhichi Dong Jianhua" [Louis Cha commented on the candidates for chief executive, and supported Tung Chee-hwa], *Ming Pao*, August 10, 1996, p. A2; "Xiagu rouchang, lun Xiangjiang fengyun" [To comment on the events in Hong Kong], *Yazhou zhoukan* [*Asia Weekly*], August 25, 1996, p. 28.

23. May Sin-mi Hon, "Tung Supporter Louis Cha Denies Acting on Orders," *South China Morning Post*, August 17, 1996, p. 6.

24. Quinton Chan, "Support for Tycoon but Anson Favourite," *South China Morning Post*, August 27, 1996, p. 4.

25. "Dong Jianhua zijielou shenbao guanlian jiaoyi" [Tung Chee-hwa revealed that he had missed reporting the deals], *Ming Pao*, September 11, 1996, p. A4; "Yang Tieliang Dong Jianhua bushu juezhu Xianggang tequ shouzhang" [Yang Ti-liang and Tung Chee-hwa plan for the chief executive competition], *Yazhou zhoukan* [*Asia Weekly*], September 16–22, 1996, p. 81.

26. Bruce Gilley, "Enter the Judge," *Far Eastern Economic Review*, September 12, 1996, p. 14.

27. "Dong Jianhua buxiang leitai" [Tung Chee-hwa climbs into the ring], *Ming Pao*, September 20, 1996, p. A2.

28. "Xingshi zhoubian, Dong Jianhua tupoxing biaotai" [The situation changed, and Tung Chee-hwa made a breakthrough by expressing his intention], *Ming Pao*, September 20, 1996, p. A4.

29. "Jingxuan chujie Dong Jianhua zan lingxian" [Tung Chee-hwa for the moment leads the race in its early stage], *Ming Pao*, September 23, 1996, p. A8.

30. "Former Top Judge Joins Hopefuls for Post-1997 Job," *South China Morning Post*, September 26, 1996, p. 5; "Jia Shiya youyi han Yang Tieliang" [Arthur Garcia intends to challenge Yang Ti-liang], *Ming Pao*, September 25, 1996, p. A2.

31. "Wu Guangzheng anshi jin xuanbu canxuan" [Peter Woo implied that he will announce to enter the election today], *Ming Pao*, September 30, 1996, p. A7.

32. "Wu Guangzheng yao jian qinmin zhengfu" [Peter Woo wants to establish a government close to people], *Ming Pao*, October 2, 1996, p. A1.

33. Chris Yeung, "Candidates Call the Tune," [*South China*] *Sunday Morning Post*, October 6, 1996, Politics, p. 10.

34. "Zha Liangyong shuo Yang Wu shi Dong duishou" [Louis Cha said that Yang Ti-liang and Peter Woo are the opponents of Tung Chee-hwa"], *Ming Pao*, October 3, 1996, p. A8.

35. "Taking the Public's Opinions into Account," [*South China*] *Sunday Morning Post*, October 6, 1996, Editorial, p. 10.

36. Chan, "Support for Tycoon but Anson Favourite," p. 4.

37. Sharon Cheung and Quinton Chan, "Sir Ti Liang Rises in Public Opinion," *South China Morning Post*, October 6, 1996, p. 1.

38. Ibid.

39. "Taking the Public's Opinions into Account," Editorial, p. 10.

40. "Jiaguan Liguan bu yu Yangguan dangxuan?" [Garcia and Li do not want Yang elected?], *Ming Pao*, October 12, 1996, p. A6.

41. "Yang Dong jiejin, Wu Li luo hou" [The competition between Yang and Tung is close, while Woo and Li fell behind], *Ming Pao*, October 20, 1996, p. A2.

42. Linda Choy, May Sin-mi Hon, and Sharon Cheung, "Confident Tung Confirms Bid for '97 Post," *South China Morning Post*, October 19, 1996, p. 1.

43. "Dong yuan dai Xianggang tiaozhan liudai weiji" [Tung Chee-hwa is willing to lead Hong Kong to face the six great challenges], *Ming Pao*, October 23, 1996, p. A2; "Dong Jianhua zhi Gang fangzhen: gongtong jianshe ershiyi shiji de Xianggang" [Tung Chee-hwa's guiding principles: to work together for Hong Kong toward the twenty-first century], *Ming Pao*, October 23, 1992, pp. A10–A11.

44. Fung Wai-kong, Linda Choy, and Chris Yeung, "Tung Stresses Consensus, Not Confrontation," *South China Morning Post*, October 23, 1996, p. 1.

45. "Chen Fang An-sheng bu canxuan xingzheng zhangguan" [Anson Chan will not run for chief executive], *Ming Pao*, October 27, 1996, p. A2.

46. Ai Kesi, "Dong Jianhua jiang miandui naxie zhongdai wenti?" [What great challenges will Tung face?], *Cheng Ming*, January 1997, p. 66.

47. "Dong Jianhua shaochao Yangguan" [Tung Chee-hwa is slightly ahead of Yang], *Ming Pao*, October 29, 1996, p. A1; "31 Bid for Chief Executive Post," *South China Morning Post*, October 29, 1996, p. 1.

48. Linda Choy and Louis Won, "Yang Overtakes Tung as People's Choice for Top Job," *South China Morning Post*, November 8, 1996, p. 1; "Yangguan zhichidu fan chaoqian Dong 2%" [The degree of support for Yang surpassed that for Tung by 2 percent], *Ming Pao*, November 8, 1996, p. A4.

49. Linda Choy and Fung Wai-kong, "Four Lesser Known Contestants Declared after Selection Body Finalised; Race for Chief Executive Down to Eight Runners," *South China Morning Post*, November 3, 1996, p. 1.

50. "Tuiwei dansheng, teshouzhan jieman" [The Selection Committee is formed, the competition for the chief executive job begins], *Ming Pao*, November 3, 1996, p. A2.

51. Chris Yeung, "Candidates in First Big Test," *South China Morning Post*, November 15, 1996, p. 1.

52. "Liguan chuju yiwai, Dong Jianhua xingqing kanzhang" [Li's defeat is a surprise, Tung's prospects look very promising], *Ming Pao*, November 16, 1996, p. A4.

53. Chris Yeung, "Public Opinion a Factor in Li Defeat," *South China Morning Post*, November 16, 1996, Analysis, p. 1.

54. "Zhengqu shangjie zhichi, Dong xianjieduan zhanyou" [To struggle for business support, Tung Chee-hwa achieves better results at this stage], *Ming Pao*, November 11, 1996, p. A4; Linda Choy, "Tung Backed by Influential Business Chief," *South China Morning Post*, November 14, 1996, p. 6.

55. Yeung, "Public Opinion a Factor in Li Defeat," Analysis, p.1.

56. Ibid.

57. "Time to Open Doors," *South China Morning Post*, November 16, 1996, Editorial, p. 16.

58. Bruce Gilley, "Shoe-In's Challenge: Prospective Chief Executive Has to Fight for Credibility," *Far Eastern Economic Review*, November 28, 1996, p. 23.

59. "Time to Open Doors," Editorial, p. 16.

60. "Dong Jianhua huo zhichidu pansheng" (The degree of support for Tung Chee-hwa increases), *Ming Pao*, November 22, 1996, p. A6.

61. "Dong huo zhichi fanchaoqian Yangguan" [The support, which Tung received, surpassed Yang's], *Ming Pao*, November 29, 1996, p. A8.

62. Frank Ching, "Hong Kong Mood Improves: Campaign for Chief Executive is More Open Than Expected," *Far Eastern Economic Review*, November 28, 1996, p. 54.

63. Ibid.

64. "Dong Jianhua buxizhu Gangdufu" [Tung Chee-hwa does not like to live in Government House], *Ming Pao*, November 29, 1996, p. A1.

65. "Dawenhui jieshu, xingshi youli Dong Jianhua" [The public forum ended, and the situation is favorable to Tung], *Ming Pao*, November 30, 1996, p. A2; Linda Choy, "'Big Boss' Tung Tipped by Yang Ally," *South China Morning Post*, November 30, 1996, p. 6.

66. "Dong huo zhichilü sheng Yang 18%" [The rate of support, Tung received, surpassed Yang's by 18 percent], *Ming Pao*, December 4, 1996, p. A4.

67. "Dong Jianhua jiaoshou minyi zhichi" [Tung Chee-hwa receives more public support], *Ming Pao*, December 9, 1996, p. A1.

68. Chris Yeung and Linda Choy, "Tung Leads the Way," *South China Morning Post*, December 12, 1996, p. 1.

69. Dorinda Elliott, "Captain Hong Kong," *Newsweek*, December 16, 1996, p. 14.

70. Sandra Burton, "China's Choice," *Time*, December 23, 1996, p. 15.

71. Ching, "A Milestone for Hong Kong," p. 28.

72. Ibid.

Chapter 8

1. Frank Ching, "Hong Kong Isn't Dead Yet," *Far Eastern Economic Review*, February 20, 1997, p. 34.

2. "Waiguo chuanmei zhizao de Xianggang" [Hong Kong as created by the foreign media], *Ming Pao*, June 1, 1997, p. A6.

3. Ibid.

4. Bruce Gilley, "Hong Kong '97: Regional Politik," *Far Eastern Economic Review*, May 29, 1997, pp. 22–23, 26.

5. "HK Media Hail New Era of Democracy," *Beijing Review*, December 9–15, 1996, p. 4; Ren Xin, "A Beginning for Democracy in Hong Kong," *Beijing Review*, January 13–19, 1997, pp. 5–7.

6. Lau Siu-kai, ed., *The First Tung Chee-hwa Administration: The First Five Years of the Hong Kong Special Administrative Region* (Hong Kong: Chinese University Press, 2002), p. xi.

7. Lau Siu-kai, "Tung Chee-hwa's Governing Strategy: The Shortfall in Politics," in *The First Tung Chee-hwa Administration*, ed. Lau Siu-kai, p. 1.

8. Ibid., p. 2.

9. "Tung Chee Hwa: A Brief Biography," *Beijing Review*, January 13–19, 1997, p. 9.

10. Pamela Baldinger, "Hong Kong Gets Its First Chinese Chief," *China Business Review*, January–February, 1997, p. 4.

11. Ibid.; "Teshou qiangshi gaoguan nanwei" [The senior officials found it hard to deal with the strong force of the chief executive], *Ming Pao*, December 16, 1996, p. D9.

12. Lau Siu-kai, ed., *The First Tung Chee-hwa Administration*, p. xi.

13. Chris Yeung, "Tung Fails to Win Over Governor," *South China Morning Post*, December 24, 1996, p. 1; "Peng Dong jueding jingchang jianmian" [Patten and Tung decided to meet regularly], *Ming Pao*, December 24, 1996, p. A1.

14. Quinton Chan, "'We Both Share A Common Objective to Maintain Confidence and Prosperity after 1997'; Chan Accepts Offer to Work with Tung," *South China Morning Post*, December 29, 1996, p. 1; "Chentai jueding ren zhengwu sichang" [Mrs. Chan decided to become the Chief Secretary], *Ming Pao*, December 29, 1996, p. A1.

15. "Looking Ahead Under Mr Tung and Mrs Chan," *South China Morning Post*, December 29, 1996, Editorial, p. 8.

16. "Dong Jianhua xiazhousi huiwu minzhudang" [Tung Chee-hwa will meet the Democratic Party next Thursday], *Ming Pao*, January 3, 1997, p. A4.

17. No Kwai-yan, "Democrats Risking HK Reputation, Says Tung," *South China Morning Post*, January 10, 1997, p. 1.

18. Ibid.

19. Ibid.

20. "Jiang Zemin xiang Dong Jianhua zuo liangxiang baozheng" [Jiang Zemin gave two guarantees to Tung Chee-hwa], *Ming Pao*, December 19, 1996, p. A1; Chris Yeung and No Kwai-yan, "Jiang Pledges Great Autonomy," *South China Morning Post*, December 19, 1996, p. 1; "Dong huo Jiang zeng bazi zhenyan" [Tung was given an eight-word promise by Jiang], *Ming Pao*, December 20, 1996, p. A2; Chris Yeung, "Tung Vows to Work Towards NPC Decision," *South China Morning Post*, December 20, 1996, p. 4.

21. Li Yi, "Deng Xiaoping qushi dui Xianggang de yingxiang" [The impact of Deng Xiaoping's death on Hong Kong], *Nineties* [Jiushi niandai yuekan], March 1997, p. 29.

22. "Decision of the National People's Congress on the Method for the Formation of the First Government and the First Legislative Council of the Hong Kong Special Administrative Region," Adopted by the Seventh National People's Congress at its Third Session on April 4, 1990, *The Basic Law of the Hong Kong Special Administrative Region of the People's Republic of China* (Hong Kong: One Country Two Systems Economic Research Institute, 1992), pp. 67–69.

23. Zhang Daming, "Wushi chuli linlihui fali wenti" [To handle the legal question of the provisional legislature in a pragmatic manner], *Ming Pao*, January 3, 1997, p. C10.

24. Hong Kong Bar Association, "The Hong Kong Bar Association States Its Case . . . No Legal Basis or Practical Necessity," *China Perspectives*, January/February 1997, pp. 33–34.

25. Ibid., p. 34.

26. "Visit to Beijing Defended by Tung," *South China Morning Post*, January 5, 1997, p. 1.

27. No Kwai-yan and Fung Wai-kong, "Beijing to Pay for Provisional Body Until July," *South China Morning Post*, January 6, 1997, p. 1.

28. "Dong yu fandui linlihui renshi 'yihe weigui'" [Tung asked the opponents of the provisional legislature "to establish a cordial relationship"], *Ming Pao*, January 9, 1997, p. A4; Linda Choy, "Less Politics Seen As An Attraction," *South China Morning Post*, January 9, 1997, p. 6.

29. "Liju buyu 16 zhiyuan 'guodang' linlihui" [Not more than 16 staff of the Legislative Council Secretariat will "move over" to the provisional legislature], *Ming Pao*, January 15, 1997, p. A4.

30. Linda Choy, "A Legal Minefield," *South China Morning Post*, January 23, 1997, p. 19.

31. Ibid.

32. "Juliuquan jiao linlihui lifa qi zhengyi" [It has caused controversies as the provisional legislature was given the right to pass laws with regard to the right of abode], *Ming Pao*, April 15, 1997, p. A2.

33. "Dongban fang Xingzhou zuofa yanzhi huiguifa" [Tung's office imitates the Singapore way in producing the reunification bill], *Ming Pao*, April 23, 1997, p. A8.

34. No Kwai-yan and others, "Mainland Preparing to Repeal 16 HK Laws," *South China Morning Post*, January 20, 1997, p. 1.

35. "Ying jiang touguo waijiao biaoda buiman feifa" [England will express its opposition toward repealing the laws], *Ming Pao*, January 21, 1997, p. A2.

36. Ibid.; Linda Choy, "Alliance Fears Door Open to Crackdown" *South China Morning Post*, April 10, 1997, p. 6.

37. "Gong'an shetuan fa 'qiyi' qian rengke jiantao" [The Public Order Ordinance and the Societies Ordinance can still be reviewed before "1 July"], *Ming Pao*, February 2, 1997, p. A2.

38. Greg Torode, "Listen to Rights Concerns, Qian Urged," *South China Morning Post*, February 13, 1997, p. 4; Fung Wai-kong and No Kwai-yan, "Rifkind Concedes Defeat," *South China Morning Post*, February 17, 1997, p. 1.

39. "Dong Jianhua ze Li Zhuming 'changshuai' Xianggang" [Tung Chee-hwa accused Martin Lee of "badmouthing" Hong Kong], *Ming Pao*, February 14, 1997, p. A2.

40. Linda Choy, "Judge Gives Backing to Civil Rights Repeal," *South China Morning Post*, February 18, 1997, p. 1.

41. Fang Su, "Dong teshou de 'miyueqi' jieshule" [Chief Executive Tung's "honeymoon" has ended], *Nineties* [Jiushi niandai yuekan], March 1997, pp. 56–57.

42. Linda Choy and Angela Li, "Pre-July 1 Review of Rights Changes," *South China Morning Post*, April 2, 1997, p. 6.

43. Chief Executive's Office, Hong Kong Special Administrative Region, the People's Republic of China, *Civil Liberties and Social Order: Consultation Document*, (Hong Kong Chief Executive's Office, Hong Kong Special Administrative Region, People's Republic of China), April 1997, p. B4.

44. Ibid., pp. 11–13, A1.

45. "Gong'an shetuan xiuli zixunqi jin zuihou, tuanti chongci biaotai" [Today is the last day of consultation for the amendments to the Public Order Ordinance and the Societies Ordinance; different groups are making use of the last opportunity to express their views], *Ming Pao*, April 30, 1997, p. A6.

46. "Gong'an shetuan cao'an zuo 11 xiang xiuding" [There are 11 amendments to the draft proposal on the Public Order and Societies Ordinances], *Ming Pao*, May 16, 1997, p. A2.

47. Ibid.

48. Ibid.

49. Ibid.

50. Ibid.; Chris Yeung, "Restraints on Protests and Political Funding Relaxed," *South China Morning Post*, May 16, 1997, p. 1.

51. Joice Pang, "National Security 'Knife Hanging Over Us,'" *South China Morning Post*, May 16, 1997, p. 3.

52. "Naming the Team," *South China Morning Post*, December 17, 1996, p. 18.

53. "Teshou gongbu tequ 23 zhuyao guanyuan mingdan" [The chief executive announced the list of 23 top officials], *Ming Pao*, February 21, 1997, p. A15.

54. Fung Wai-kong, "Tung's Popularity on the Rise, Says Opinion Poll," *South China Morning Post*, March 3, 1997, p. 1.

55. Ibid.

56. David Bottomley, "Polls Point to a New-Found Confidence," *South China Morning Post*, March 16, 1997, p. 13. This article reports on the Asian Commercial Research (ARC) poll of 586 people conducted from February 22 to 26. This poll is that which is cited in notes 53 and 54.

57. Ibid.

58. Ibid.

59. Ibid.

60. Chris Yeung, "Faith in Tung Drops Amid Freedom Fears," *South China Morning Post*, April 14, 1997, p. 1.

61. "Dong Jianhua shangren wuyue minwang weisheng" [Tung Chee-hwa's popularity slightly increased five months after he took up the job], *Ming Pao*, May 12, 1997, p. A3.

62. Fung Wai-kong, "Handover Optimism Wavers, Survey Shows," *South China Morning Post*, April 15, 1997, p. 6.

63. Dorinda Elliott, "The Best Man for the Job," *Newsweek*, June 9, 1997, p. 14.

64. Ibid.

65. Chris Yeung, "Anson Chan's Words 'Indicate Looming Crisis,'" *South China Morning Post*, June 4, 1997, p. 6.

66. "Ye Guohua: buzhengsi quanli hui bei 'tiaozheng'" [Paul Yip said that the power of the Chief Secretary will be "modified"], *Ming Pao*, June 4, 1997, p. A6.

67. Song Ligong, "Cong zhengce guocheng kan gaoguan miandui de tiaozhan" [How the policy process reflected on the challenges the top officials faced], *Hong Kong Economic Journal Monthly* [Xinbao caijing yuekan], March 1997, p. 26.

Bibliography

Archives

Basic Law Drafting History Online, Digital Initiatives, University of Hong Kong Libraries.

Contemporary China Research Collection, Special Collections & Archives, Hong Kong Baptist University Library.

FCO 40/113, Microfilm, Special Collections, Main Library, University of Hong Kong.

Foreign Broadcast Information Service. *China Report: Political, Sociological, and Military Affairs* (JPRS-CPS-86-010). 1986.

Hong Kong Collection, Main Library, University of Hong Kong.

Universities Service Centre for China Studies, Chinese University of Hong Kong.

Books

A Draft Agreement between the Government of the United Kingdom of Great Britain and Northern Ireland and the Government of the People's Republic of China on the Future of Hong Kong. Hong Kong: Government Printer, September 26, 1984.

Allen, Jamie. *Seeing Red: China's Uncompromising Takeover of Hong Kong.* Singapore: Butterworth-Heinemann Asia, 1997.

Armstrong, J. D. *Revolutionary Diplomacy: Chinese Foreign Policy and the United Front Doctrine.* Berkeley: University of California Press, 1977.

Beazer, William F. *The Commercial Future of Hong Kong.* New York: Praeger Publishers, 1978.

Beijing Shehui Zhuyi Xueyuan, ed. *Zhongguo Gongchandang tongyi zhanxian shi* [A history of the united front of the Chinese Communist Party]. Beijing: Zhongguo wenshi chubanshe, 1993.

Beijing Shehui Zhuyi Xueyuan Bangongshi, ed. *Gandan xiangzhao rongru yugong: shehui zhuyi chuji jieduan tongyi zhanxian yu duodang hezuo* [Mutual understanding, mutual support: the united front and multi-party collaboration in the early stage of socialism]. Beijing: Shishi chubanshe, 1989.

Buckley, Roger. *Hong Kong: The Road to 1997.* Cambridge: Cambridge University Press, 1997.

Burns, John P., Victor C. Falkenheim, and David M. Lampton. *Hong Kong and China in Transition*. Canada and Hong Kong Papers No. 3. Toronto: University of Toronto – York University Joint Centre for Asia Pacific Studies, 1994.

Carroll, John M. *A Concise History of Hong Kong*. Hong Kong: Hong Kong University Press, 2007.

Chan Lau Kit-ching. *China, Britain and Hong Kong 1895–1945*. Hong Kong: Chinese University Press, 1990.

———. *From Nothing to Nothing: The Chinese Communist Movement and Hong Kong, 1921–1936*. Hong Kong: Hong Kong University Press, 1999.

Chan, Ming K., ed. *Precarious Balance: Hong Kong Between China and Britain, 1842–1992*. Armonk, NY: M. E. Sharpe, 1994.

Chan, Ming K., and David J. Clark, eds. *The Hong Kong Basic Law: Blueprint for "Stability and Prosperity" under Chinese Sovereignty?* Armonk, NY: M. E. Sharpe, 1991.

Chan, Ming K., and Gerard A. Postiglione, eds. *The Hong Kong Reader: Passage to Chinese Sovereignty*. Armonk, NY: M. E. Sharpe, 1996.

Chang, David Wen-wei, and Richard Y. Chuang. *The Politics of Hong Kong's Reversion to China*. New York: St. Martin's Press, 1998.

Chen Xin, and Guo Zhikun, eds. *Xianggang quanjilu* [Illustrated chronicle of Hong Kong]. Vol. 1. Hong Kong: Zhonghua shuju, 1997–1998.

Chief Executive's Office, Hong Kong Special Administrative Region, the People's Republic of China. *Civil Liberties and Social Order: Consultation Document*. Hong Kong: Chief Executive's Office, April 1997.

Chung Sze-yuen. *Hong Kong's Journey to Reunification: Memoirs of Sze-yuen Chung*. Hong Kong: Chinese University Press, 2001.

Cottrell, Robert. *The End of Hong Kong: The Secret Diplomacy of Imperial Retreat*. Hong Kong: John Murray, 1993.

Courtauld, Caroline, and May Holdsworth. *The Hong Kong Story*. Hong Kong: Oxford University Press, 1997.

Deng Xiaoping wenxuan 1975–1982 [Selected works of Deng Xiaoping 1975–1982]. Hong Kong: renmin chubanshe, 1983.

Dimbleby, Jonathan. *The Last Governor: Chris Patten & the Handover of Hong Kong*. London: Little, Brown, 1997.

Domes, Jürgen, and Yu-ming Shaw, eds. *Hong Kong: A Chinese and International Concern*. Boulder: Westview Press, 1988.

Dongjiang zongdui zhi [Anecdotes of the East River Column]. Beijing: Jiefangjun chubanshe, 2003.

Evans, Richard. *Deng Xiaoping and the Making of Modern China*. London: Penguin Books, 1995.

Flowerdew, John. *The Final Years of British Hong Kong: The Discourse of Colonial Withdrawal*. Houndmills: Macmillan, 1998.

Guangdongqu dang, tuan yanjiu shiliao, 1937–1945 [Research materials on the party and the league in Guangdong region, 1937–1945]. Vols. 1 & 2. Guangzhou: Guangdong renmin chubanshe, 1988.

Hong Kong: Economic Prospects to 1987, Special Report No. 156. London: Economist Intelligence Unit, 1983.

Hong Kong in Transition 1992. Hong Kong: One Country Two Systems Economic Research Institute, 1993.

Hughes, Richard. *Borrowed Place, Borrowed Time: Hong Kong and Its Many Faces*. 2nd rev. ed. London: André Deutsch, 1976.

Jibenfa de dansheng [The birth of the Basic Law]. Xianggang [Hong Kong]: Wenhui chubanshe, 1990.

Kan Tang. *Hongkong and Macao: History in Search of a Future*. Taipei (Taibei): World Anti-Communist League, China Chapter: Asian Peoples' Anti-Communist League, Republic of China, 1989.

Lane, Kevin P. *Sovereignty and the Status Quo: The Historical Roots of China's Hong Kong Policy*. Boulder: Westview Press, 1990.

Lau Siu-kai, ed. *The First Tung Chee-hwa Administration: The First Five Years of the Hong Kong Special Administrative Region*. Hong Kong: Chinese University Press, 2002.

Li Changdao and Gong Xiaohang. *Jibenfa toushi* [A look into the Basic Law]. Hong Kong: Chung Hwa Book, 1990.

Li Guoqiang and Zhang Peixin. *Xianggang zai kang Ri qijian* [Hong Kong's anti-Japanese period]. Hong Kong: Xianggang wenshi chubanshe, 2005.

Li Jiayuan. *Xianggang baoye zatan* [Essays on the newspaper industry in Hong Kong]. Hong Kong: Joint Publishing (HK), 1989.

Li Kwok-sing, comp. *A Glossary of Political Terms of the People's Republic of China*. Translated by Mary Lok. Hong Kong: Chinese University Press, 1995.

Li Pang-kwong, ed. *Political Order and Power Transition in Hong Kong*. Hong Kong: Chinese University Press, 1997.

Liang Shangyuan. *Zhonggong zai Xianggang* [The Chinese Communists in Hong Kong]. Hong Kong: Wide Angle Press, 1989.

Liao Chengzhi wenji [Collected works of Liao Chengzhi]. Vol. 1. Hong Kong: Joint Publishing (HK), 1990.

Liu Zhipeng and Zhou Jiajian. *Tunsheng renyu: Rizhi shiqi Xianggangren de jiti huiyi* [Fell silent: the collective memory of Hong Kong people during the Japanese occupation]. Hong Kong: Chung Hwa Book, 2009.

Lo, Sonny Shiu-Hing. *The Dynamics of Beijing-Hong Kong Relations: A Model for Taiwan?* Hong Kong: Hong Kong University Press, 2008.

Loh, Christine. *Underground Front: The Chinese Communist Party in Hong Kong*. Hong Kong: Hong Kong University Press, 2010.

Lu Fanzhi. *Lu Fanzhi lun Xianggang qiantu (2): Ping Zhong Ying shuangfang yu jibenfa wenti* [A discussion on Sino-British Relations and the Basic Law question] Hong Kong: Beichen xueshe, Jixianshe, 1985.

Lu Ping. *Lu Ping koushu Xianggang huigui* [Lu recounted the return of Hong Kong]. Hong Kong: Joint Publishing (HK), 2009.

Lu Weiluan. *Xianggang wenzong—Neidi zuojia nanlai ji qi wenhua huodong* [Hong Kong's literary circles: the arrival of mainland writers and their cultural activities]. Hong Kong: Wah Hon Publishing, 1987.

Mao Dun. *Wo zouguo de daolu* [My path]. Vol. 3. Hong Kong: Chung Hwa, 1981.

Mao Tse-tung. *Selected Works of Mao Tse-tung*. Vol. 2. Peking (Beijing): Foreign Language Press, 1965.

————. *Selected Works of Mao Tse-tung*. Vol. 4. Peking (Beijing): Foreign Language Press, 1975.

McGurn, William, ed. *Basic Law, Basic Questions: The Debate Continues*. Hong Kong: Review Publishing Co., 1988.

Ng Lun Ngai-ha and Yee Yim Kwong. *Zhongguo mingren zai Xianggang: 30, 40 niandai zai Gang huodong jishi* [China's celebrities in Hong Kong: a record of their activities in Hong Kong in the 1930s and 1940s]. Hong Kong: Hong Kong Educational Publishing, 1997.

Patten, Chris. *East and West: The Last Governor of Hong Kong on Power, Freedom and the Future*. London: Macmillan, 1998.

Patrikeeff, Felix. *Mouldering Pearl: Hong Kong at the Crossroads*. London: George Philip, 1989.

Pepper, Suzanne. *Civil War in China: The Political Struggle, 1945–1949*. Berkeley: University of California Press, 1978.

————. *Keeping Democracy at Bay: Hong Kong and the Challenge of Chinese Political Reform*. Lanham: Rowman & Littlefield Publishers, 2008.

Qian, Yin. *Dynamics vs. Tradition in Chinese Foreign Policy Motivation: Beijing's Fifth Column Policy in Hong Kong as a Test Case*. Commack, NY: Nova Science Publishers, 1999.

Qiao Songdu. *Qiao Guanhua and Gongpeng: wo de fuqing muqing* [My parents Qiao Guanhua and Gongpeng]. Beijing: Zhonghua shuju, 2008.

Qin Yefeng, Bai Yuwu, and Feng Lianju. *Guogong hezuo de guoqu yu weilai* [The past and future of the Guomindang-CCP collaboration]. Harbin: Heilongjiang jiaoyu chubanshe, 1991.

Radtke, Kurt W. *China's Relations with Japan 1945–83: The Role of Liao Chengzhi*. Manchester: Manchester University Press, 1990.

Ride, Edwin. *BAAG: Hong Kong Resistance, 1942–1945*. Hong Kong: Oxford University Press, 1981.

Roberti, Mark. *The Fall of Hong Kong: China's Triumph and Britain's Betrayal*. New York: John Wiley & Sons, 1994.

Scott, Ian. *Political Change and the Crisis of Legitimacy in Hong Kong*. Honolulu: University of Hawaii Press, 1989.

Segal, Gerald. *The Fate of Hong Kong: The Coming of 1997 and What Lies Beyond*. New York: St. Martin's Press, 1993.

Shambaugh, David, ed. *Greater China: The Next Superpower?* Oxford: Oxford University Press, 1995.

Shum Kui-Kwong. *The Chinese Communists' Road to Power: The Anti-Japanese National United Front, 1935–1945*. Hong Kong: Oxford University Press, 1988.

Snow, Philip. *The Fall of Hong Kong: Britain, China and the Japanese Occupation*. New Haven & London: Yale University Press, 2003.

So, Alvin Y. *Hong Kong's Embattled Democracy: A Societal Analysis*. Baltimore & London: John Hopkins University Press, 1999.

Tang, James Tuck-Hong. *Britain's Encounter with Revolutionary China, 1949–54*. New York: St. Martin's Press, 1992.

Thatcher, Margaret. *The Downing Street Years 1979–1990*. London: HarperCollins Publishers, 1993; New York: HarperPerennial, 1995.

The Basic Law of the Hong Kong Special Administrative Region of the People's Republic of China. Hong Kong: One Country Two Systems Economic Research Institute, 1992.

Tsai Jung-fang. *Xianggangren zhi Xianggangshi 1841–1945* [The Hong Kong people's history of Hong Kong]. Hong Kong: Oxford University Press, 2001.

Tsang, Steve. *Hong Kong: An Appointment with China*. London: I. B. Tauris, 1997.

Uhalley, Stephen, Jr. *A History of the Chinese Communist Party*. Stanford: Hoover Institution Press, 1988.

Van Ness, Peter. *Revolution and Chinese Foreign Policy: Peking's Support for Wars of National Liberation*. Berkeley: University of California Press, 1970.

Van Slyke, Lyman P. *Enemies and Friends: The United Front in Chinese Communist History*. Stanford: Stanford University Press, 1967.

Vienna Convention on the Law of Treaties 1969. Done at Vienna on May 23, 1969. Entered into force on January 27, 1980. United Nations, Treaty Series, Vol. 1155, p. 331. United Nations, 2005.

Wang Gungwu and John Wong, eds. *Hong Kong in China: The Challenges of Transition*. Singapore: Times Academic Press, 1999.

Welsh, Frank. *A History of Hong Kong*. London: Harper Collins *Publishers*, 1994.

Wesley-Smith, Peter, and Albert H. Y. Chen, eds. *The Basic Law and Hong Kong's Future*. Hong Kong: Butterworths, 1988.

Wu Guoguang, ed. *Jiuqi xiaoying: Xianggang, Zhongguo yu Taipingyang* [The 1997 effect: Hong Kong, China and the Pacific]. Hong Kong: Taipingyang shiji yanjiusuo, 1997.

Xie Yongguang. *Sannian ling bageyue de kunan* [Misery of three years and eight months]. Hong Kong : Mingbao chubanshe, 1994.

———. *Xianggang kang Ri fengyunlu* [A record of Hong Kong's anti-Japanese activities]. Hong Kong: Cosmos Books, 1995.

Xu Jiatun. *Xu Jiatun Xianggang huiyilu* [Xu Jiatun's Hong Kong memoirs]. Vols. 1 & 2. Hong Kong: Xianggang lianhebao, 1994.

Xu Yueqing, ed. *Yuan Dongjiang zongdui Gang Jiu duli dadui* [The original independent force of Hong Kong and Kowloon of the East River Column]. Hong Kong: Gang Jiu dadui (jianshi) bianjizu, 1999.

Xuanyuan Lu. *Xinhuashe toushi* [An insight into the Xinhua News Agency]. Hong Kong: Wide Angle Press, 1987.

Yahuda, Michael. *Hong Kong: China's Challenge*. London: Routledge, 1996.

Yee, Albert H. *A People Misruled: Hong Kong and the Chinese Stepping Stone Syndrome*. Hong Kong: API Press, 1989.

Youngson, A. J., ed. *China and Hong Kong: The Economic Nexus*. Hong Kong: Oxford University Press, 1983.

Yuan Lizhou. *Tongzhan zhishi yu zhengce* [Facts and policies of the united front]. Harbin: Harbin gongye daxue chubanshe, 1985.

Yuan Qiushi, ed. *Xianggang guodu shiqi zhongyao wenjian huibian* [A collection of the important documents of Hong Kong in the transitional period]. Hong Kong: Joint Publishing (HK), 1997.

Yuan Xiaolun. *Yue Gang kangzhan wenhuashi lungao* [A history of anti-Japanese war effort among cultural circles in Guangdong and Hong Kong]. Guangzhou: Guangdong renmin chubanshe, 2005.

Zhang Hanzhi and others. *Wo yu Qiao Guanhua* [Qiao Guanhua and I]. Beijing: Zhongguo qingnian chubanshe, 1994.

Zhang Huizhen and Kong Qiangsheng. *Cong shiyiwan dao sanqian: lunxian shiqi Xianggang jiaoyu koushu lishi* [From 110,000 to 3,000: An oral history on Hong Kong's education under the Japanese occupation]. Hong Kong: Oxford University Press, 2005.

Zhang Jiefeng and others. *Bubian, wushi nian?: Zhong Ying Gang jiaoli Jibenfa* [No change for fifty years?: China, Britain and Hong Kong wrestled with the Basic Law]. Hong Kong: Langchao chubanshe, 1991.

Zhao Chunyi, Sun Youkui, and Bai Yuming, eds. *Xinshiqi tongyi zhanxian lilun yu shijian* [The theory and practice of the new era's united front]. Changchun: Jilin daxue chubanshe, 1986.

Zheng Canhui, Ji Hongsheng, and Wu Jingping. *Song Qingling yu kang Ri jiuwang yundong* [Song Qingling and the anti-Japanese movement for national survival]. Fuzhou: Fuzhou renmin chubanshe, 1986.

Zhonggong dangshi ziliao zhuanti yanjiuji: kan Ri zhanzheng shiqi (2) [Historical materials on the history of the Chinese Communist Party: anti-Japanese war period (2)]. Beijing: Zhonggong dangshi ziliao chubanshe, 1989.

Zhonggong Sichuan Shengwei Dangshi Yanjiushi and others, eds. *Nanfangju dangshi yanjiu lunwenji* [A collection of essays on the history of the Southern Bureau]. Chongqing: Chongqing chubanshe, 1993.

Zhonggong Zhongyang Tongyi Zhanxian Gongzuobu and Zhonggong Zhongyang Wenxian Yanjiushi, eds. *Deng Xiaoping lun tongyi zhanxian* [Deng Xiaoping discusses the united front]. Beijing: Zhongyang wenxian chubanshe, 1991.

Zhonggong Zhongyang Tongzhanbu Yanjiushi, ed. *Tongyi zhanxian zhishi wenda* [Questions and answers for the knowledge of united front]. Beijing: Zhongguo wenshi chubanshe, 1988.

Zhongguo tongyi zhanxian quanshu [The complete book on China's united front]. Beijing: Guoji wenhua, 1993.

Zhou Shuzhen. *1949 piaoyao Gangdao* [Hong Kong and 1949]. Beijing: Shishi chubanshe, 1996.

Zong Daoyi and others, eds. *Zhou Nan koushu: shen zai jifeng zhouyu zhong* [Zhou Nan recounted: in strong winds and rain]. Hong Kong: Joint Publishing (HK), 2007.

Articles

"Accord Brings Stability to Hongkong." *Beijing Review*, December 24, 1984, p. 8.

Ai Kesi, "Dong Jianhua jiang miandui naxie zhongdai wenti?" [What great challenges will Tung face?], *Cheng Ming*, January 1997, pp. 66–67.

Baldinger, Pamela. "Hong Kong Gets Its First Chinese Chief." *China Business Review,* January–February, 1997, p. 4.

"Beijing dachu 'liangyuanzhi' xinpai?" [Has Beijing showed its new card of a "bicameral system"?]. *Yazhou zhoukan* [*Asia Weekly*], September 10, 1989, p. 16.

Bowring, Philip. "Heaven's Command: Index Arise." *Far Eastern Economic Review,* February 23, 1984, p. 77.

———. "Elec and Eltek—El-cheapo." *Far Eastern Economic Review,* March 8, 1984, p. 101.

———. "Peking's Little List." *Far Eastern Economic Review,* May 17, 1984, pp. 18–19.

Bowring, Philip and Teresa Ma. "Promises, Promises: Britain and China Talk on about an Agreement, but without Guarantees It Is Not Likely to Mean Much." *Far Eastern Economic Review,* May 17, 1984, pp. 18–19.

Burns, John P. "The Structure of Communist Party Control in Hong Kong." *Asian Survey* 30, no. 8 (August 1990): 748–65.

Burton, Sandra. "The Tycoon in a Taxi." *Time,* November 11, 1996, pp. 25–28.

———. "China's Choice." *Time,* December 23, 1996, pp. 14–16.

Business and Professional Group, Consultative Committee for the Basic Law of the Hong Kong Special Administrative Region. "How to Elect the Chief Executive of the Future Hong Kong SAR Government: A Proposal by the Business and Professional Group of the BLCC." Gift from Shui On Group Ltd.; Hong Kong Collection, Main Library, University of Hong Kong, 1986.

Chan, Gordon Y. M. "Hong Kong and Communist Guerilla Resistance in South China, 1937–1945." *Twentieth-Century China* 29, no. 1 (November 2003): 39–63.

Chen Xiaoman. "Shijia caituan jiebanren, nianqing wushi qiyejia: zhengtan xinxing yaobuyao minzhu?" [The successors of big families and big corporations, the young and practical entrepreneurs: Do the new political stars want democracy?]. *Pai Shing Semi-monthly,* November 16, 1986, pp. 18–20.

Cheng, Elizabeth. "Lending Credibility: The Bank of China Moves Further into the International Capital Markets by Arranging a Hongkong Property Loan." *Far Eastern Economic Review,* May 9, 1985, pp. 84–85.

Cheung, Anthony Bing-leung and Kin-sheun Louie. *Social Conflicts in Hong Kong, 1975–1986: Trends and Implications.* Occasional Paper No. 3. Hong Kong: Hong Kong Institute of Asia-Pacific Studies, Chinese University of Hong Kong, April 1991.

Ching, Frank, and Stacy Mosher. "Shaken and Stirred: Governor Patten Unveils New Political Programme." *Far Eastern Economic Review,* October 15, 1992, p. 13.

Ching, Frank. "Choosing Hong Kong's Leader: Chief Executive Must Understand 'One Country, Two Systems.'" *Far Eastern Economic Review,* July 18, 1996, p. 34.

———. "Tung: A Reluctant Candidate." *Far Eastern Economic Review,* July 25, 1996, p. 40.

———. "Hong Kong Mood Improves: Campaign for Chief Executive Is More Open Than Expected." *Far Eastern Economic Review,* November 28, 1996, p. 54.

———. "A Milestone for Hong Kong." *Far Eastern Economic Review,* December 26, 1996 & January 2, 1997, p. 28.

————. "Hong Kong Isn't Dead Yet." *Far Eastern Economic Review,* February 20, 1997, p. 34.

Chu Yik-yi. "Tung Chee-hwa and His Challenges: A Look at Hong Kong's Last Colonial Days, December 1996–June 1997." *Asian Perspective* 22, no. 2 (1998): 169–91.

————. "Overt and Covert Functions of the Hong Kong Branch of the Xinhua News Agency, 1947–1984." *Historian* 62, no. 1 (Fall 1999): 31–46.

————. "The Failure of the United Front Policy: The Involvement of Business in the Drafting of Hong Kong's Basic Law, 1985–1990." *Asian Perspective.* 24, no. 2 (2000): 173–98.

Chu, Cindy Yik-yi. "The Origins of the Chinese Communists' Alliance with the Business Elite in Hong Kong: The 1997 Question and the Basic Law Committees, 1979–1985." *Modern Chinese History Society of Hong Kong Bulletin* nos. 9–10 (October 1999): 51–67.

————. "The Chinese Communists, Hong Kong, and the Sino-Japanese War." *American Journal of Chinese Studies* 7, no. 2 (October 2000): 131–45.

————. "Back to the Masses: The Historiography of Hong Kong's Recent Political Developments and the Prospects of Future Scholarship." *American Journal of Chinese Studies* 10, no. 1 (April 2003): 29–42.

Davies, Derek. "China Earns from Hongkong." *Far Eastern Economic Review,* June 20, 1963, pp. 689–95.

————. "A Leap into the Dark: Britain Concedes Sovereignty but Wants All Agreements Guaranteed." *Far Eastern Economic Review,* May 3, 1984, pp. 14–16.

"Deng on Problems About Hong Kong." *Beijing Review,* June 4, 1984, pp. 6–7.

"Deng Xiaoping on Hongkong Issue." *Beijing Review,* July 23, 1984, pp. 16–17.

do Rosario, Louise. "The Door Opens Wide: Entrepreneurial Entrepôt Hongkong Profits from the Opening of China's Trade with the World." *Far Eastern Economic Review,* February 28, 1985, pp. 96–97.

Du Junhua. "Liao Chengzhi yu Xianggang kangzhan baozhi" [Liao Chengzhi and anti-war newspapers in Hong Kong]. *Wenshi zazhi* [Journal of literature and history], 1 (2002): 60–62.

Elliott, Dorinda. "Captain Hong Kong." *Newsweek,* December 16, 1996, pp. 14–19.

————. "The Best Man for the Job." *Newsweek,* June 9, 1997, pp. 14–15.

"Examples of Constituents for the Grand Electoral College Proposed by the Business & Professional Group (BPG) of Members of BLCC for the Election of the Chief Executive and 25% of the Legislature." Gift from the BPG; Hong Kong Collection, Main Library, University of Hong Kong, received in 1988.

Fang Su. "Dong teshou de 'miyueqi' jieshule" [Chief Executive Tung's 'honeymoon' has ended]. *Nineties* [Jiushi niandai yuekan], March 1997, pp. 56–59.

Gilley, Bruce. "Enter the Judge." *Far Eastern Economic Review,* September 12, 1996, pp. 14–15.

————. "Shoe-In's Challenge: Prospective Chief Executive Has to Fight for Credibility." *Far Eastern Economic Review,* November 28, 1996, pp. 23 & 26.

———. "Hong Kong '97: Regional Politik." *Far Eastern Economic Review,* May 29, 1997, pp. 22–23, 26.

He Yumian. "'Gongshang jie,' 'minzhu pai': zhengzhi lunzhan maixiang gaochao" [The "industrial and business sectors," the "pro-democracy party": The debates over the political system reaches the high wave]. *Pai Shing Semi-monthly,* November 16, 1986, p. 12.

———. "Zhengzhi yingxiangli shei yu shangjia bi" [Who could compete with the political influence of the business elite?]. *Pai Shing Semi-monthly,* November 16, 1986, pp. 16–17.

Healy, Tim and Law Siu Lan. "'Highest Honor': A Landslide Vaults Tung Chee Hwa into the 1997 Leader's Hot Seat." *Asiaweek,* December 20, 1996, pp. 26 & 28.

"HK Agreement Hailed Worldwide." *Beijing Review,* October 8, 1984, pp. 10–11.

"HK Media Hail New Era of Democracy." *Beijing Review,* December 9–15, 1996, p. 4.

Hong Kong Bar Association. "The Hong Kong Bar Association States Its Case . . . No Legal Basis or Practical Necessity." *China Perspectives,* January/February, 1997, pp. 33–35.

Huang Kangxian. "Cong lianhe zhenxian dao huaqing jiexian: Zhonggong dui Xianggang zhengdang tongzhan de jibenfa" [From united front to drawing the line: the basic principles of the Chinese Communists' united front work among political parties in Hong Kong]. *Hong Kong Economic Journal Monthly* [Xinbao caijing yuekan], April 1993, pp. 45–49.

Jin Yaoru. "Chongwen Zhou Enlai zongli Xianggang zhengce: kan jinri Gang-Ao gongzuo zhi 'zuo'—wo de huiyilu zhi er" [To look at the "leftism" of today's Hong Kong and Macao work: remembering Premier Zhou Enlai's Hong Kong policy, the second part of my memoirs]. *Dangdai yuekan* [Contemporary monthly], June 15, 1992, pp. 32–35.

King, Ambrose Y. C. "The Hong Kong Talks and Hong Kong Politics." *Issues & Studies* 22, no. 6 (June 1986): 52–75.

Lau, Emily. "Left, Right and Centre." *Far Eastern Economic Review,* September 13, 1984, pp. 29–30.

———. "Scramble for Power: The Territory's Non-Civil Servant Leaders Begin the Race to the Top." *Far Eastern Economic Review,* April 18, 1985, pp. 43–46.

———. "Basic-Law Makers: Peking Announces the Make-Up of a Drafting Committee Geared to Develop a Mini-Constitution for the British Territory." *Far Eastern Economic Review,* July 4, 1985, p. 16.

———. "The Rising Red Tide: Under the Surface China Is Establishing Its Own Structure." *Far Eastern Economic Review,* August 1, 1985, pp. 22–23.

———. "Capitalist Delegates to People's Congress." *Far Eastern Economic Review,* August 1, 1985, pp. 24 & 26.

———. "Shadow in the Wings: Peking's Xinhua Sets Up Power Centre in the Territory." *Far Eastern Economic Review,* January 9, 1986, p. 32.

Lau, Emily, and Michael Malik. "Modern Politics Come Late to Colonial Legco." *Far Eastern Economic Review,* April 16, 1987, pp. 40–43.

"Leaders: HK Policy Will Not Be Altered." *Beijing Review,* October 15, 1984, p. 6.

Li Yi. "Deng Xiaoping qushi dui Xianggang de yingxiang" [The impact of Deng Xiaoping's death on Hong Kong]. *Nineties* [Jiushi niandai yuekan], March 1997, pp. 28–29.

Lin Piao. "Long Live the Victory of People's War! In Commemoration of the 20th Anniversary of Victory in the Chinese People's War of Resistance Against Japan." *Peking Review* 8, no. 36 (September 3, 1965): 9–30.

Lu Jingli. "Zhongzi jigou zai Gang fazhan de xin zhuanbian" [New changes of mainland companies in Hong Kong]. *Economic Digest* [*Jingji yizhou*], February 13, 1984, pp. 4–6.

Ma, Teresa and Philip Bowring. "Amber, But Not Green: An Upsurge of Optimism over the Future May Be Premature." *Far Eastern Economic Review*, February 9, 1984, pp. 10–11.

Ma, Teresa. "Capitalism, China-style: 'Big Boss' Wang Outdoes Hongkong Entrepreneurs with a Series of Deals Which Shake Up the Territory." *Far Eastern Economic Review*, March 1, 1984, pp. 68–69.

———. "Debatable Proposition: The Territory's Usually Docile Councillors Want At Least A Say in What the Future Is to Be." *Far Eastern Economic Review*, March 8, 1984, pp. 26–27.

Ren Xin. "A Beginning for Democracy in Hong Kong." *Beijing Review*, January 13–19, 1997, pp. 5–7.

Situ Huifen. "Meiguo, Xianggang jingyan he Zhongguo de gaige" [The United States, Hong Kong experience and China's reform]. *Guangjiaojing yuekan* [*Wide Angle* monthly], September 1988, pp. 58–64.

Song Ligong. "Cong teshou zhengba kan zhi Gang banzi de guanjian weizhi" [The chief executive competition and its implications for the ruling elite of Hong Kong]. *Hong Kong Economic Journal Monthly* [Xinbao caijing yuekan], October 1996, pp. 10–12.

———. "Cong zhengce guocheng kan gaoguan miandui de tiaozhan" [How the policy process reflected on the challenges the top officials faced]. *Hong Kong Economic Journal Monthly* [Xinbao caijing yuekan], March 1997, pp. 25–27.

Specter, Michael. "Colonial Constituency: An Election Proposal May Mean a New Phase in Sino-British Talks." *Far Eastern Economic Review*, January 19, 1984, pp. 12–14.

"Taiwan Not Same Issue as Hongkong." *Beijing Review*, August 27, 1984, p. 8.

Tan Li. "Gongshang zhuanyejie ziwei chunqiang shejian hui jizhe" [The BLCC members of the industrial, business, and professional sectors met with the reporters and skillfully answered the questions]. *Pai Shing Semi-monthly*, November 16, 1986, pp. 13–14.

Tsang, Steve. "Maximum Flexibility, Rigid Framework: China's Policy Towards Hong Kong and Its Implications." *Journal of International Affairs* 49, no. 2 (Winter 1996): 413–33.

"Tung Chee Hwa: A Brief Biography." *Beijing Review*, January 13–19, 1997, p. 9.

Wong Wai-kwok. "Can Co-optation Win Over the Hong Kong People? China's United Front Work in Hong Kong Since 1984." *Issues & Studies* 33, no. 5 (May 1997): 102–37.

"Xiagu rouchang, lun Xiangjiang fengyun" [To comment on the events in Hong Kong]. *Yazhou zhoukan* [*Asia Weekly*], August 25, 1996, pp. 26 & 28.

Xuanyuan Lu. "Xinhuashe Xianggang fenshe de zaoqi lishi" [The early history of the Hong Kong Branch of Xinhua News Agency]. *Guangjiaojing yuekan* [*Wide Angle* monthly], June 16, 1986, pp. 19–21.

Yang Sen. "Cong gongshang zhuanye renshi jiaodu ping 'yihui liangju' fang'an" [Comment on the "bicameral legislature" model from the point of view of the industrialists, businessmen and professionals]. *Mirror* [Jingbao yuekan], October 1989, pp. 12–13.

"Yang Tieliang Dong Jianhua bushu juezhu Xianggang tequ shouzhang" [Yang Ti-liang and Tung Chee-hwa plan for the chief executive competition]. *Yazhou zhoukan* [*Asia Weekly*], September 16–22, 1996, p. 81.

Yu Jiwen. "Zhonggong zai Gang de gongzuo xitong" [The Chinese Communist work system in Hong Kong]. *Nineties* [Jiushi niandai yuekan], October 1985, pp. 56–59.

Zeng Zhongrong and Chen Shaojuan. "Yao fanrong buyao minzhu: Shangjia zhuanzheng shi qilu? shi tantu?" [Prosperity but not democracy: Is the business monopoly of politics a rough road? A smooth journey?]. *Pai Shing Semi-monthly,* November 16, 1986, pp. 9–11.

Zeng Zhongrong. "Kan! shangjiamen zai xiang shenme?" [Look! What are the businessmen thinking?]. *Pai Shing Semi-monthly,* November 16, 1986, pp. 14–15.

Zhang Han. "Lishi shang de Zhonggong Xianggang fenju" [The Hong Kong Central Branch Bureau in history]. *Wenshi zazhi* [Journal of literature and history] 3 (1997): 14–15.

Zhong Shimei. "Zhonggong ruhe guanli Xianggang?" [How did the Chinese Communists administer their work in Hong Kong?]. *Dangdai shishi zhoukan* [*Contemporary* weekly], November 25, 1989, p. 20.

————. "Gongwei qian Gang tongyi lingdao—Zhonggong ruhe guanli Xianggang?" [The work committee moved to Hong Kong and consolidated the leadership—how did the Chinese Communists administer their work in Hong Kong?]. *Dangdai shishi zhoukan* [*Contemporary* weekly], December 2, 1989, pp. 20–21.

————. "Dui Gang fangzhen, zheng chu duo men—Gang Ao Ban yu Gongwei de maodun" [Different policies toward Hong Kong: conflicts between the Hong Kong and Macao Affairs Office and the Hong Kong and Macao Work Committee]. *Dangdai shishi zhoukan* [*Contemporary* weekly], December 9, 1989, pp. 20–21.

Zhong Zheng. "Qianxi Song Qingling de kang Ri guoji tongyi zhanxian sixiang" [An analysis of Song Qingling's thought on the anti-Japanese international united front]. *Luoyang shifan xueyuan xuebao* [Newsletter of Luoyang Normal School] 4 (2003): pp. 97–99.

"Zhonggong kan Xianggang jieji jiegou" [The Chinese Communist Party looks at the Hong Kong class structure]. *Dangdai yuekan* [*Contemporary* monthly], October 15, 1991, pp. 16–18.

Dissertations

Chu, Cindy Y. Y. "'The New Era's Patriotic United Front,' the Hong Kong Question, and Implications for China's Reform." PhD diss., University of Hawaii at Manoa, 1996.
Wong Wai Kwok. "China's United Front Work in Hong Kong since the 1980s." MPhil. thesis, Hong Kong University of Science and Technology, 1996.

Newspapers

Dagongbao (Ta Kung Pao)
Ming Pao
Sing Tao Daily
South China Morning Post
Wah Kiu Yat Po
Wenhuibao (Wen Wei Po)

Index